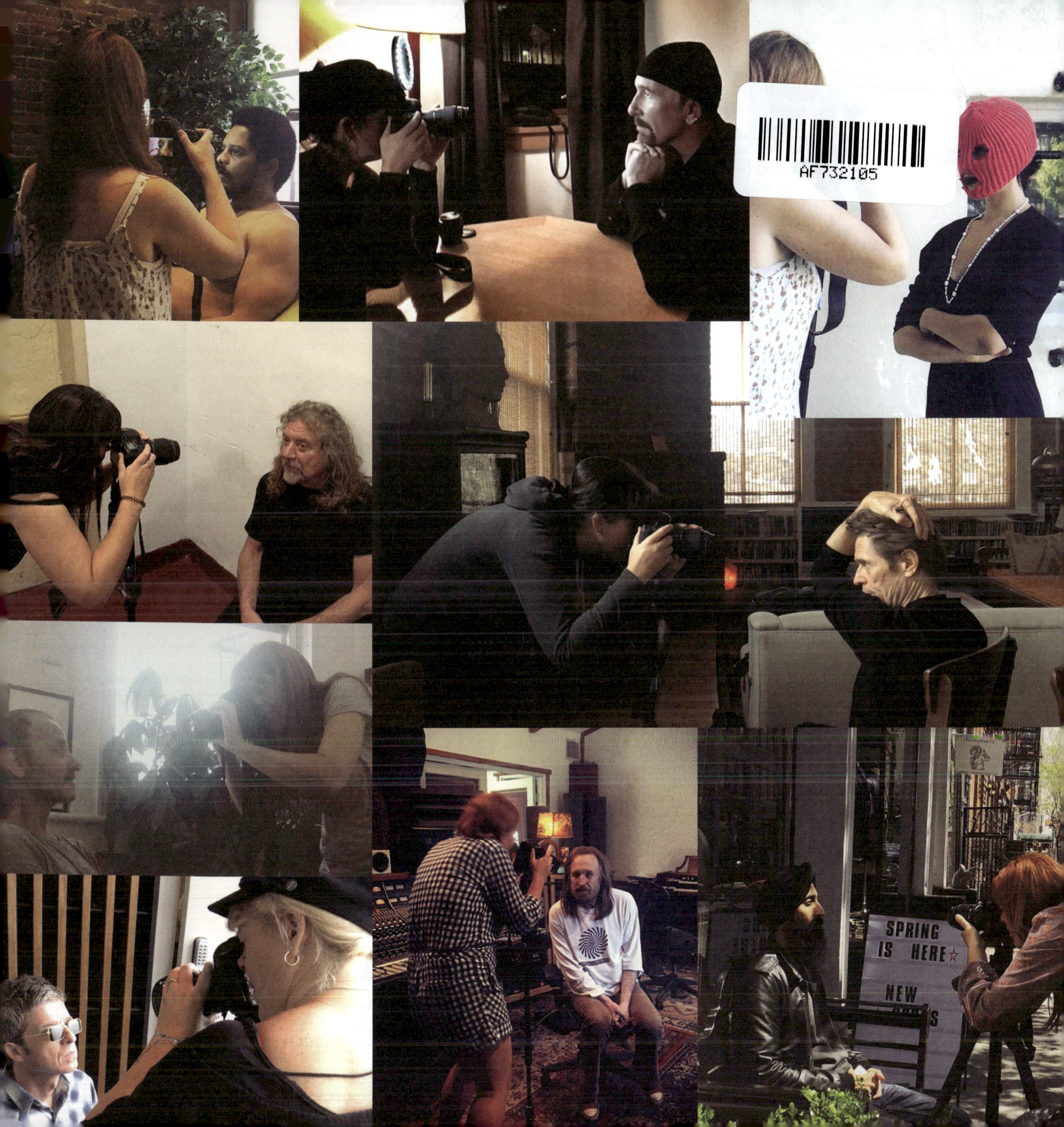
SPRING
IS HERE
NEW

EYE-D

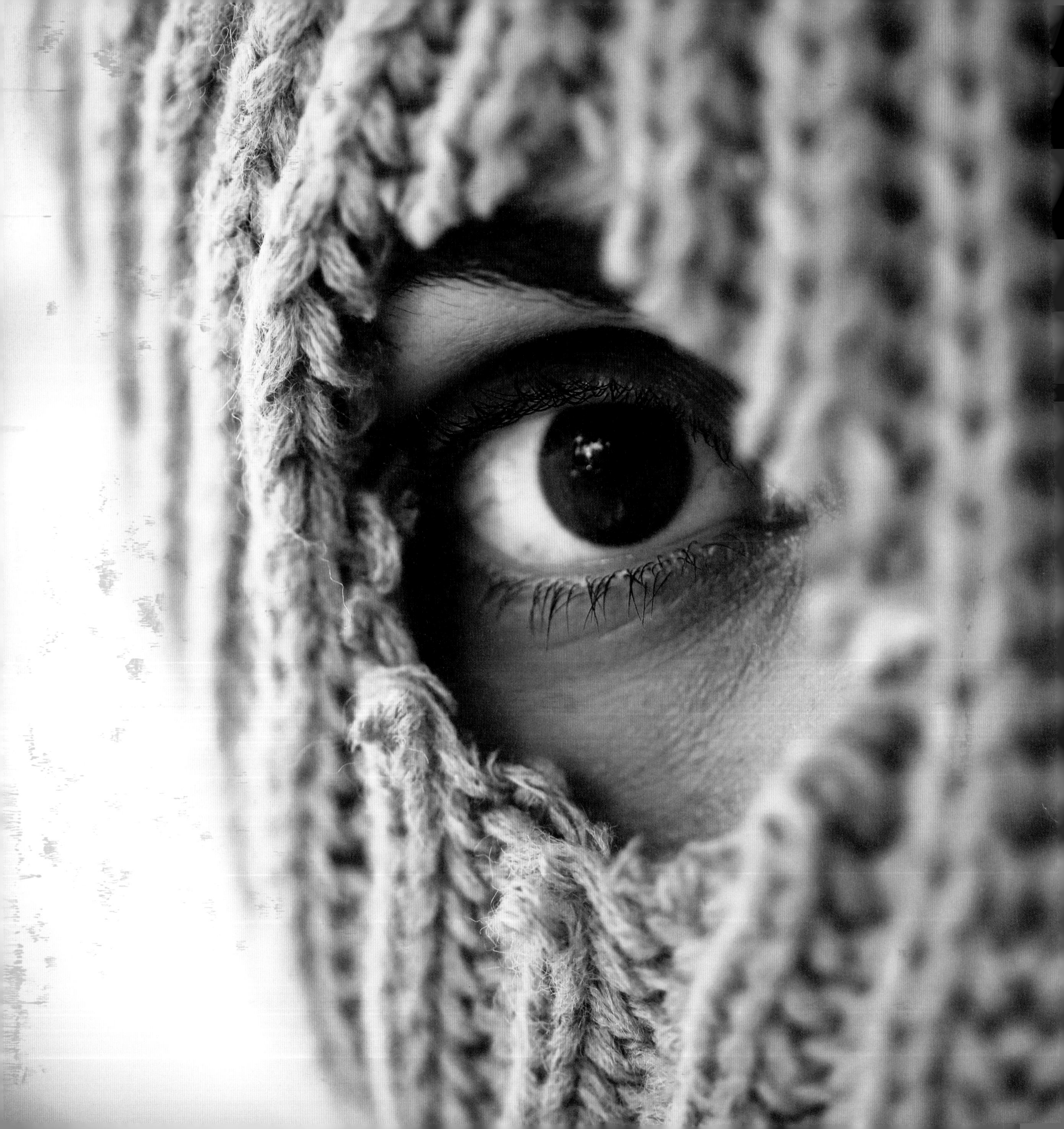

ANNA GABRIEL

EYE-D

ACC ART BOOKS

CONTENTS

PREFACE by Peter Gabriel

You only need

two dots

● ●

and the brain

tells you they are

eyes.

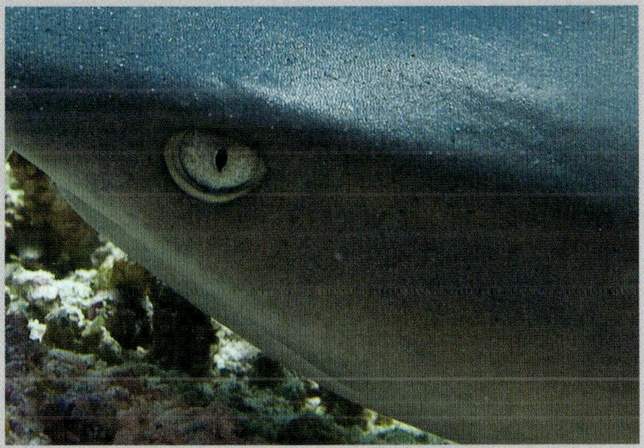 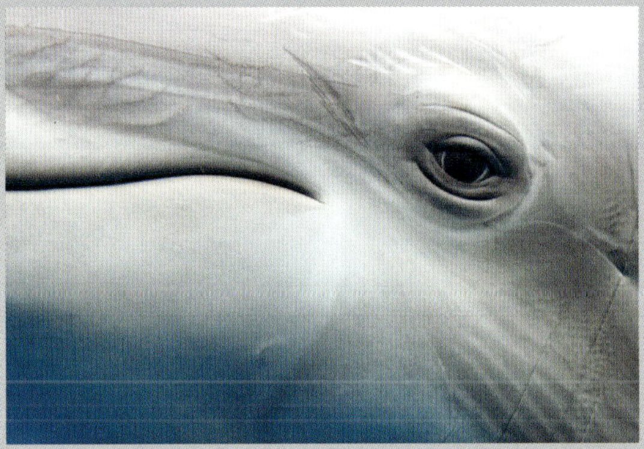

Take a look at the eye of this shark and then the eye of this dolphin. Quite apart from their historical PR, the messaging coming from the eyes alone is very different.

And playing Peek-a-Boo – concealing your eyes – is one of the games I love to play with my favourite small people. As soon as your eyes are hidden, you have gone, disappeared – you just don't exist.

There are good reasons why the eye is this important. The retina at the back of the eye is effectively an extension of the brain, formed from neural tissue from when we are embryos in the womb and connected directly to the brain by the optic nerve. It is the only external part of our bodies that tells you something of what is really going on, inside the core of who you are.

One of the functions of art should be to allow you to see in a new way what you already know well. This is what Anna has done so well in this book. Many of these people will be familiar, but these photos are neither carefully constructed portraits nor casual snaps. They are original close-ups – like peering through a door left a little open, they allow us a glimpse of a private interior world.

Anna has always shown an ability to do things differently and it's easy to look back and see the path that led her to *Eye-D*. From her film and photographic work she would always have a distinctive way of seeing and doing things, like painting a primitive house to enclose her self portrait.

One of my favourite moments working with Anna was when she directed a video for the song I had written for my own father, "Father Son". She used the old Super 8 format to film my father and I, walking up the little hill outside of the studio, and then she brought my young son Isaac into the video. What she captured was both very natural and very precious.

Beginning *Eye-D* was not an easy job. It was a new approach to portraiture and was not designed to be flattering. The first few subjects were there on trust; I happily helped with the invitations, but the more images Anna took, the clearer the work became and the easier it was for those Anna was approaching to see what on earth they were getting themselves into. Most were generous enough to be a part of this project and were very encouraging when they saw the results.

Although Anna's film and video work has been seen by many, her photographic work has not. I am delighted to see this project finally assembled into a beautiful book, the first of many, a book which makes me such a proud dad.

Peter Gabriel

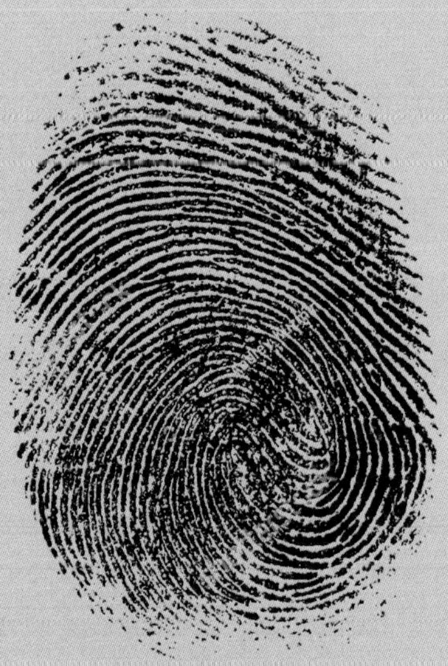

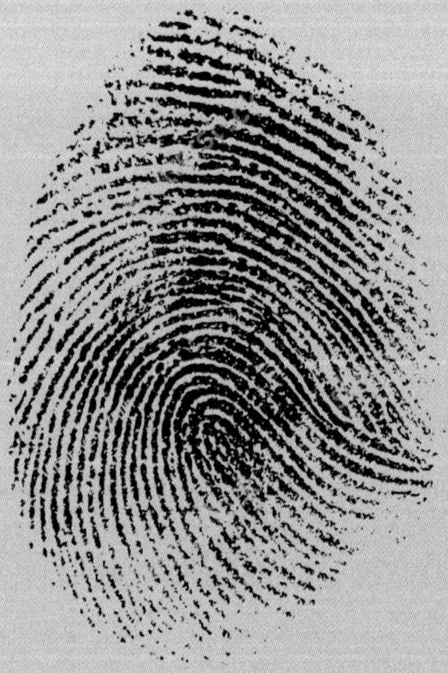

THE ISOLATED EYE

First of all, thanks so much Anna for asking me to contribute to this soulful project.

Maybe because things seem to be happening so fast these days here in the beginning of 2021, with such mind-boggling and game-changing consequences, I'm finding it hard to remember days and events from an era that seems to have disappeared. The eyes in your book were all seeing a very different world.

But – regardless of what time it is – what a wonderful collection of photographs!

When the eye is isolated like this I always think of lizards. The skin that folds and wraps and sags around and under the eye and the way we peer out from within this wrapping of skin is miraculous, as is the contrast between the glistening eyeball and the surrounding skin.

I don't remember the photo session with you very well but I'm sure that the sensation of being lens-to-lens with you was a little unnerving. The mechanical lens between two biological ones is a truly remarkable arrangement!

I don't really remember the circumstances of Lou Reed's self-portrait either, but I'm guessing it could have been a logistical solution? Lou was shooting many portraits around this time and any chance to use his new Leica cameras and test lenses must have seemed irresistible. Lou was someone who could take cameras apart.

Lou was mad for lenses and had a huge collection of cameras and lenses. Keep in mind he also wrote a song called "I'll Be Your Mirror" and even though he sometimes used himself as a subject, he was most often the one behind the camera.

I'll be your mirror, reflect what you are
In case you don't know....
Let me be your eyes
A hand in your darkness
So you wont be afraid.

Laurie Anderson

INTRODUCTION

Eye-D began quite modestly as an album insert for my father's covers album *And I'll Scratch Yours*. Musical legends like Brian Eno, David Byrne, Lou Reed and Paul Simon contributed to the album. My father and I had the idea to shoot close-ups of each contributor. It's a bit of a clichéd phrase at this point, but I identified strongly with the idea that the eyes are the windows to the soul, and I thought it would be much more special – rather than taking a standard photo of the subject leaning languidly against a wall or sitting inertly in a chair – to shoot a close-up of the subject's eye. I was hopeful that these photographs would capture the emotions that I saw running so deeply in my subjects, longing, pain and joy. When the physical photos were finally in my hands, I wasn't disappointed.

My fascination with eyes stretches all the way back to my childhood with my father. When he would walk through the door, the tip-off about his mood wouldn't necessarily be from the tenor of his voice or the words that would spill out of his mouth. I would know immediately by looking up into his eyes whether he was happy or annoyed or sad.

I've always been very close with my father and now that I'm a parent, I understand that the bond you share with your child when you look into their eyes is one of the deepest human connections you will ever share. So it felt fitting that the first eye I shot for this project was my father's.

Each participant – Eddie Vedder, Tom Petty, Randy Newman – had a story to tell spoken through their eyes alone. With each click of the camera, I gained new insights into who these people really were. Some of these much-photographed

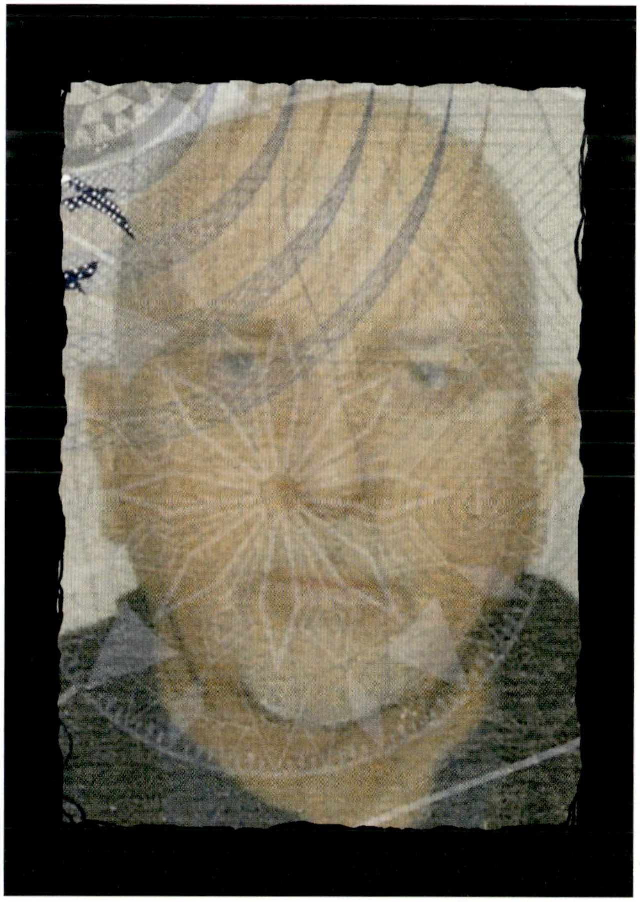

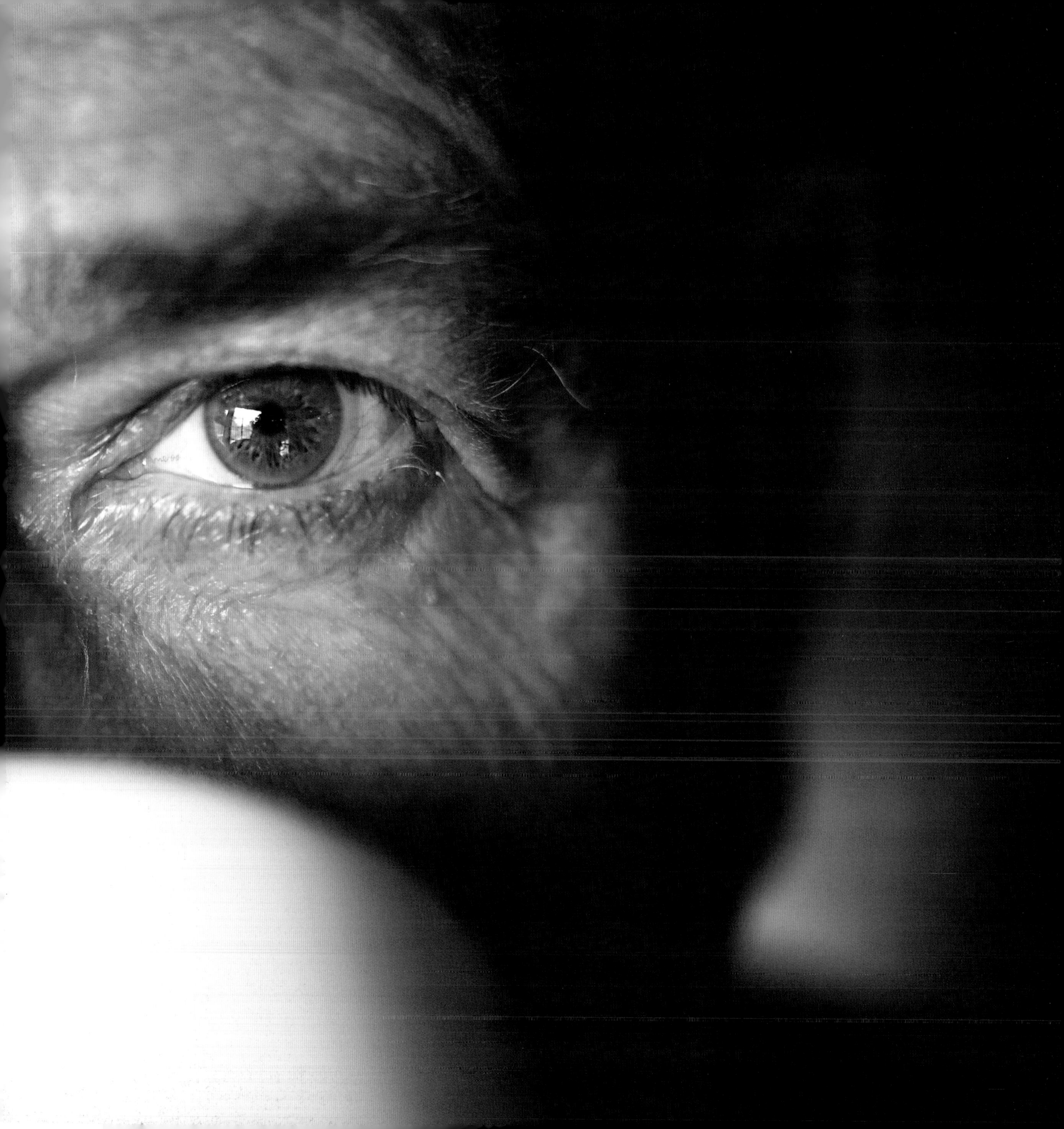

GRAHAM NASH

Born in Blackpool, England; February 2, 1942
Eyes: green

Graham lives in the East Village of New York, not too far from me at the time. In contrast to the neighbourhood, which is generally artsy and gritty, his apartment has an elegant British air about it. Partly because of the surroundings, I immediately felt like I knew him. He and his wife offered me tea and I felt at home.

I had met Graham at a fundraiser for a charity my dad helped found, called Witness, which helps people to document human rights abuses through video and photography.

In addition to being an iconic musician, Graham is a photographer and had an extensive collection of photography books. Photography is clearly something he is passionate about. He was showing me some of his favorite images, and we discovered we shared a similar taste in photography. I could also tell he was genuinely interested about the shoot and my work.

I wanted to do something dramatic with him, so while I shot with natural light, I used a dark black background and did a close up of his eye. It's always a little different when you're shooting a photographer because you can begin to imagine how they might have chosen to create the image. Graham was happy and complimentary about the final image so I was happy.

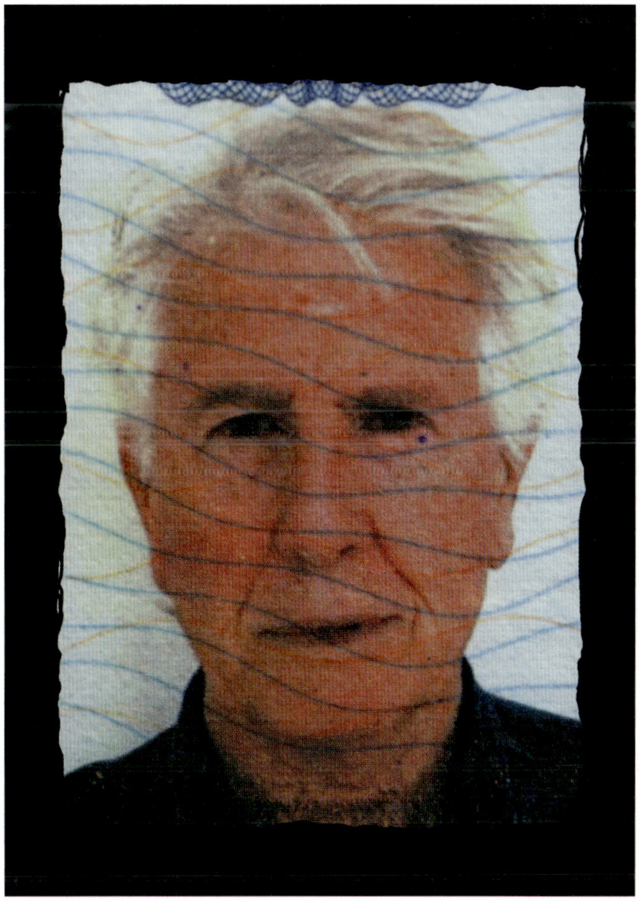

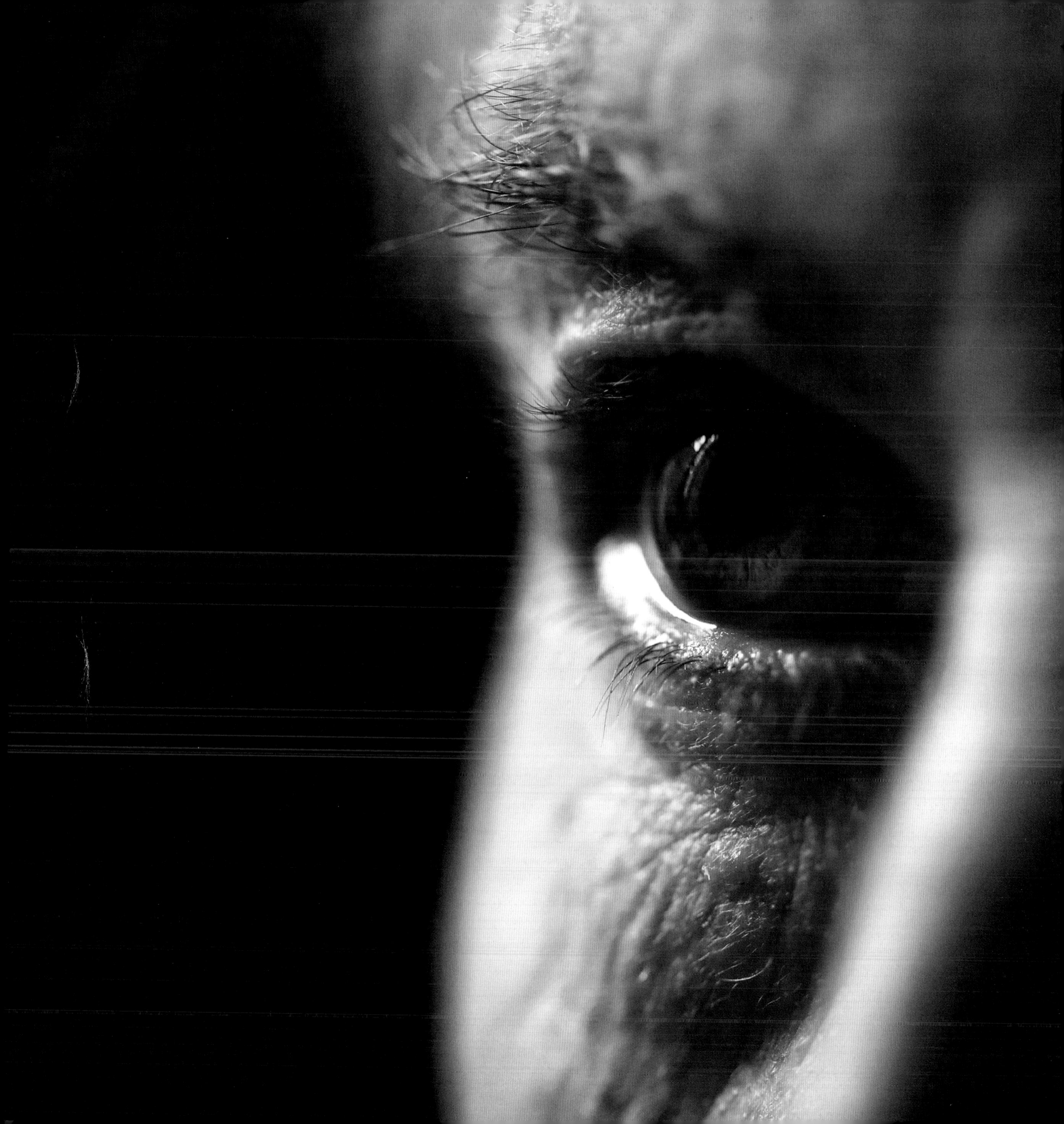

NADYA TOLOKONNIKOVA
from PUSSY RIOT

Born in Norilsk, Russia; November 7, 1989
Eyes: brown

This may be one of my favorite photographs in the book. I met Nadya through The Voice Project, which I co-founded with Hunter Heaney. The Voice Project is a non-profit advocacy group that promotes freedom of artistic expression as an agent of social change. While Pussy Riot was in jail, The Voice Project started taking in donations on their behalf.

I went to LA to shoot Nadya. I told her, "I'd love you to have a balaclava on and take your photo through the hole". She didn't have a balaclava so we bought a bright pink hat and she cut holes in it. We went across the street and shot her against a brick wall. Pussy Riot is known for their balaclavas so it was an obvious choice but I love the way it frames her eye. Nadya lives her life without fear. In person she can be almost intimidating. She has a soft, young, fragile side but is also incredibly tough. She's been imprisoned and yet she remains determined. And she continues to stand up and speak out against oppression, knowing she's risking her life to do so.

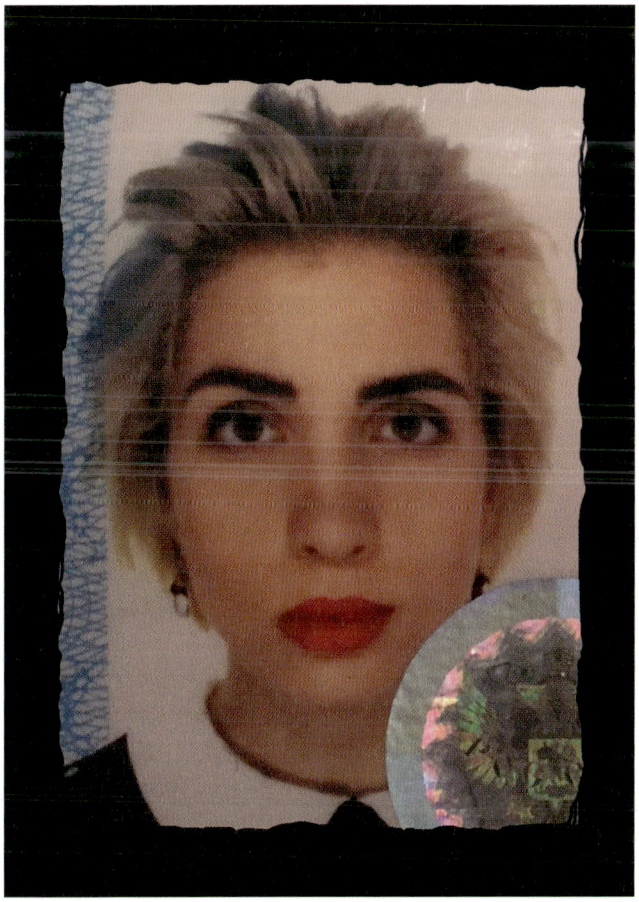

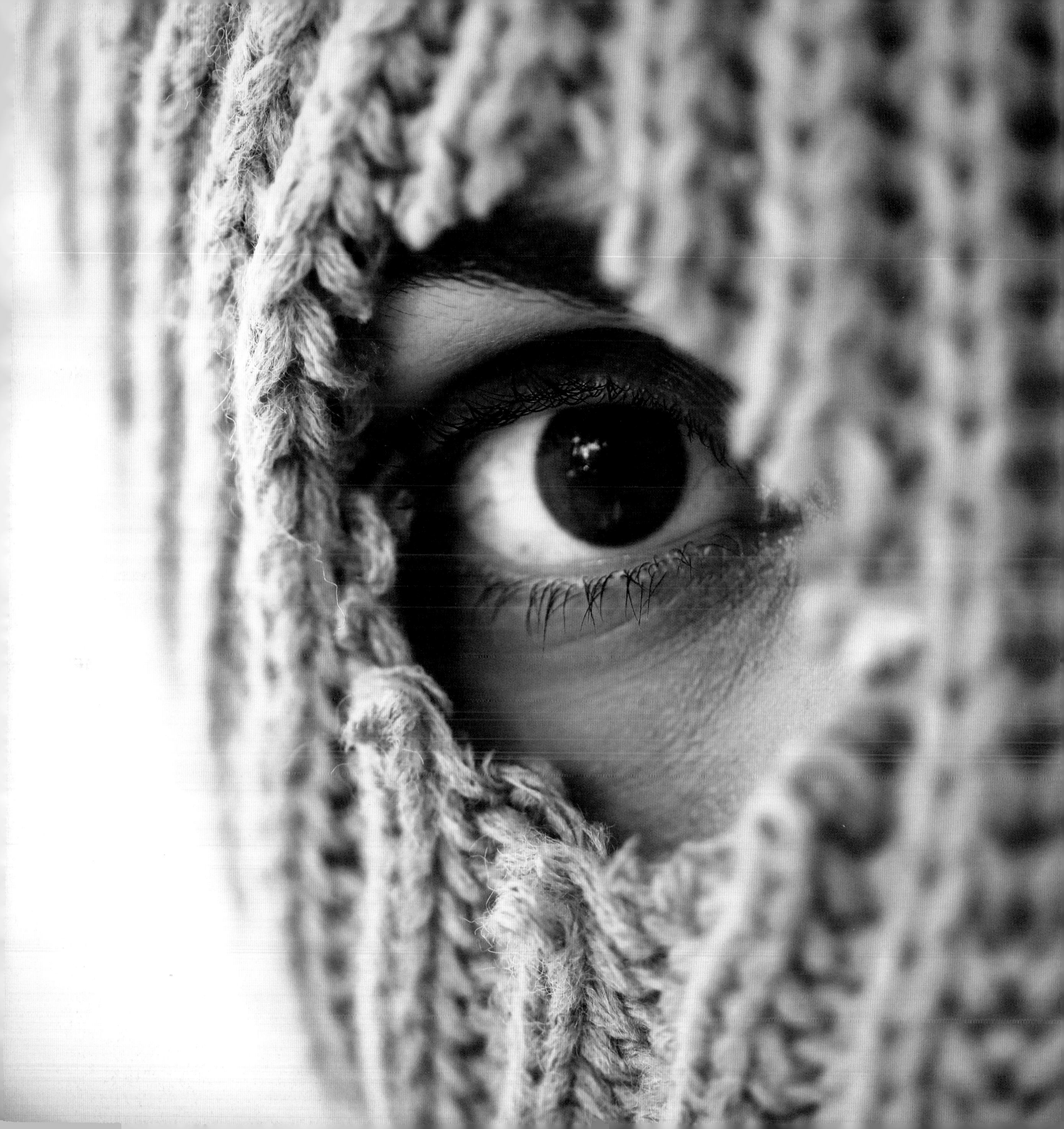

YOUSSOU N'DOUR

Born in Dakar, Senegal; October 1, 1959
Eyes: dark brown

Youssou is one of my favorite people in the world. I've known him since I was a teenager. He is godfather to my half-brother Isaac, and my dad is godfather to Youssou's son. My dad helped Youssou at the beginning of his career to get his name out there, but Youssou is a massive star in his own right all over the world. When you visit Dakar, everyone treats Youssou like a king.

I shot this photo in New York. He was performing at the Brooklyn Academy of Music. I shot him outside in the street, right before the show. I wanted to get the smile in his eyes, because one of his defining characteristics is his emotional generosity. He's always treated me and my sister as family and it felt like I was taking a photo of someone very close to my family. I think I captured his warmth.

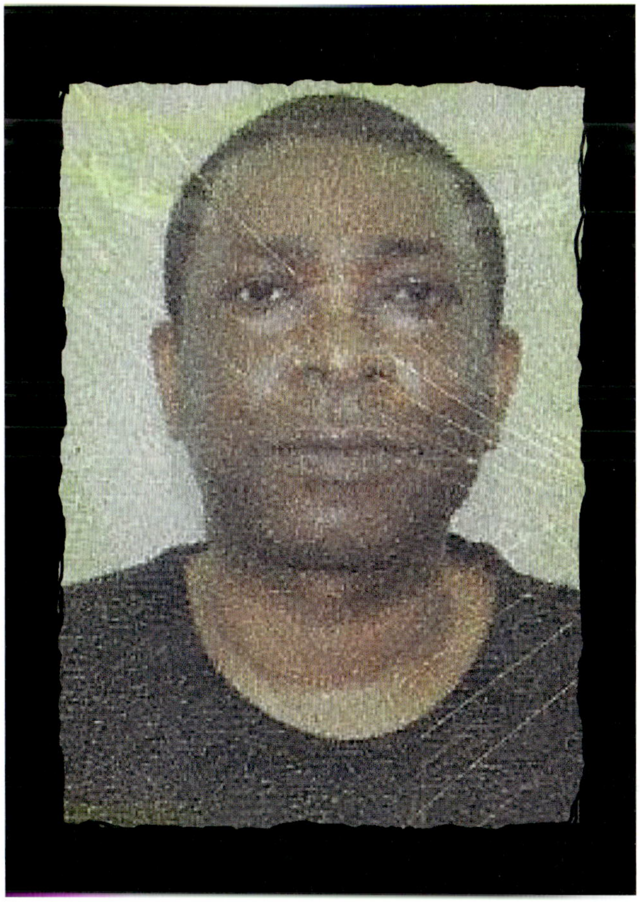

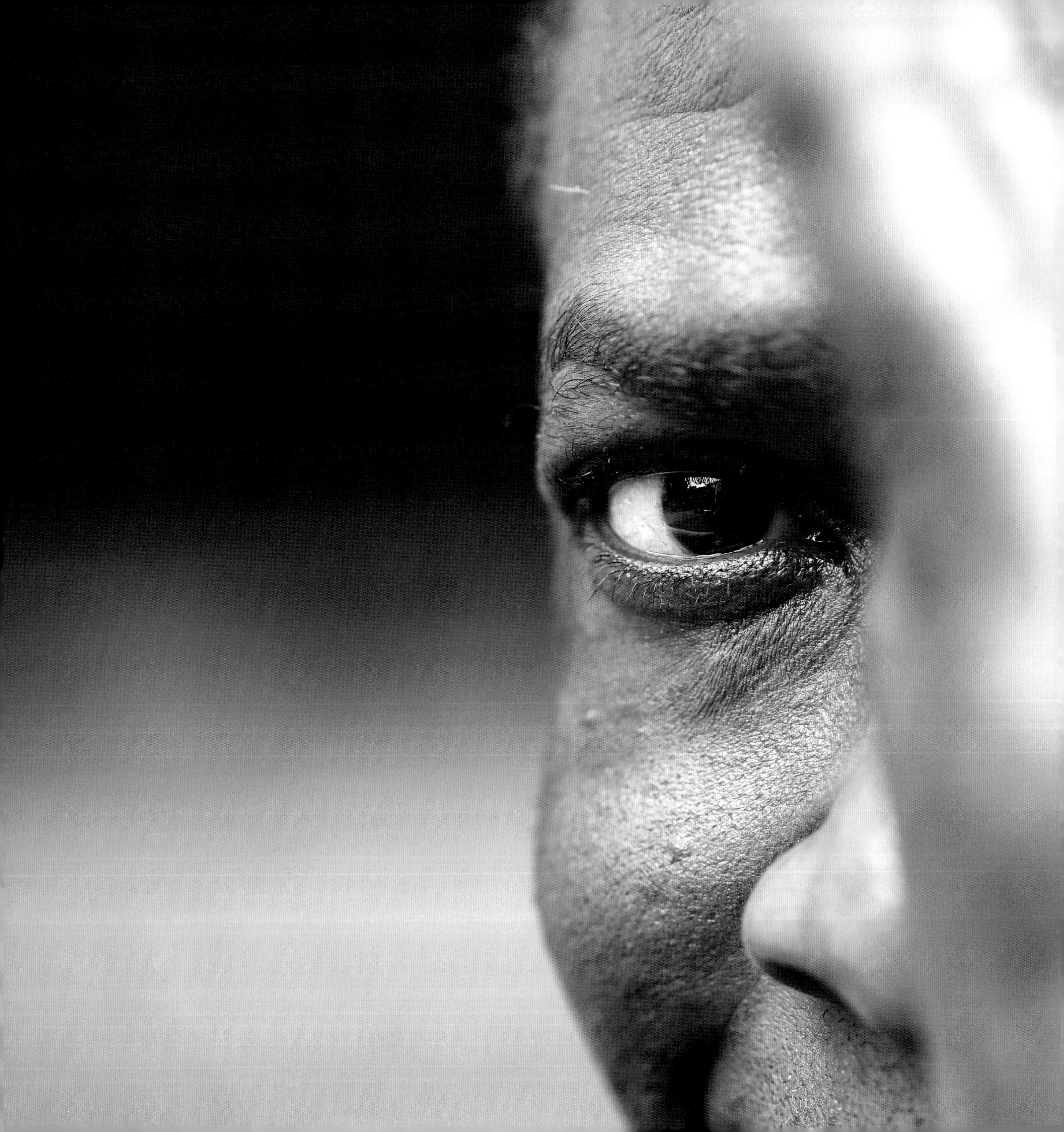

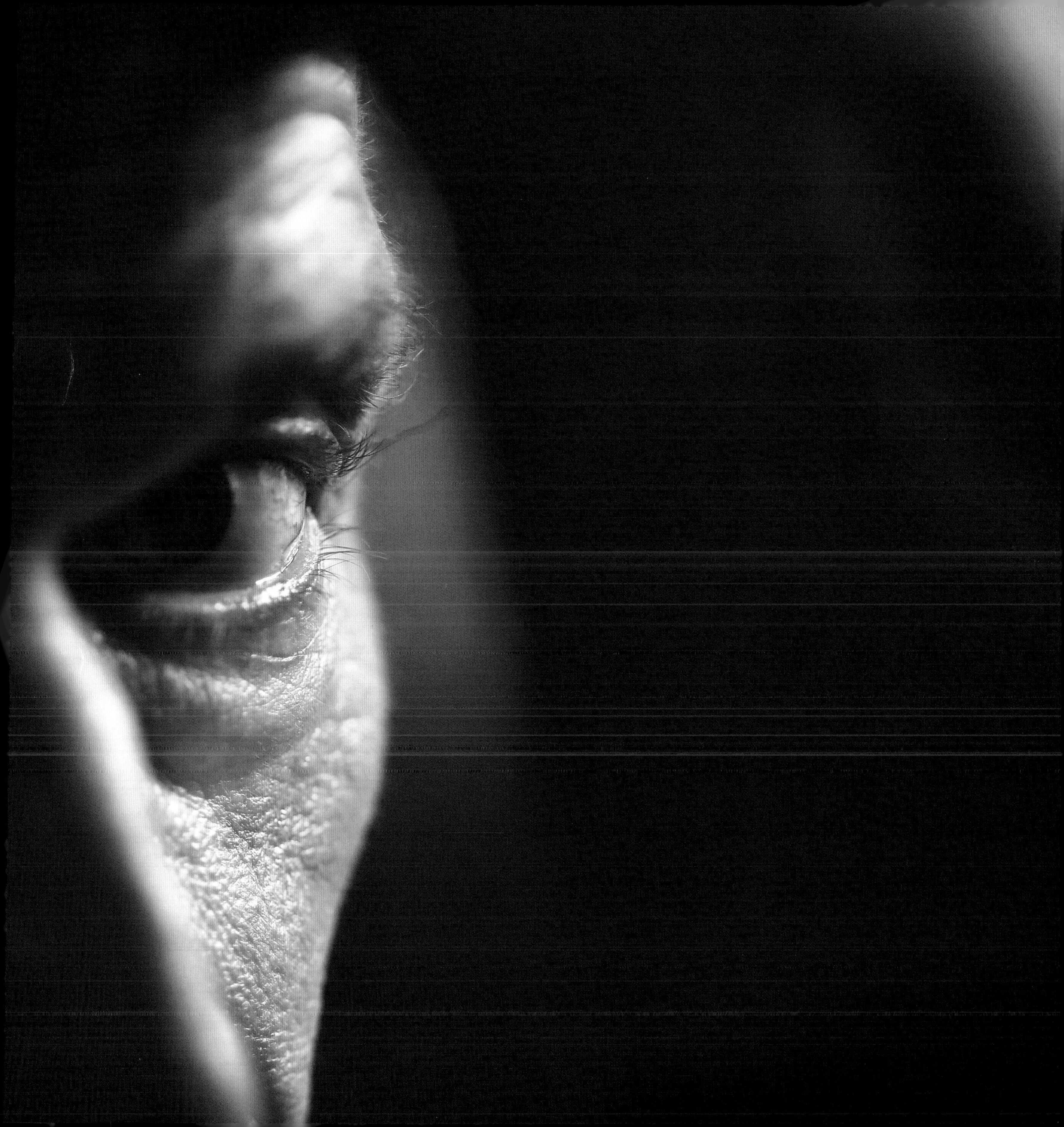

WILLEM DAFOE

Born in Appleton, Wisconsin; July 22, 1955
Eyes: blue

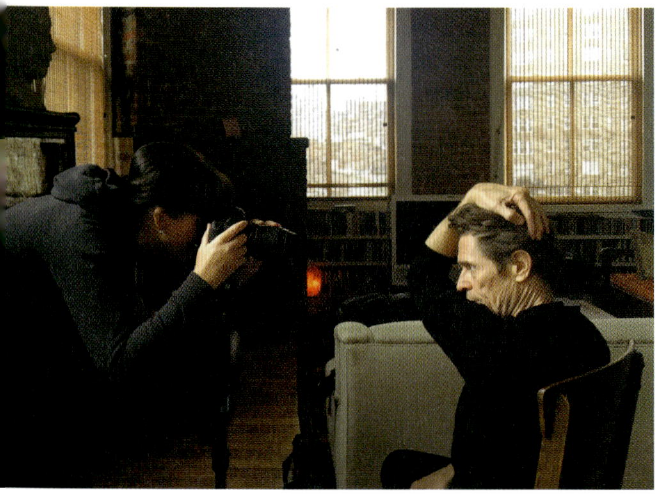

As a teenager, I always associated Willem Dafoe with Jesus. My dad composed the score to Scorsese's *Last Temptation of Christ*, in which Willem starred. During post-production, dad went to New York to work in the same building that Scorsese was editing in. This way he was able to watch the film as it all came together with the music.

I shot Willem at his apartment in the West Village. A lot of the characters he has played are quite dark and maniacal and even though he's not like that at all as a person, I thought it would be cool to try to get a more moody shot. I shot him looking through his arms, to create an interesting shape.

He has very intense eyes, and it's easy to understand why he would get cast as the Messiah. Ironically, as soon as I was done I asked for his passport photo, and he grabbed it and drew devil horns on it, turning himself into the devil.

JUL 55

NOEL GALLAGHER

Born in Manchester, England; May 29, 1967
Eyes: blue

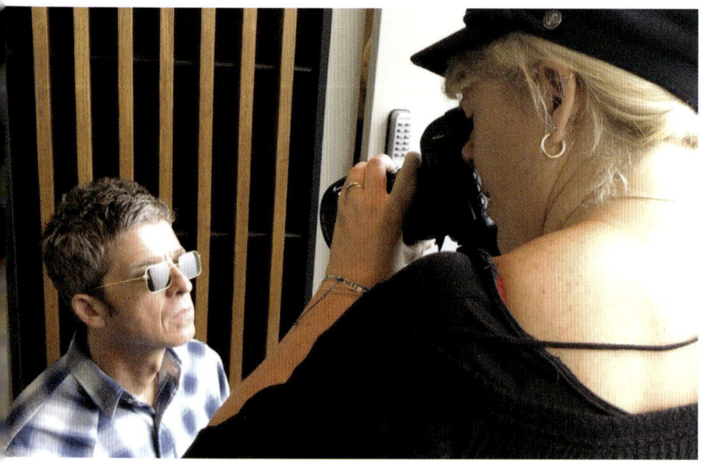

I met Noel through a mutual friend of my husband. He put us in touch directly and in our online exchanges Noel was perfectly charming and accommodating. Not unlike the Eddie Vedder shoot there was no publicist or manager involved so organising the shoot took on the uncanny feeling of texting a mate.

We met at Noel's brand new studio in London. To my surprise, the first thing he told me was, he was a massive fan of *From Genesis to Revolution*, particularly the song "The Conqueror". I never had Noel down as a Genesis fan!

The studio was perfect for photographing. Noel's very into feng shui and the studio had a vermillion psychedelic feel, but I ended up settling on an office room with natural daylight. Out of everyone I photographed for this book, no one else had been able to hold his eye open without blinking for as long or as effortlessly as Noel did. When I mentioned this to him he joked that it must have been all the drugs he took in the Nineties.

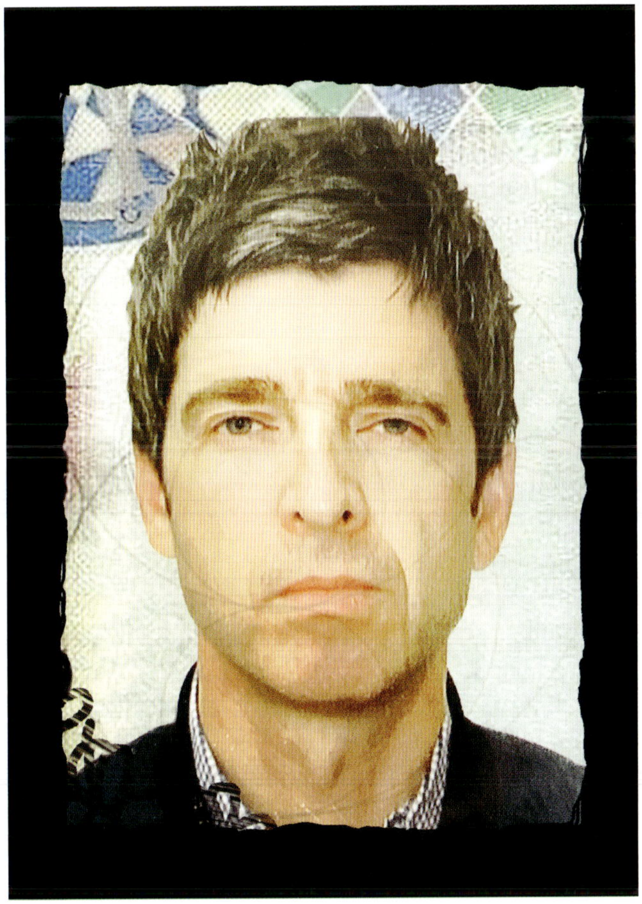

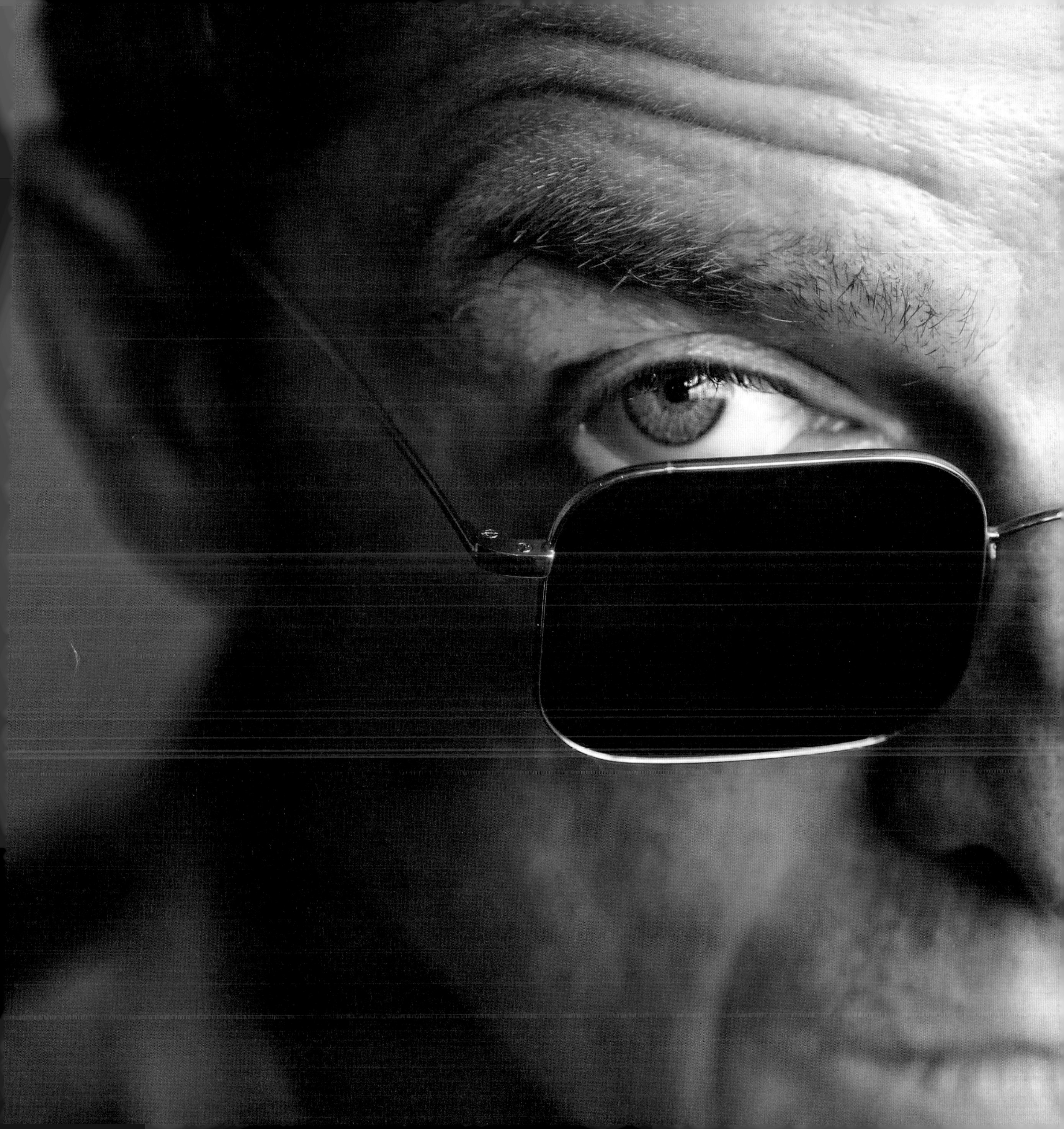

GRIFFIN DUNNE

Born in New York City, New York; June 8, 1955
Eyes: brown

I first heard of Griffin because he co-starred in the movie *After Hours* with Rosanna Arquette, and she began a long-term relationship with my father not long after the film came out. Although Griffin has gone on to have an illustrious career and has done many films and TV shows since then, in my mind, I guess I always associate him with that mid-Eighties period. It was a time when my sister and I were just getting to know Rosanna. She had a beautiful cabin in the woods near Big Sur, where she kept a massive VHS collection of movies. It was on one of her video tapes that I first saw *After Hours*, which is one of his first major roles, and is a sort of dystopian Kafkaesque cult classic. But Griffin will always represent a connection to Rosanna and to that period of my life.

I took this photo of him in Tompkins Square Park, which was next door to where I lived at the time. We have several overlapping social connections and could have talked about a lot of people we know in common, but for whatever reason, we didn't really talk much during the shoot. I can't say I know him that well, but I feel like as an actor, Griffin has a kind of intriguing emotional opacity, which I think this image reflects.

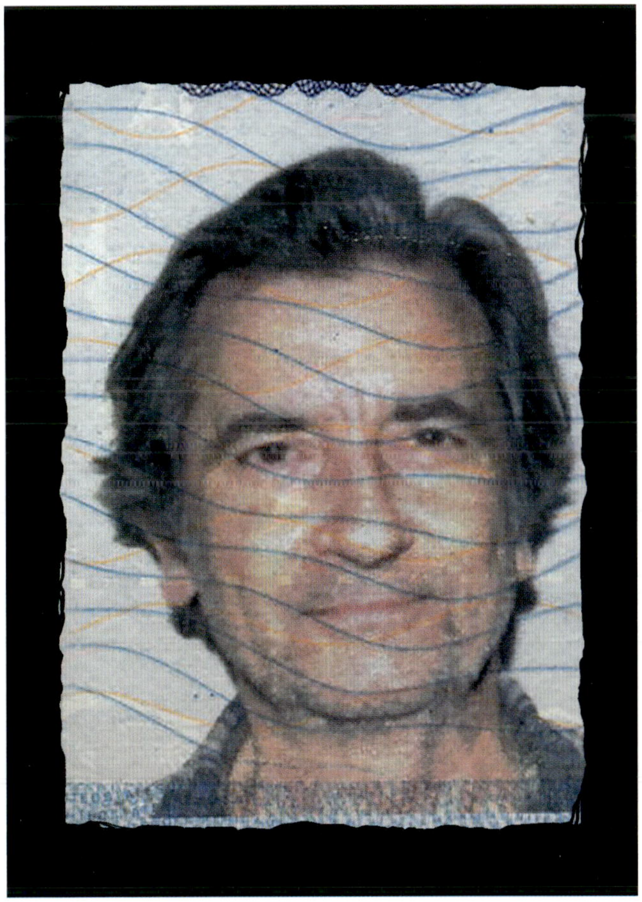

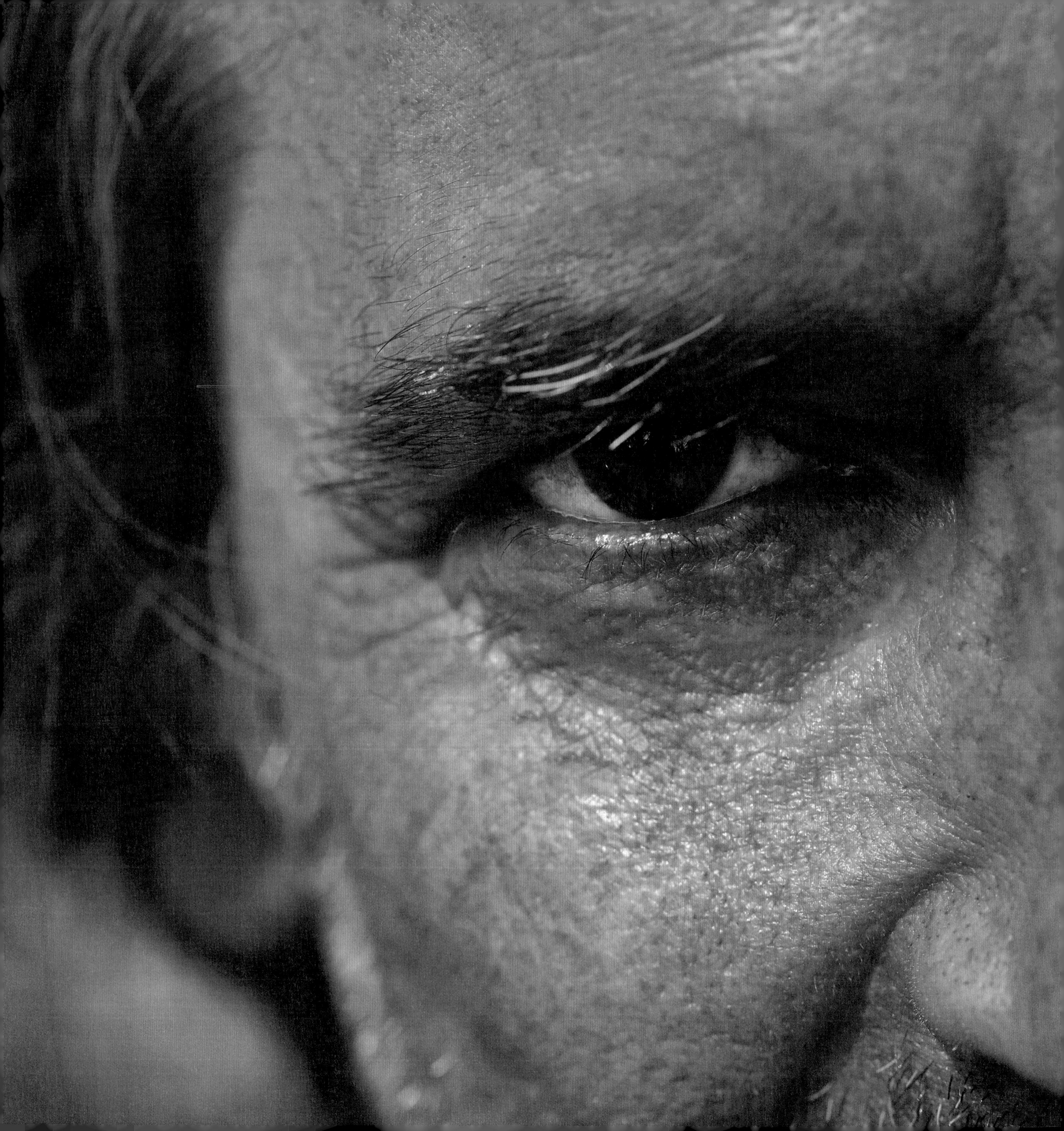

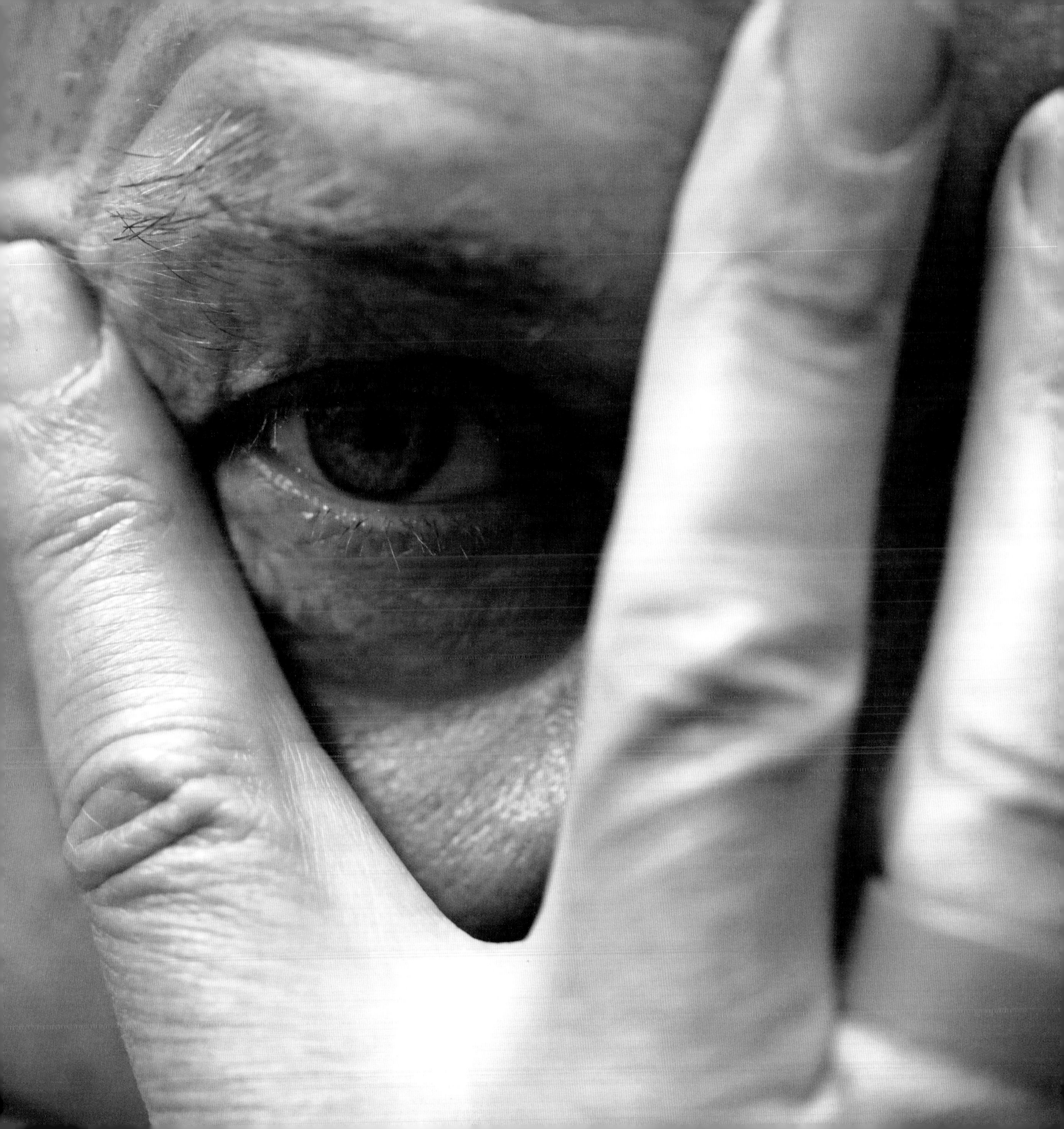

BRIAN ENO

Born in Woodbridge, England; May 15, 1948
Eyes: blue

I am a massive fan of many of the albums Brian Eno has produced with some of my favorite artists. He covered dad's song 'Mother of Violence', which is a track my mother helped write the lyrics for and has always been a personal favorite of mine.

I don't know him personally, although he lives right around the corner from my dad, and they've worked together and see each other socially. Even though he visits my father every now and then, to me he's always remained a kind of enigmatic figure.

He has an amazing combination art and music studio in Notting Hill, with skylights and windows everywhere. It's a photographer's dream. When I arrived, he was working on an art project. He invited me but was absorbed in his work, which was amazing to watch for a moment. We quickly took the shot and he got back to work. He's an inspiring person and obviously extremely creative. A man who inhabits his own magical world.

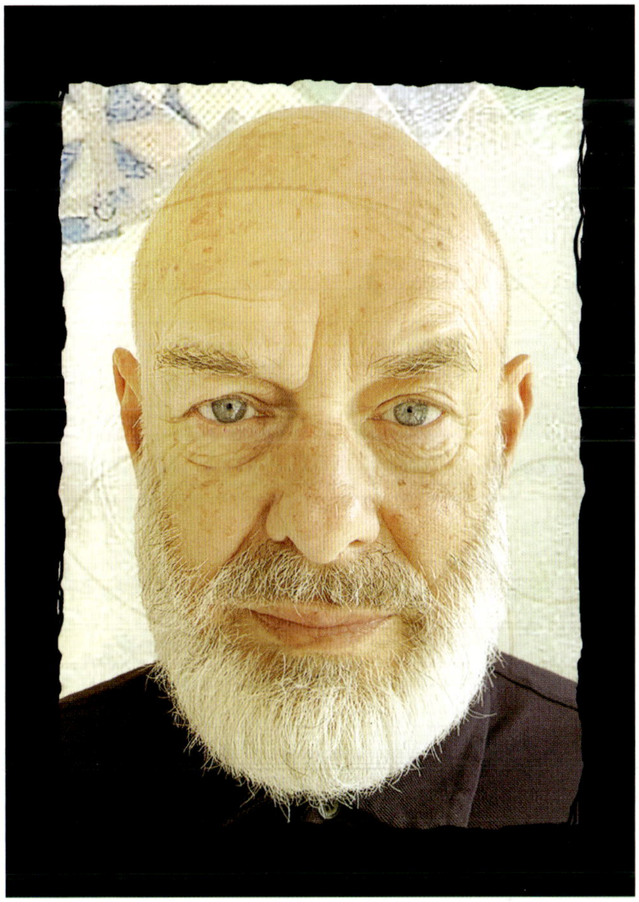

ROSANNA ARQUETTE

Born in New York City, New York; August 10, 1959
Eyes: blue

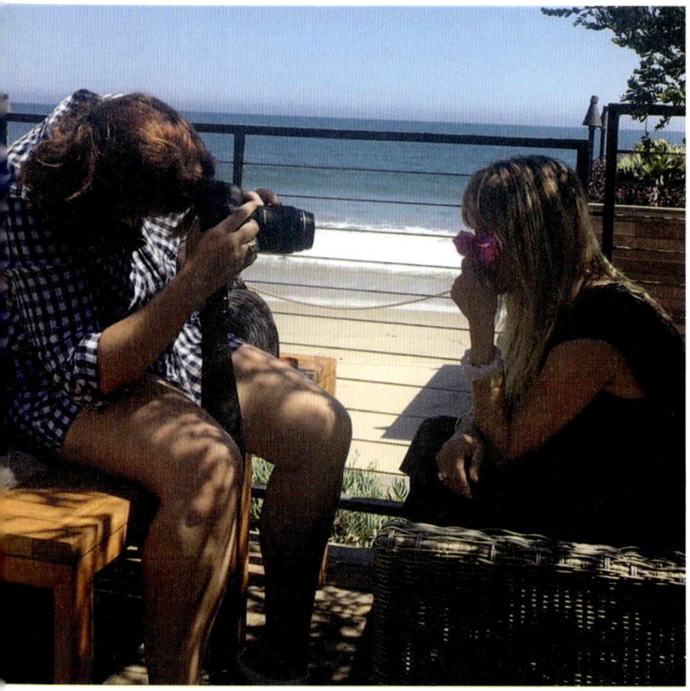

My sister and I spent our early childhood in the countryside. Up until then, we had been building fires, making dams and playing in the woods. It was a life utterly removed from the LA world of music and movies. The first time we met Rosanna was at dad's studio. She put on a Prince song. We stared at this strange beautiful woman dancing around in these super cool clothes, and were in awe of this unknown world she represented. Rosanna had recently starred opposite Madonna in *Desperately Seeking Susan*. As 13-year-old Madonna superfans, this made it hard for us not to be fascinated with her and the glamorous Hollywood lifestyle Rosanna embodied.

Looking back, her approach to life was kind, grounded and authentic, in a scene that was often shallow. She became a big influence in my life and was instrumental in encouraging me to choose a college in New York, the place I still live to this day. She remains a close friend.

I went to shoot her in California, at the beach in front of the Soho House in Malibu. We sat outside among these beautiful purple flowers. I wanted to shoot her with the flowers in front of her eyes. I always thought Rosanna was very beautiful but she also has a quirky side and a very warm heart. I wanted to create a slightly blurry, almost painterly image. It's difficult to photograph someone you know really well, so I thought perhaps something a little more abstract would be interesting.

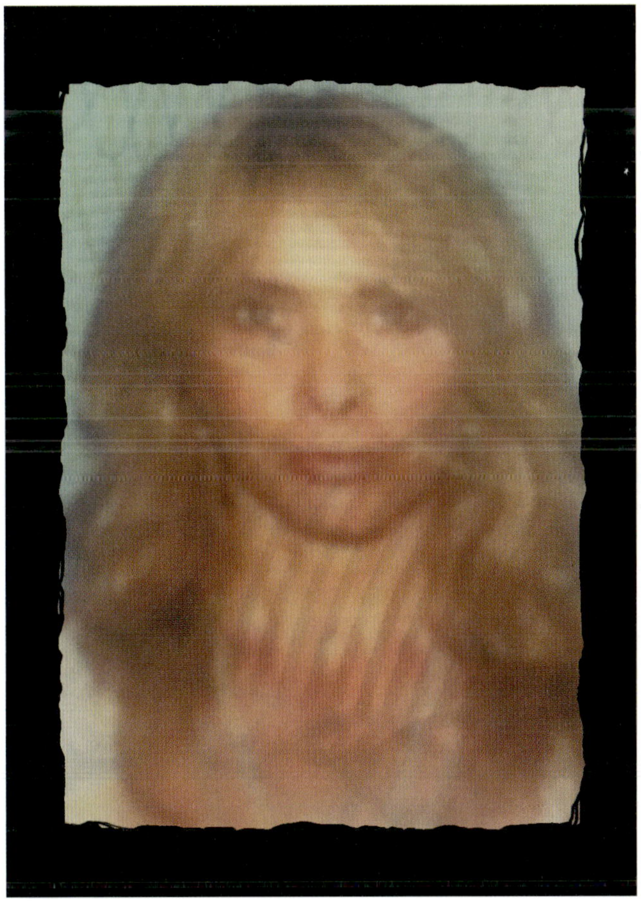

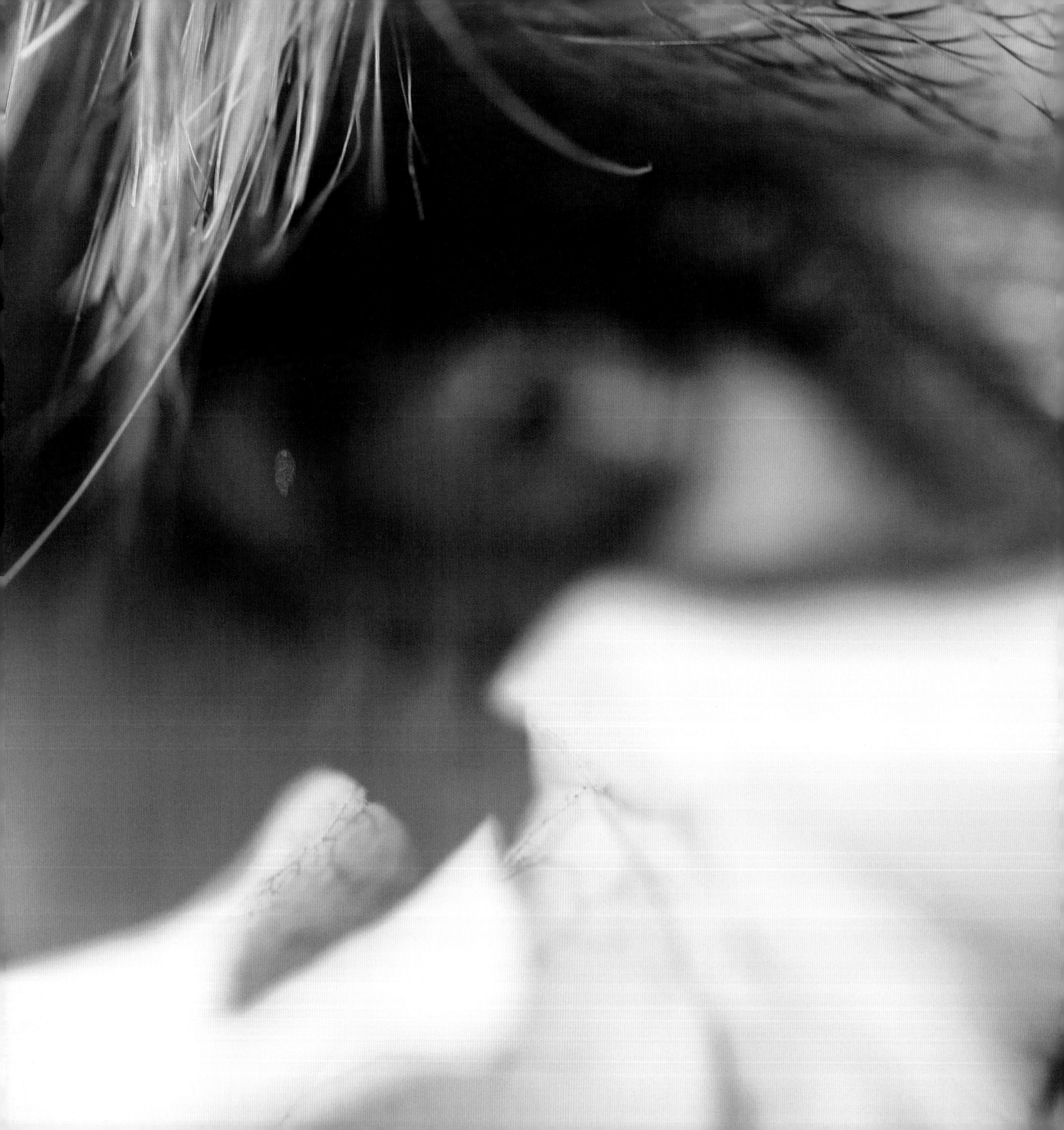

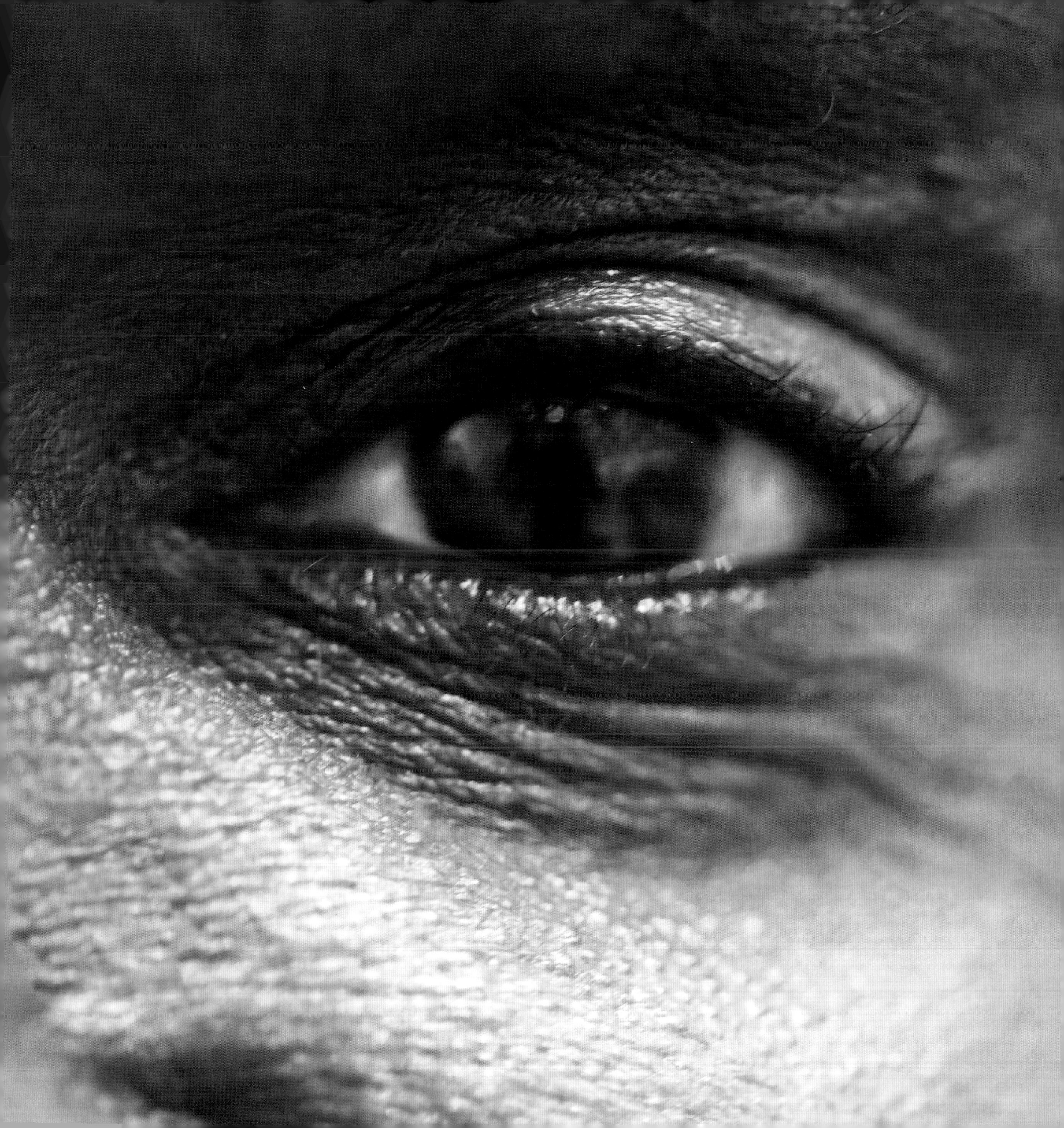

ANGÉLIQUE KIDJO

Born in Ouidah, Benin; July 14, 1960
Eyes: dark brown

They say good things come in small packages, and that's certainly true of Angelique Kidjo. The Grammy-award-winning singer was born in the city of Ouidah, on the coast of Benin in West Africa. She is a tornado of life force, smiles and infectious laughter.

Angelique has a vivid *joie de vivre* to her that's impossible to ignore. She radiates light, and she puts her warm-heartedness into action: she is a Unicef good will ambassador, and through her Batonga Foundation she helps make education available to African girls.

Growing up, I spent a great deal of time in Africa, as we had a family home in Senegal for several years. The infectious feeling of the music and dance that comes from the Senegalese people is something I love. Angelique brings that same feeling out in me. When you see her perform – you just can't sit down. You have to get up and dance. If you aren't dancing, she will come into the crowd and make you get up. I love that about her. She brings out the best in people.

For this shoot, I visited her at her home in Brooklyn, which she shares with her husband and songwriting collaborator, Jean Hébrail. Angelique is an amazing cook. I walked in and it smelled incredible. You immediately feel like you're at home with her. She has a great sense of humor and she's always joking.

I had her sit on the couch. I wanted to capture that joyous feeling in her, but, of course, you have to sit still for a photograph, and there wasn't a lot of daylight left, so it was a struggle to photograph her – but I finally got the shot I was looking for and the energy in her eyes.

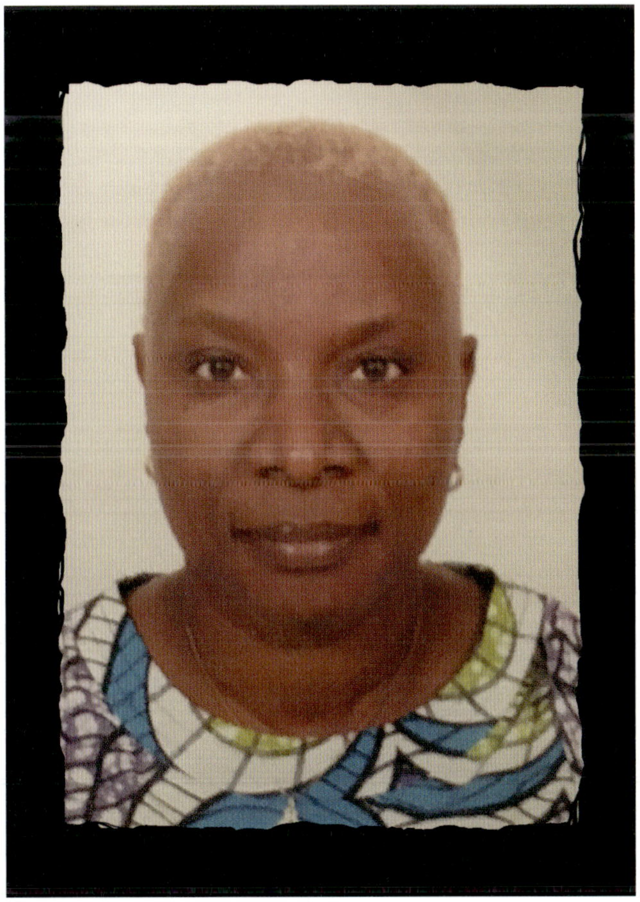

PAUL SIMON

Born in Newark, New Jersey; October 13, 1941
Eyes: brown

Paul Simon is one of my favorite artists of all time. I went to his house in New Canaan, Connecticut, which is a beautiful estate with a winding driveway nestled in a forest of trees.

Edie Brickell answered the door and told me Paul was in the studio. He was recording a cover version of my dad's song "Biko" when I arrived, and I got to listen in on the session. It was fascinating watching Paul do a cover of one of dad's songs and making it his own. Paul Simon is of course renowned as an incredible guitar player, whereas my dad wrote the song on piano and it was especially interesting to see how Paul re-voiced the chords on the guitar, exploring several harmonic variations. It was a real privilege to see that process unfold in real time.

I did a quick interview with him about why he chose "Biko" and we talked about the influence of South African music. He spoke about recording *Graceland* and how that album changed his life. The entire experience was fascinating but unfortunately it's one of my least favorite photos. But he ended up loving the photograph and wanted to use it as an album cover. You can't see his eye, it's just his thumb. It's such a close up that you can see he has a callus on his thumb from playing guitar. In a sense it's nice to have a hidden eye in the book.

After spending about two hours at his studio, he drove me to the train station. In the car, he asked if I wanted to hear some new songs he was working on and he started playing me stuff and talking about it. He was very excited and happy to share and it was almost as if he became a different person, when he began talking about his music. It reminded me of being in the car with my dad as a child and him playing me tracks he was working on. He always said the car is the best place to listen to the music. The whole visit to Paul's was an unforgettable experience.

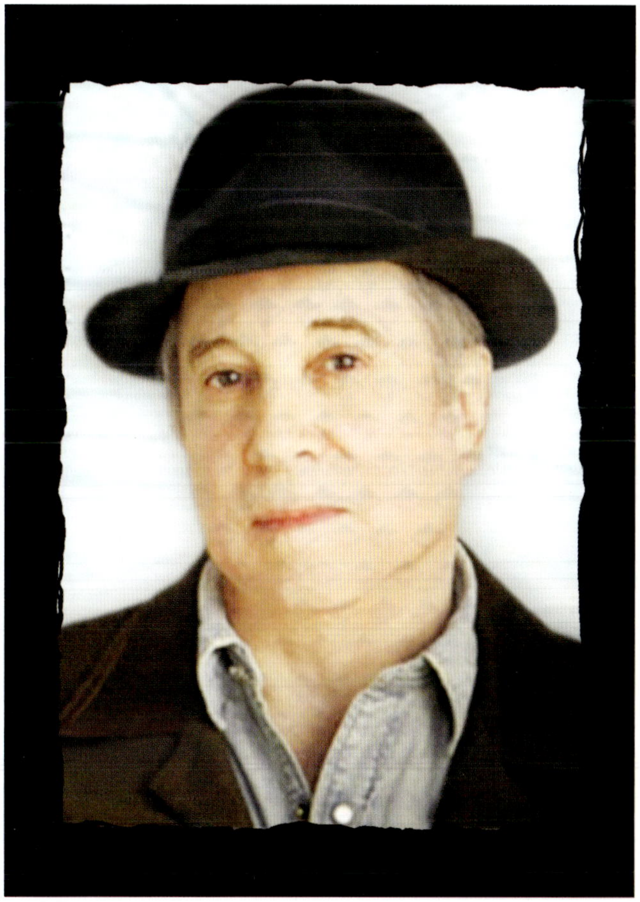

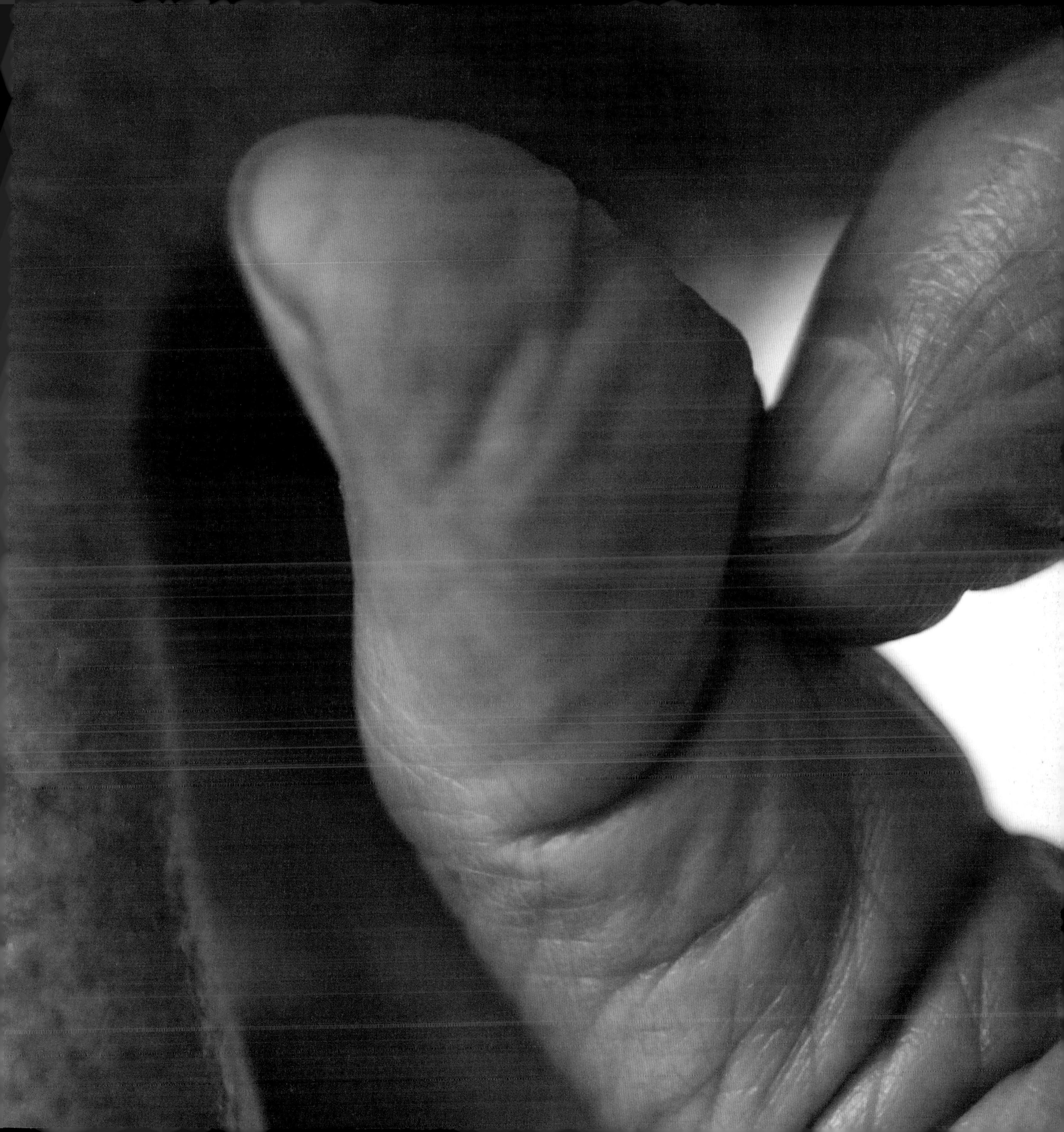

ANNIE LENNOX

Born in Aberdeen, Scotland; December 25, 1954
Eyes: blue

Effortlessly cool and imbued with magnetic allure, Annie Lennox is the kind of person who would attract attention even if she weren't famous. Although she has met my dad a few times, I had never met her myself. I'd grown up loving her in Eurythmics music videos but to meet her in person is something entirely different.

I got in touch with her through my friend Bill Shipsey at Art for Amnesty, and it turned out she was coming to New York for 24 hours and staying at a hotel near where I lived. It was a small room, dimly lit. Her physical presence immediately conveys a quiet sense of power and yet she is disarmingly warm and lively in conversation. Her wide-mouthed smile exudes enthusiasm but it's those piercing blue-grey eyes that stop you in your tracks. She's from Aberdeen and has a wonderful brogue. We chatted for a few minutes and then put a chair by the window and quickly took the photo.

She was completely lovely and easygoing. Although her face has a few lines and wrinkles she was utterly unconcerned. I found her refreshingly centered. She's one of those rare people who just knows exactly who she is.

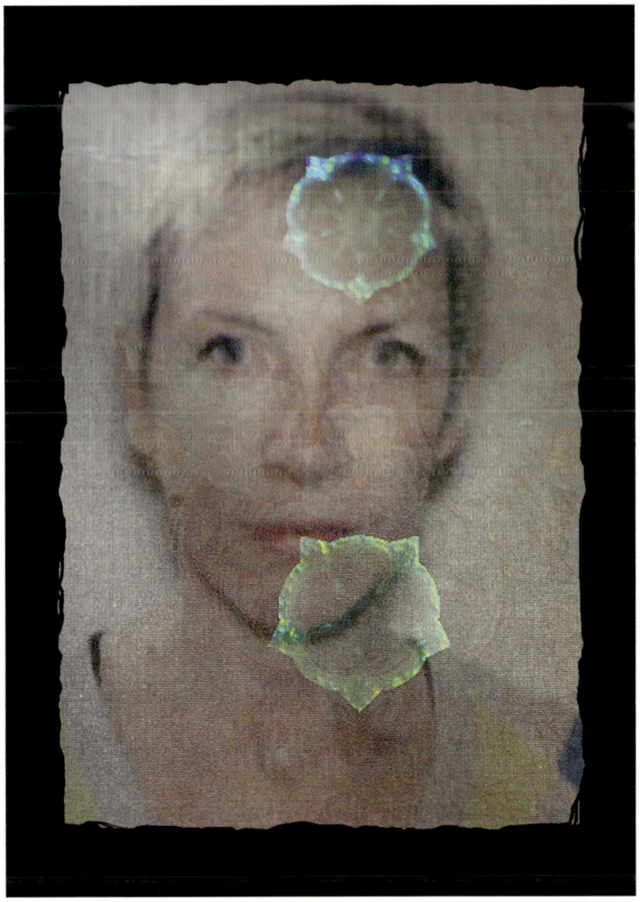

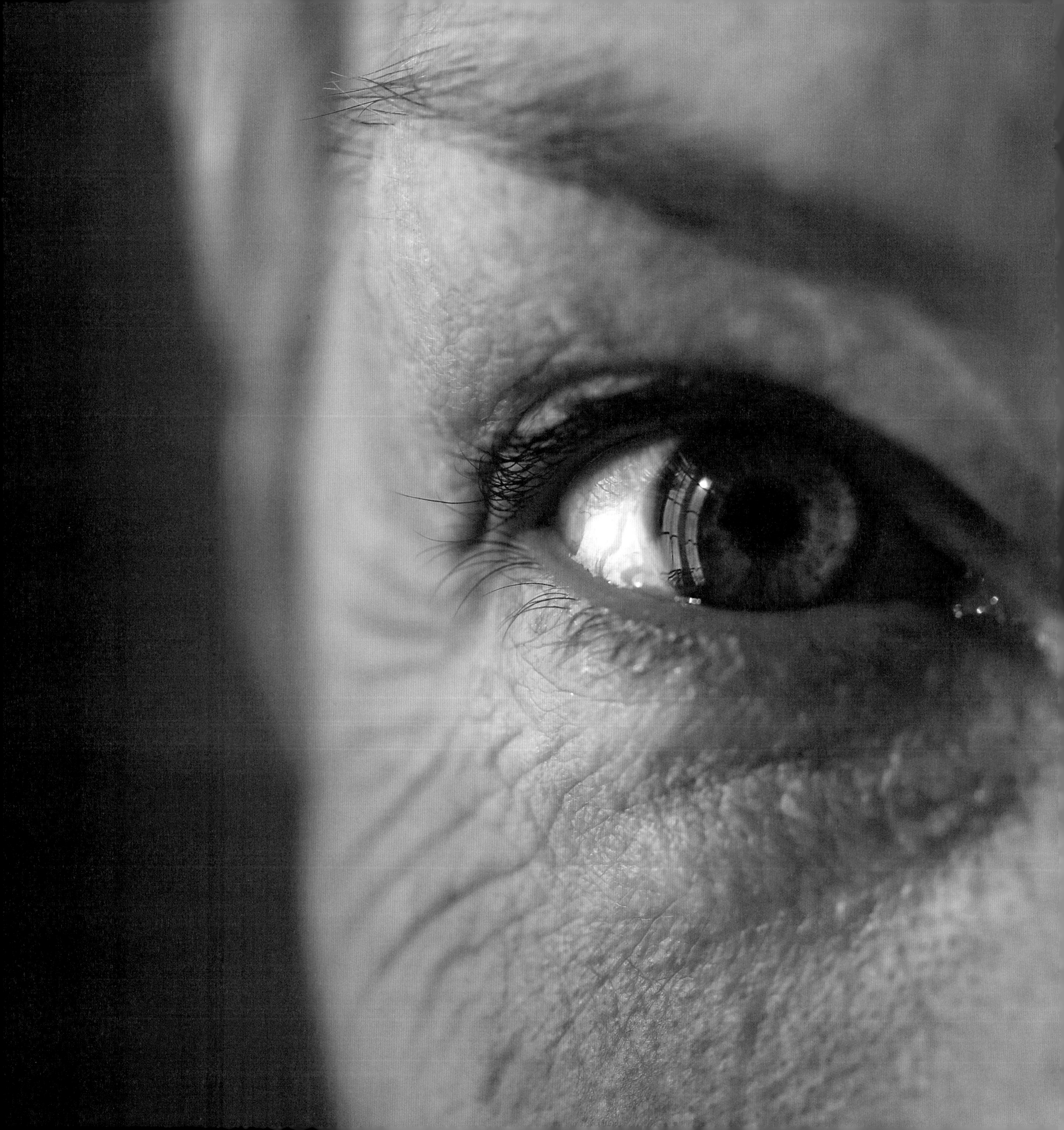

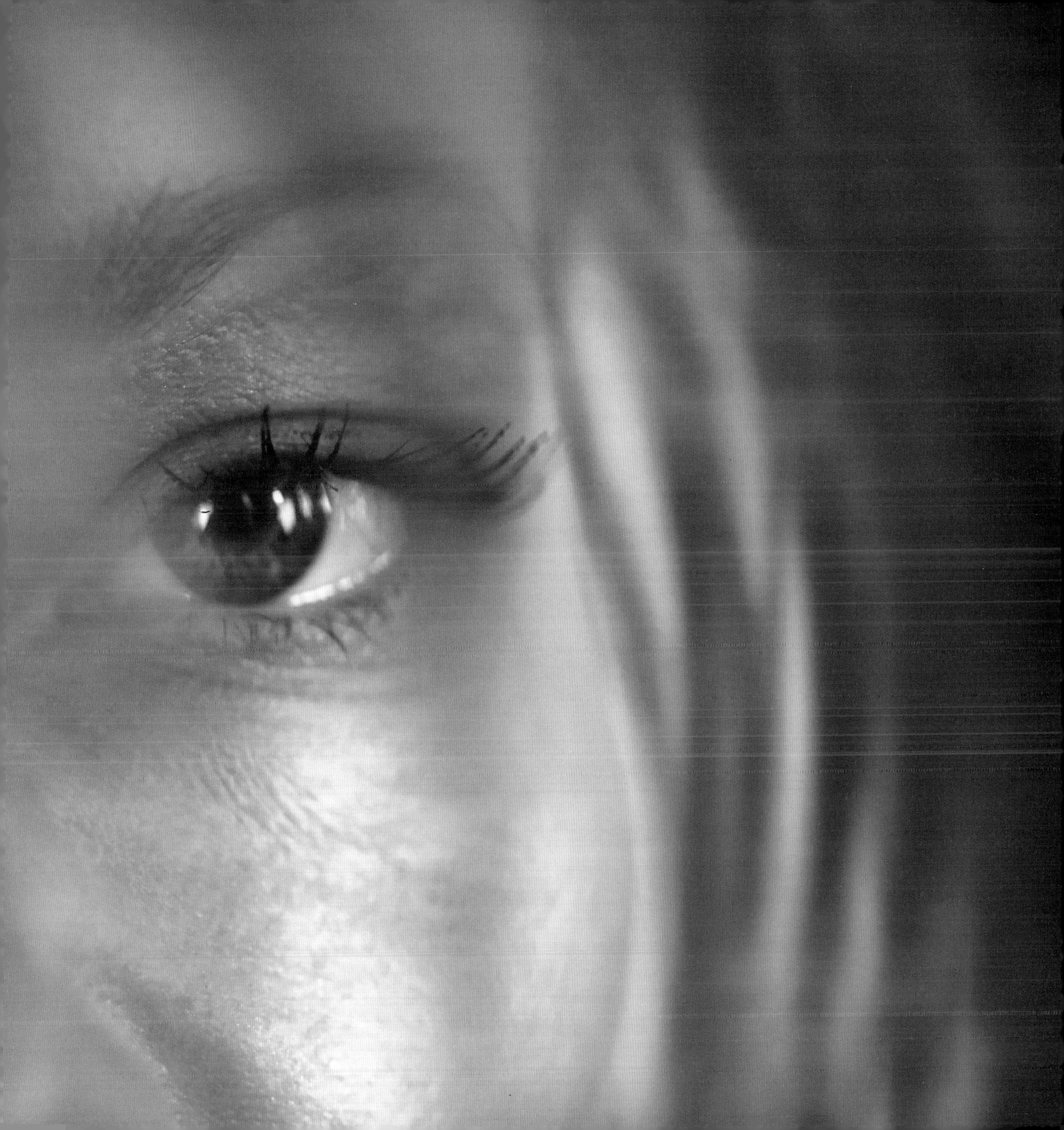

SAMANTHA MATHIS

Born in New York City, New York; May 12, 1970
Eyes: blue

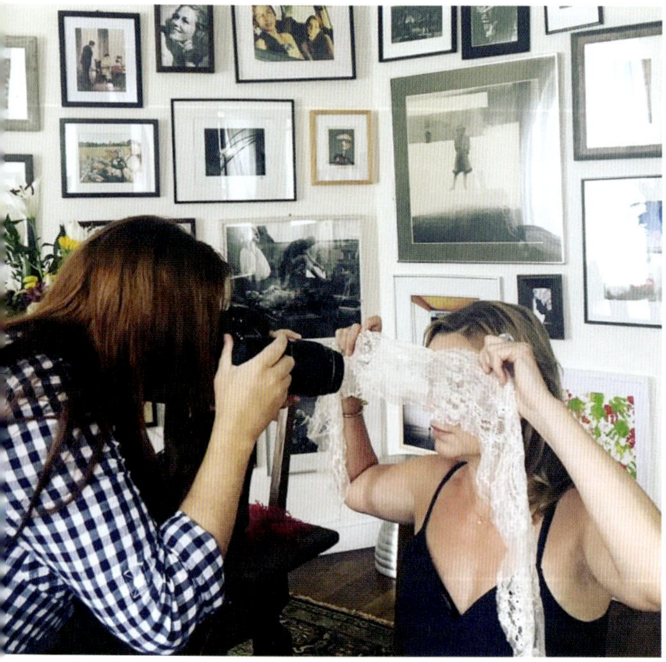

In addition to being a great actress, Samantha is a lovely person. We first met at a dinner about 10 years ago through our mutual friend Reyna Mastrosimone. She is a beautiful spirit: very grounded, and we share similar values.

We did this shoot at my house, and because she's a friend, I felt comfortable being a bit more experimental. This image was also taken during the beginning phase of this project so I didn't yet have a definite sense of the style of the book.

We experimented with layering different props. Because there aren't a lot of women in the book, it was important to me to make this a very feminine image. I wanted to do something soft, so I layered her with lace and feathers and beads. I feel like this image expresses her character and her subtle, inner beauty. You can see her goodness. It's sort of abstract, but I think it's a beautiful image of a beautiful person.

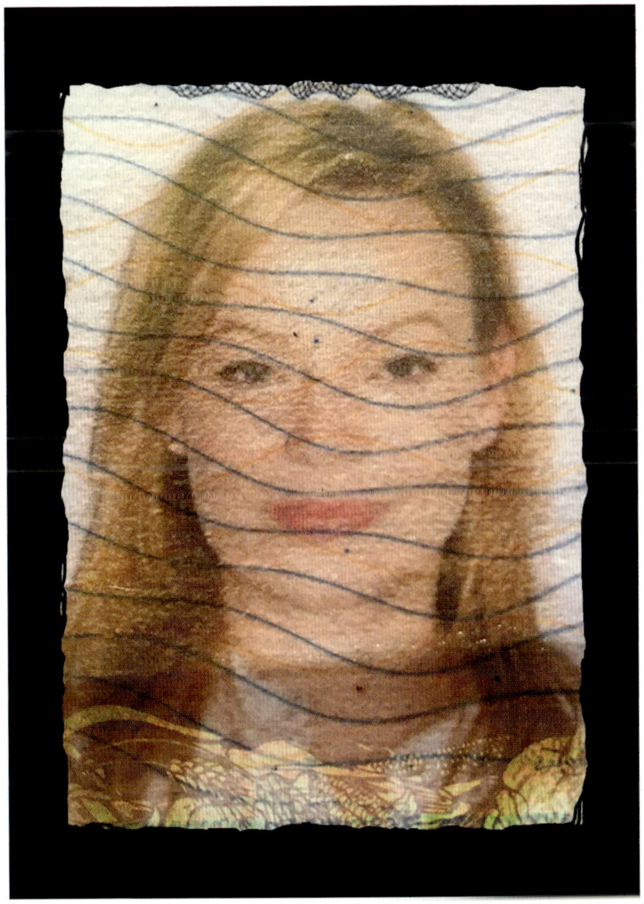

BETH ORTON

Born in East Dereham, England; December 14, 1970
Eyes: blue

When I did this shoot, Beth was coming through New York on tour, and had a show that night near my home in Williamsburg, Brooklyn. She was doing a rehearsal in South Brooklyn, in a little room with a back garden. The building had a tiny door that was unmarked; you wouldn't know it was a rehearsal studio. I went in and it was pitch black. I thought, there's no way I can shoot in such a dark place; I'll have to take her out in the street. But Beth told me there was a back garden, and I wanted to try something different, so I asked her to write out the lyrics to one of her songs on a piece of paper. Then I cut a hole in the paper and shot her eye through it.

A lot of these people who I have shot before a show are squeezing me in while they were in the middle of doing something. And if it's pre-show, I find people are nervous or hyped up trying to get themselves ready. It can be a hard time to get someone to focus. But it's an interesting time, because you're seeing a side of them that's more vulnerable or nervous, which is why most artists don't want to do anything until after the show.

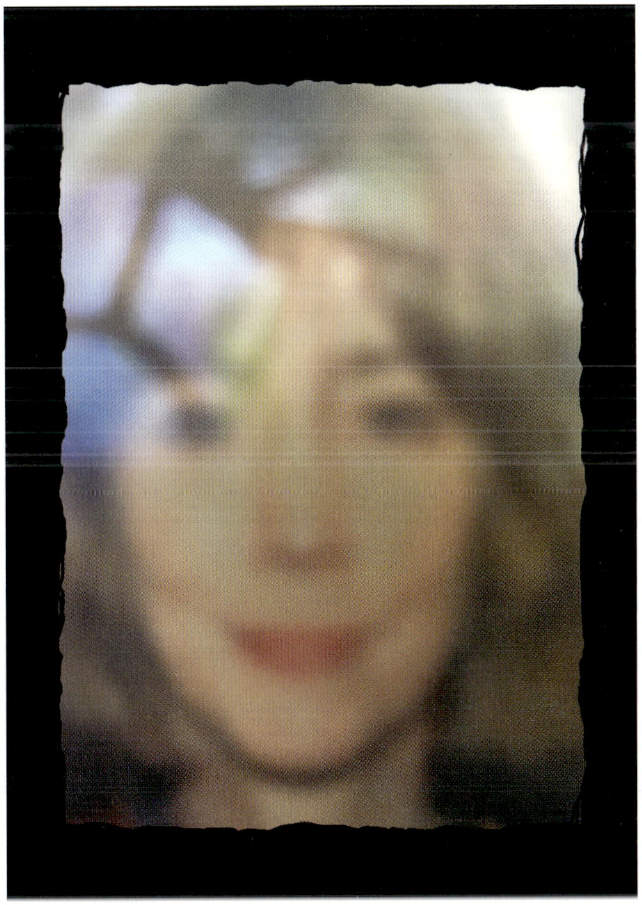

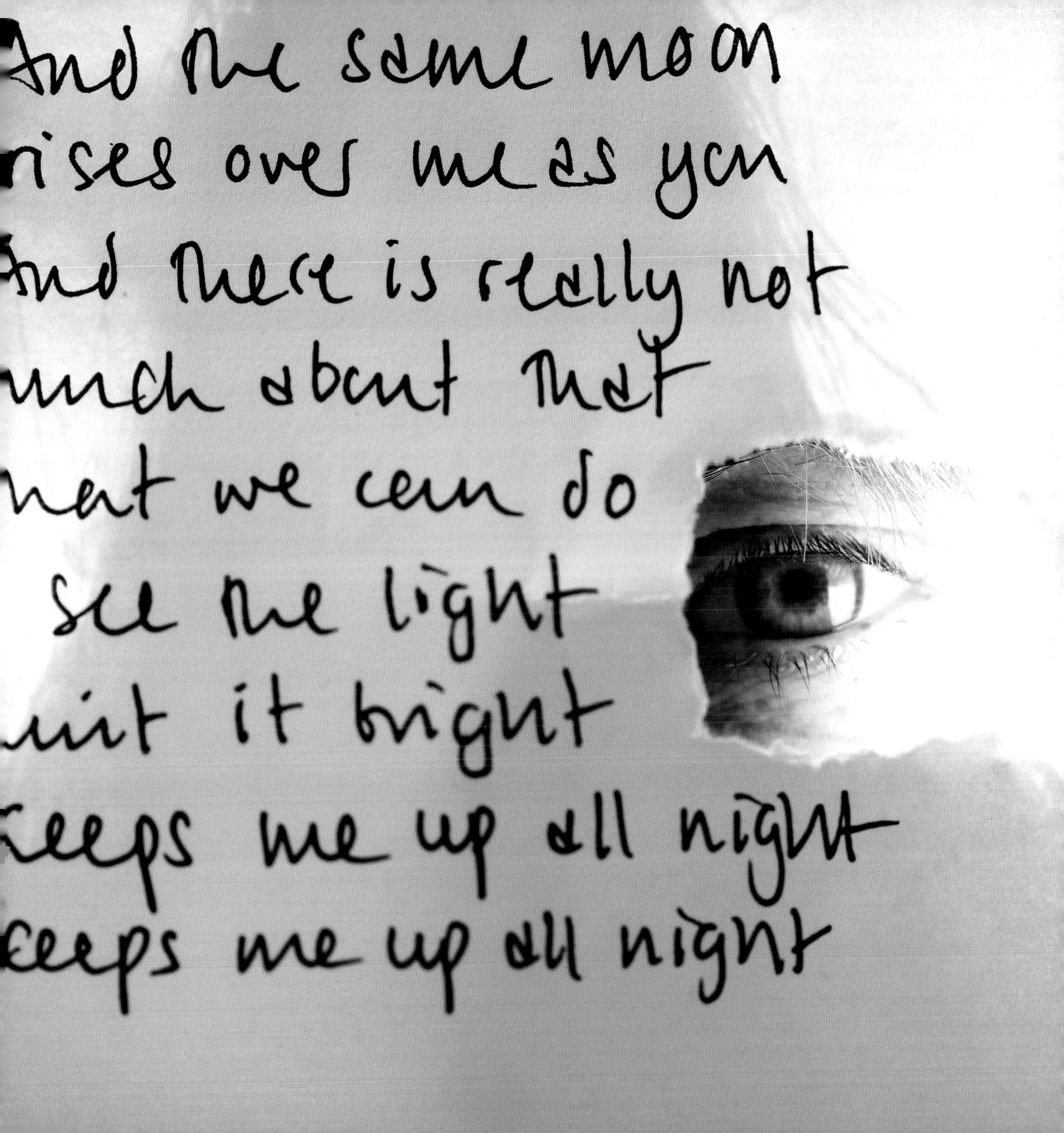
And the same moon
rises over me as you
And there is really not
much about that
hat we can do
see the light
uit it bright
eeps me up all night
eeps me up all night

KEVIN BACON

Born in Philadelphia, Pennsylvania; July 8, 1958
Eyes: blue

Before meeting him to take this photo, I had heard many stories about what a great guy Kevin Bacon is. I am pleased to say that those stories are true.

He lives on the Upper West Side, in a beautiful apartment, overlooking Central Park. In order to arrange this photo shoot, I had been texting with Kevin's assistant, but never had any direct contact with him. When I arrived at his apartment and told the doorman I was there to see Kevin Bacon, the doorman said: "Oh, he just stepped out".

I called his assistant, and 10 minutes later I got a call back and she said there was a miscommunication of some kind and apparently he'd gone to brunch with his friends. With almost anyone else, that would have been the end of it, and we would have simply rescheduled the shoot. But Kevin said he felt bad, immediately left his friends in the restaurant, jumped in a cab and came to meet me. His first words were a profuse apology about the mix up. It was not a big deal to me, as I hadn't waited long but he seemed genuinely sorry about it.

I like this shot of him because it looks very dreamlike. It's like he's in a serene and blissful world. The moment was all the more remarkable since right up until the actual photo, it was all rush, rush, rush. Then there was this sudden overwhelming sense of calm, which you can see in the picture, like that moment after a thunderstorm when everything is still.

And then he rushed off back to his brunch again.

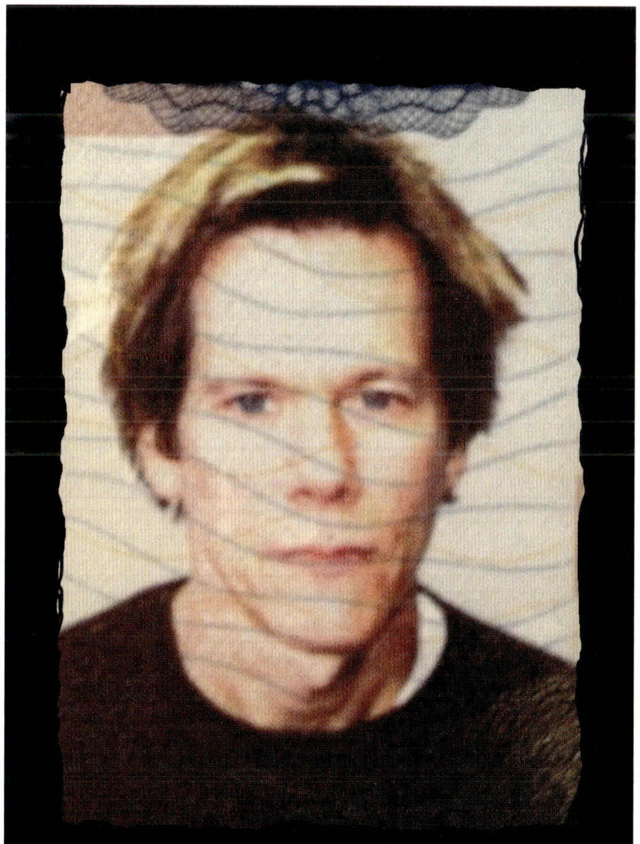

It’s like he’s in a serene
and blissful world.
The moment was all the more
remarkable since right up
until the actual photo, it was
all rush, rush, rush.

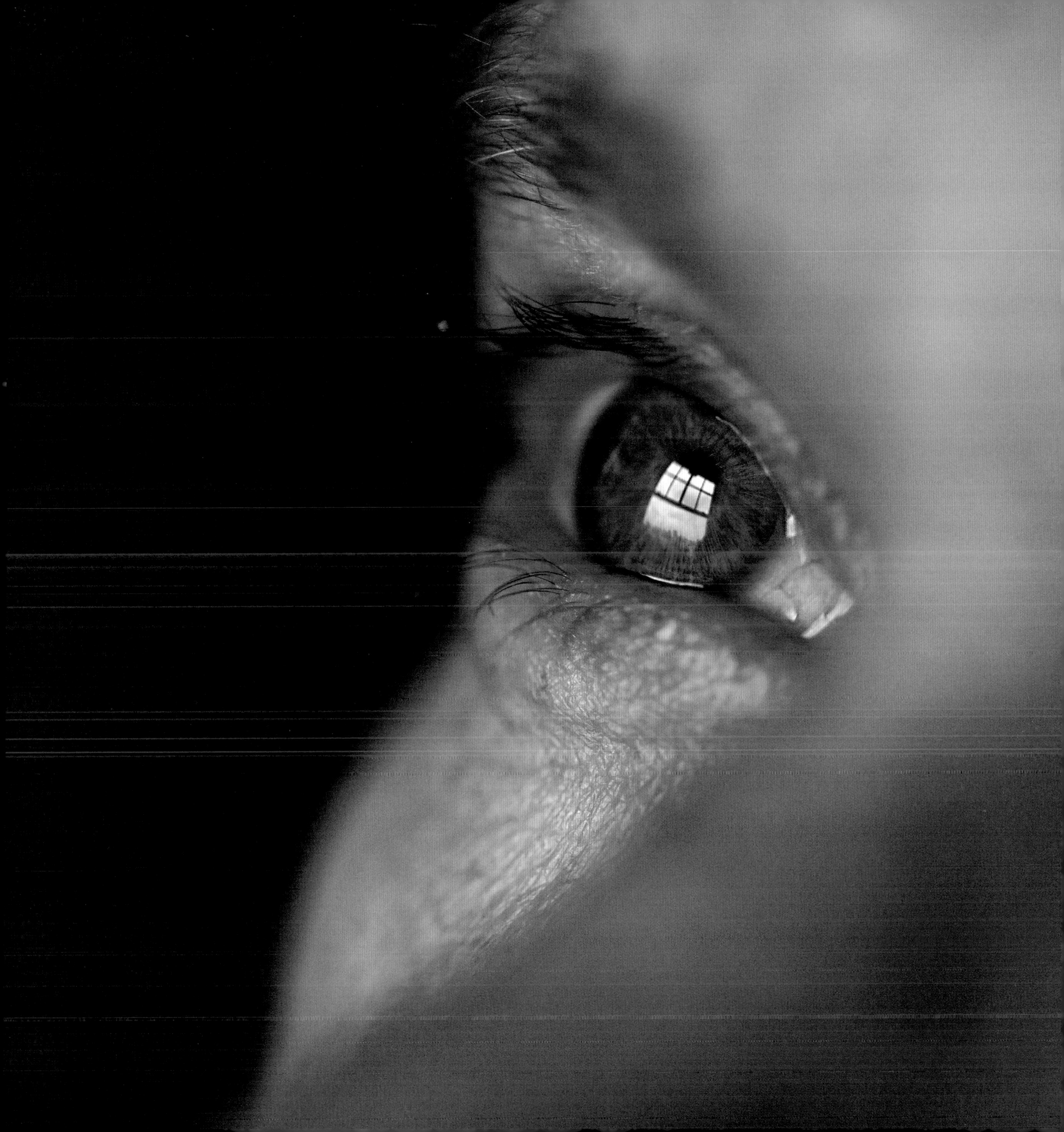

JOHNNY DEPP

Born in Owensboro, Kentucky; June 9, 1963
Eyes: dark brown

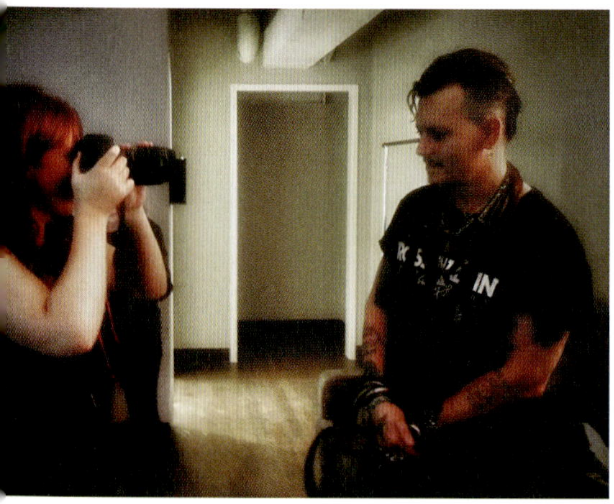

In general, I don't get nervous around celebrities but as I walked into the backstage area in Coney Island to shoot Johnny Depp I had butterflies in my stomach.

Johnny was scheduled to perform with his band, the Hollywood Vampires that night. I wasn't there to photograph him for this book. Instead, he had agreed to participate in another shoot I was doing for an organisation called The Voice Project, which aims to bring attention to political prisoners and promote artistic expression as an agent of social change.

I found myself backstage in a dressing room, where Ian Hunter, Alice Cooper and Joe Perry were among the revellers. A lot of people were coming and going. Smoke, laughter and loud music filled the air. It was more like a party than a typical backstage experience, and I waited, quietly watching everyone around me.

Finally, Johnny walked up to me and said, "Let's do it." We took the photos for The Voice Project, and then somehow I mustered the courage to ask him to pose for this book.

I wasn't sure if he would say yes, but I had bought a pair of glasses in a thrift store in the East Village, and taken them along in case he would to pose in them. It was an antique pair of old spectacles, with one lens missing. Ironically, he told me he was partially blind out of that eye that had no lens.

The moment we started shooting, although we could still hear the backstage rumblings outside, it was like he flipped a switch and suddenly became completely focused on what we were doing. I felt we captured a great moment.

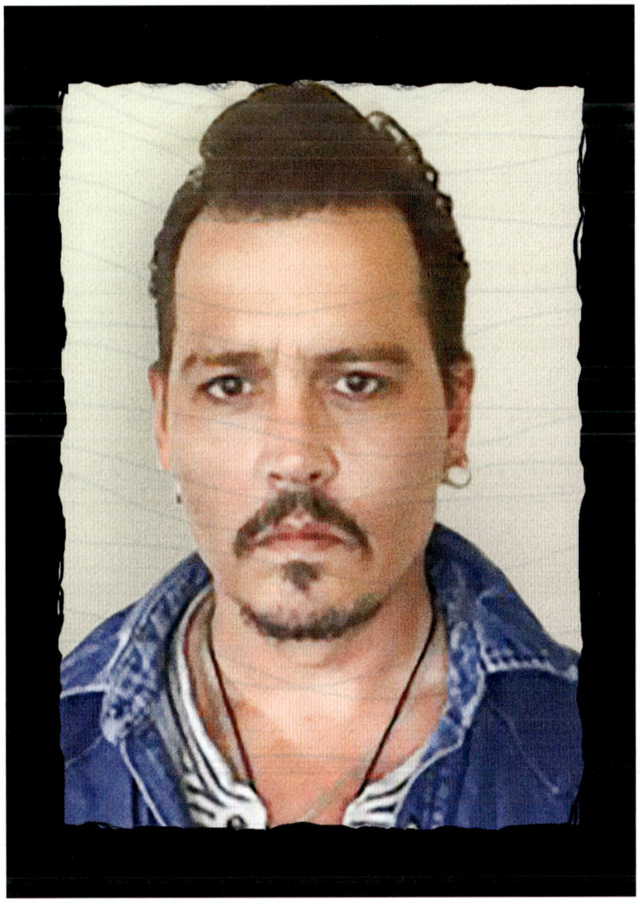

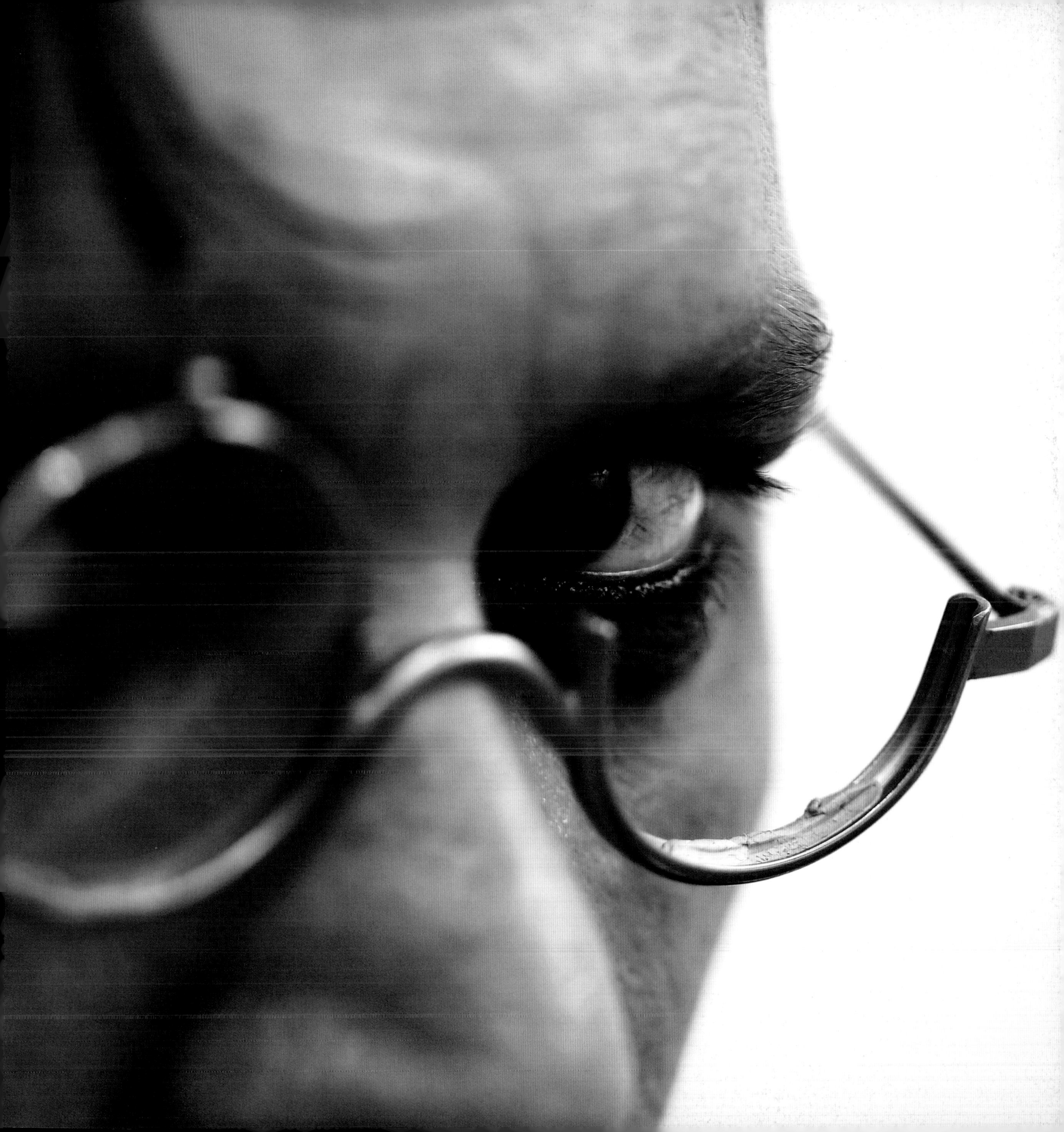

MARY GAUTHIER

Born in New Orleans, Louisiana; March 11, 1962
Eyes: blue

I had a wonderful couple of days in Key West where I travelled from NYC to shoot Mary. She is a songwriter and author and was taking part in a writing residency at The Studios of Key West.

Mary is an incredible musician with an authentic sound that cuts right to the heart of her storytelling. I got to see her perform with her partner, Jaimee Harris, on the roof of the studios. I was transported into the lives and stories of the characters that inhabit her songs. Just as they finished, the skies opened up and it started to rain almost as if I was now anointed into the world of Mary Gauthier.

This photo was taken at her work desk, a place of intense focus for Mary, and it resonated with that energy. I wanted to get in tighter and shoot this moment of thought.

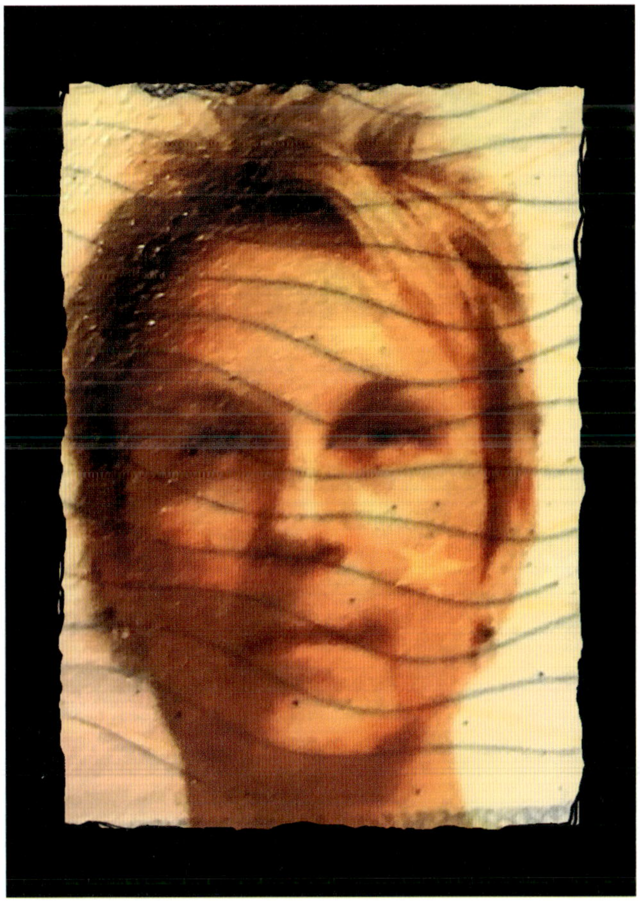

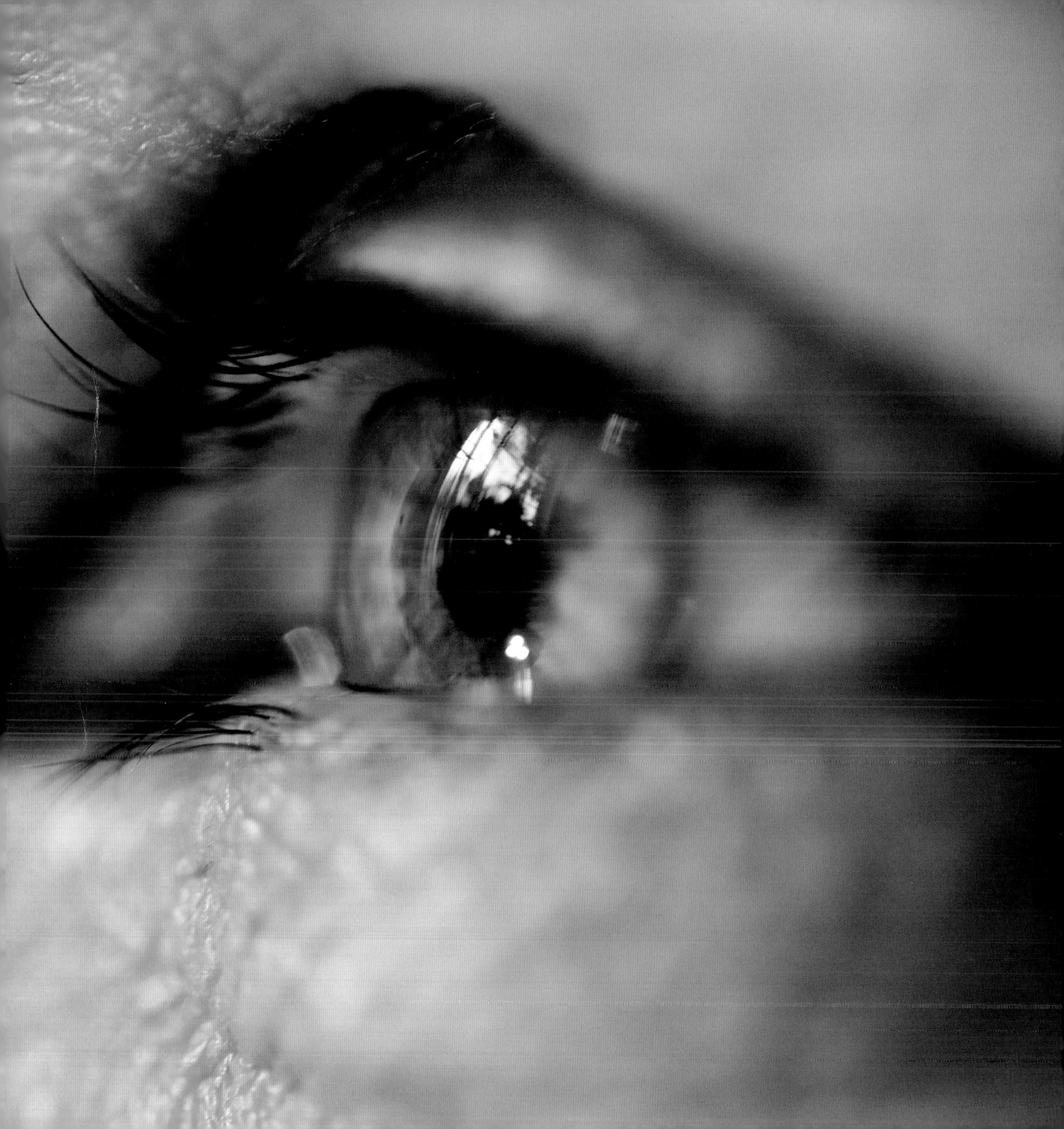

RANDY NEWMAN

Born in Los Angeles, California; November 28, 1943
Eyes: blue

Randy Newman straddles two different eras. We know him more recently for composing hit songs for animated films such as *Toy Story*, but a generation of fans fell in love with Randy Newman decades earlier for his mordant but tender songwriting. My dad co-wrote a song with Randy called "That'll Do, Pig" for the animated movie *Babe: Pig In The City*.

Randy was one of the artists featured on the *And I'll Scratch Yours* album covering dad's song "Big Time" and dad enlisted me to take a shot of him for the album. Dad's original concept was taking shots of fingerprints and eyes. So this was one of the first photos I took and I wasn't completely clear of the artistic direction I wanted to take. I began shooting his finger and as I asked him to put it up to his eye, I saw that the true strength of the project lay in the eyes alone, they told more of a story, and *Eye-D* was born.

After the shoot Randy showed me around his house and sat down at his grand piano and played for a little while. It was during this moment that I could feel the way he almost disappears into the music, immersing himself like a classical piano composer in a world of his imagination.

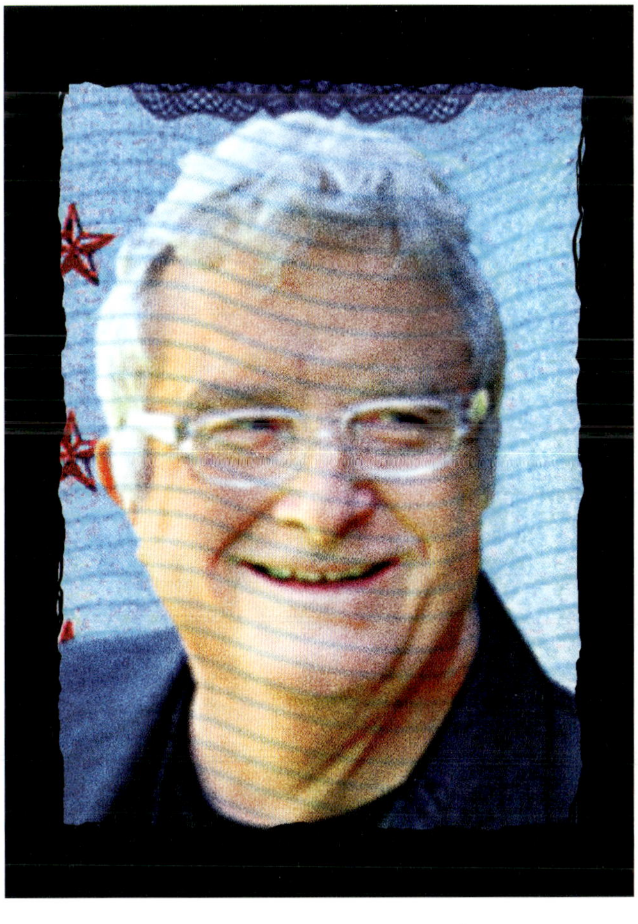

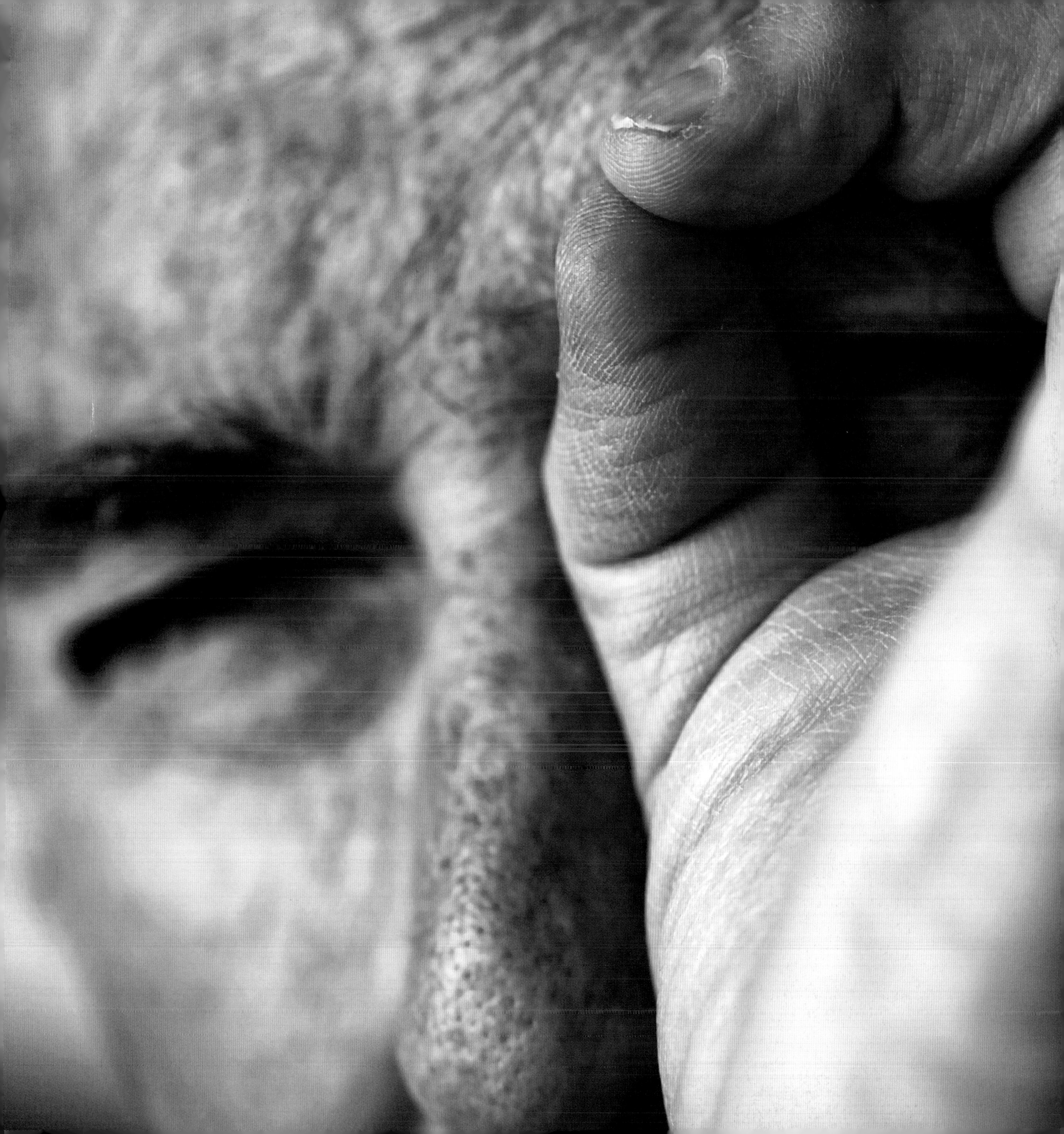

ROHAN MARLEY

Born in Kingston, Jamaica; May 19, 1972
Eyes: dark brown

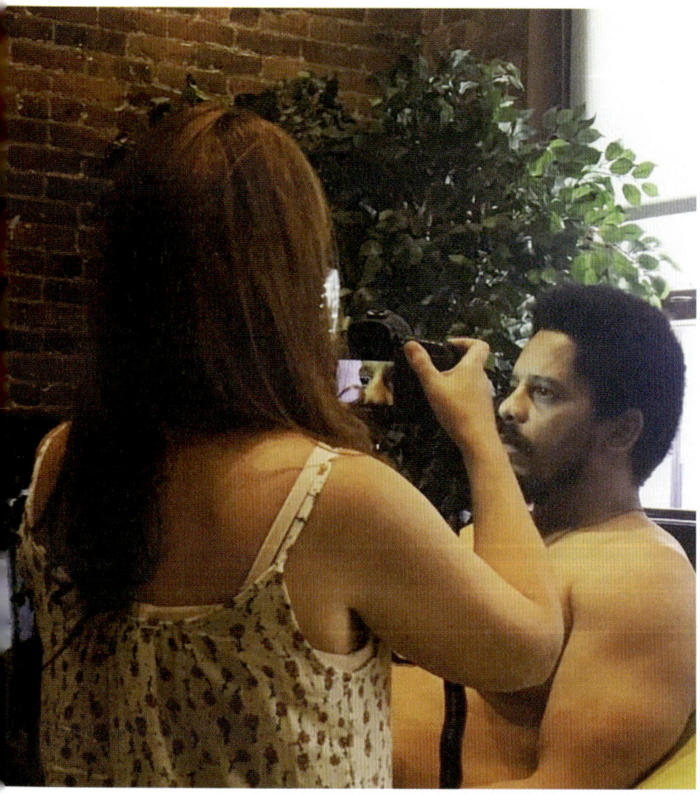

As anyone who is the son or daughter of a celebrity knows, it's not easy to do something that sets you apart from your famous parent and makes a name for yourself. Rohan Marley is clearly very much his own person. As the son of Bob Marley, Rohan has strived to achieve success on his own terms, from his role as a professional athlete (he played American football for the Miami Hurricanes and the Ottawa Rough Riders) to his entrepreneurial ventures (he runs his own coffee company).

I went to shoot him at his apartment in Tribeca, New York. Rohan was just getting out of bed, so it was an informal setting. I sat him by the window and took a close up of his eye. The way he was looking away from the camera made me think of the stoic look a sportsman has when their nation's anthem is being played before a game. Perhaps this is something a sportsman always keeps.

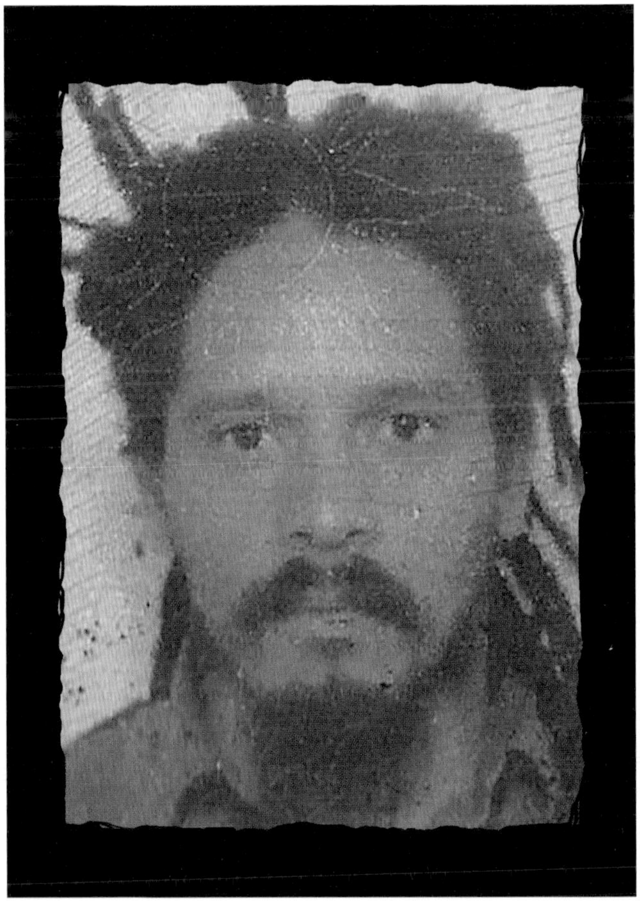

The way he was looking away
from the camera made me think
of the stoic look a sportsman
has when their nation's anthem
is being played before a game...

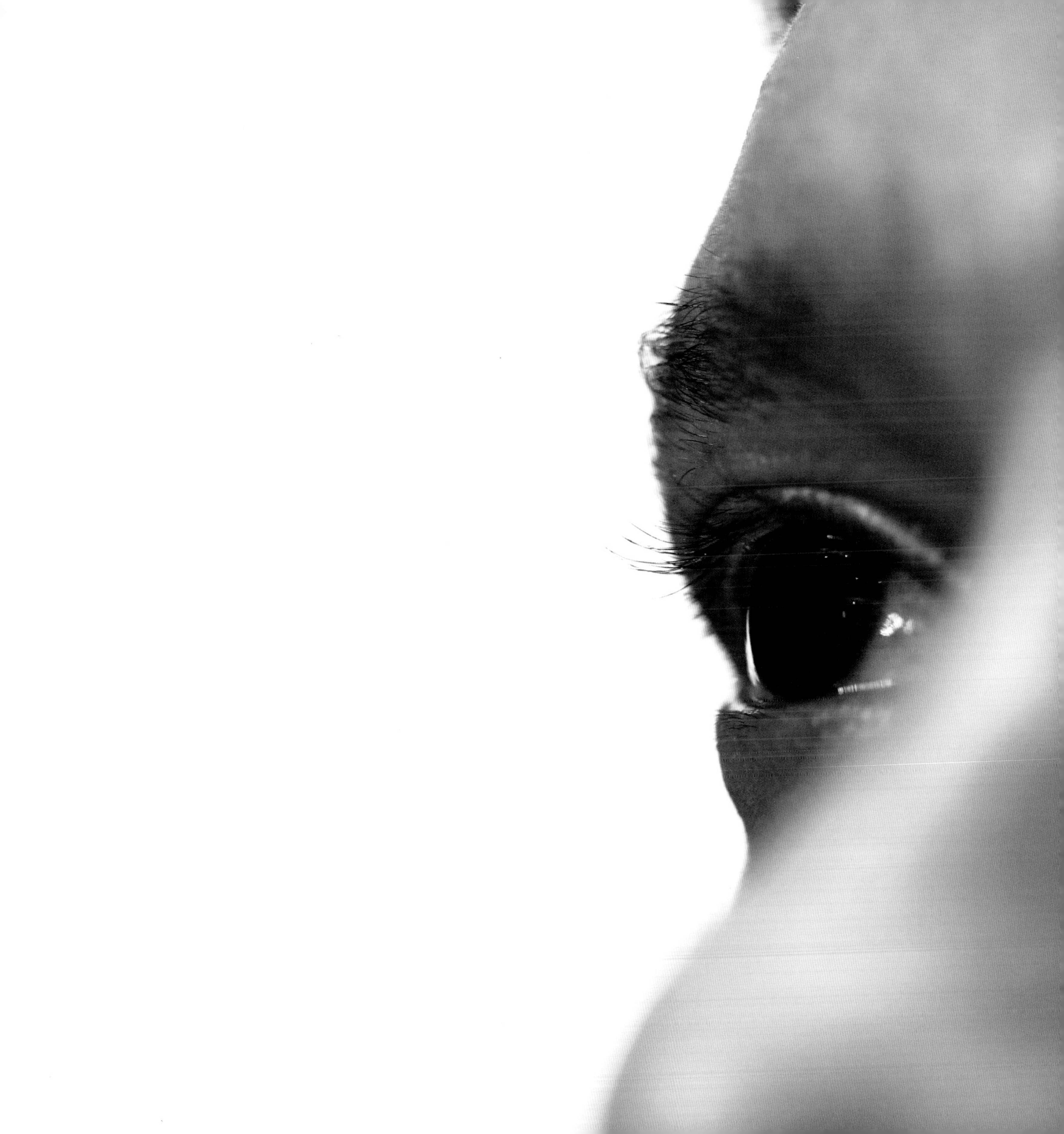

GLEN HANSARD

Born in Dublin, Ireland; April 21, 1970
Eyes: blue

Glen's starring role in the movie and Broadway play *Once* was an enormous phenomena. I've long been a fan of Glen's solo material and his band The Frames.

I have experienced a lot of Irish culture in my time, in which music and storytelling are an integral part of life. Melody and a love of language are just part of who they are in Ireland; it's the way you grow up. It's somewhat similar to what I experienced during my time in Senegal. That kind of seamless integration of musicality with life means music isn't just a profession or a passion, it's really a part of who you are. Storytelling is a part of their life.

My friend Bill Shipsey at Art for Amnesty connected Glen and I while he was visiting New York. Glen came over to my house to take the photos. At the time, I was living in the East Village. Glen arrived with his guitar and I thought it would be nice to shoot him with the neck of the guitar in the background and experimented with this as I liked the graphic of the guitar. However I felt in the end it may be a little cliched and wanted to cut straight to Glen's soul using a simple close up of his eye.

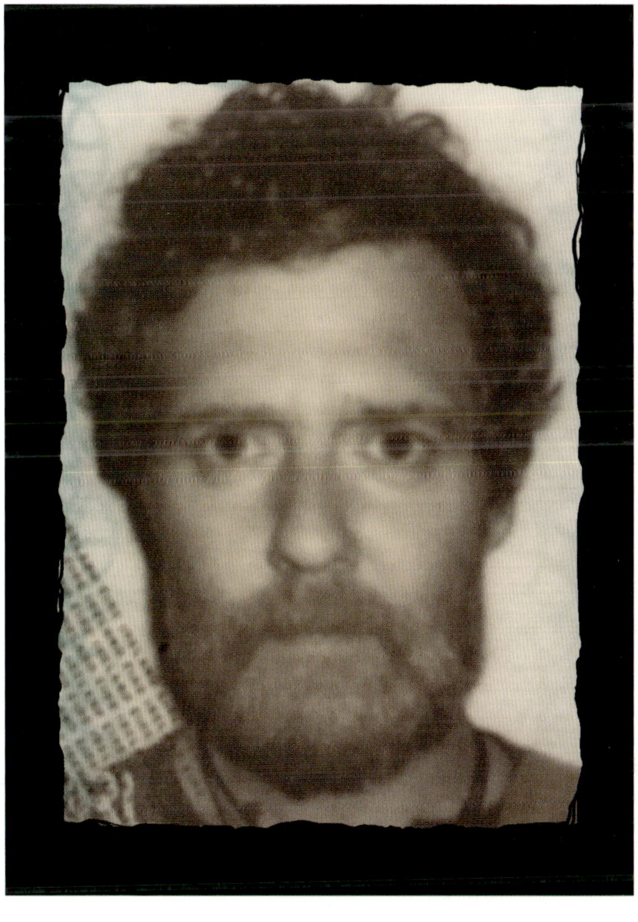

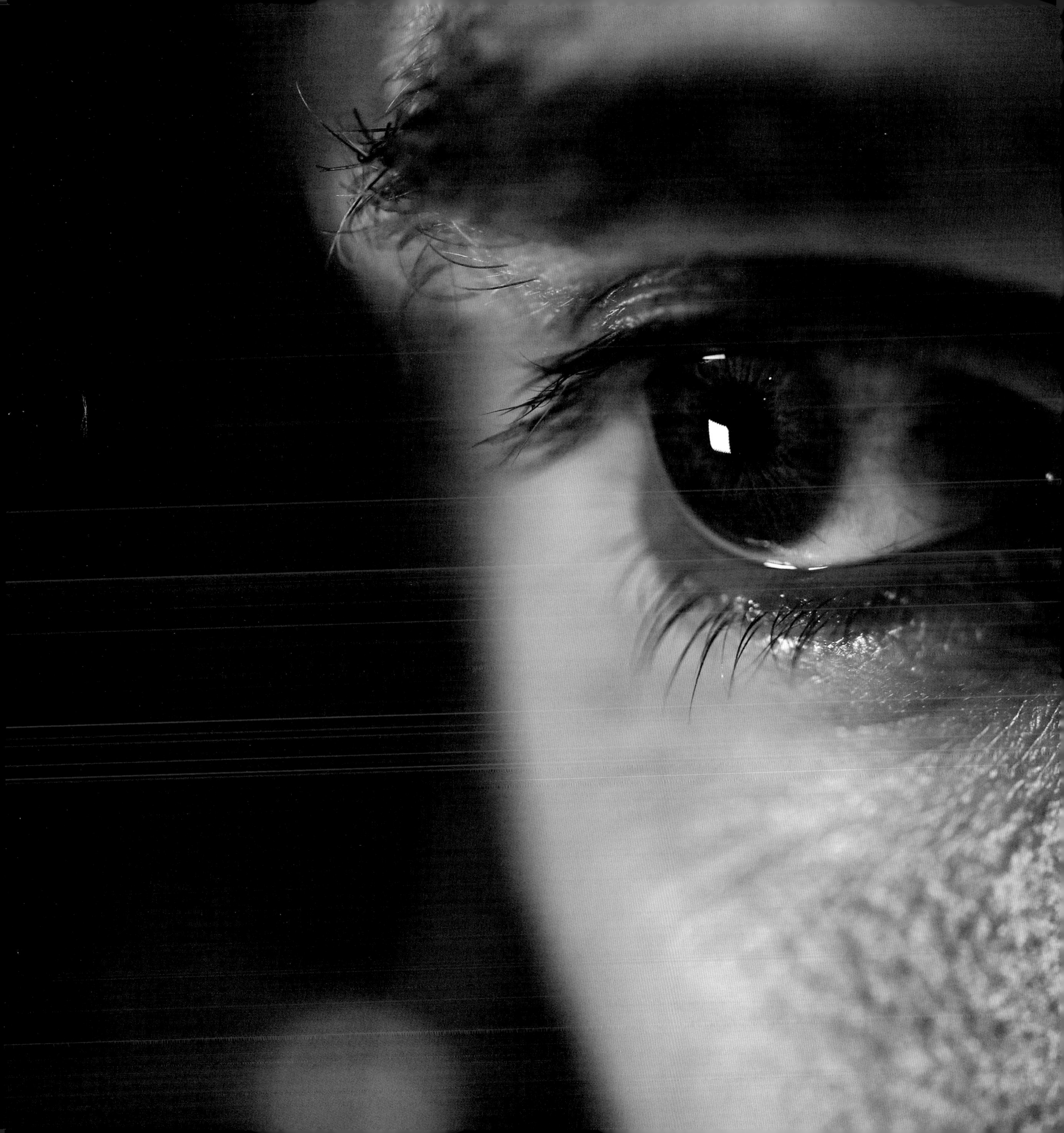

DAVID BYRNE

Born in Dumbarton, Scotland; May 14, 1952
Eyes: brown

David Byrne reminds me of my dad. They are both unafraid to be different. Even the way he moves is so distinctive. He is insatiably curious, which is why in addition to being an iconic songwriter, musician and record producer, he's also an artist, actor, writer, music theorist and filmmaker. He is able to do all of these things at the highest level.

When I went to shoot him, I was excited because I knew he has a reputation for being endlessly creative and playful in his approach to visual work, and I wasn't disappointed.

As soon as I pointed the camera at him, he began grabbing his eyelid and pulling it, making interesting shapes. The shapes of his eyes were all over the place and it was really fun. It's nice for me to let someone else take the lead, because then you really get their personality. So his photo is one of my favorites.

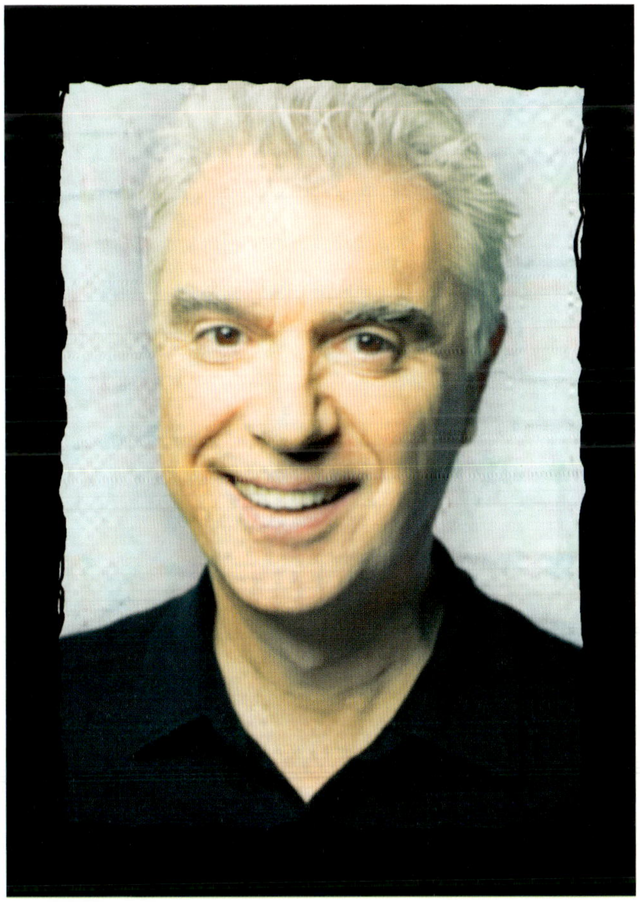

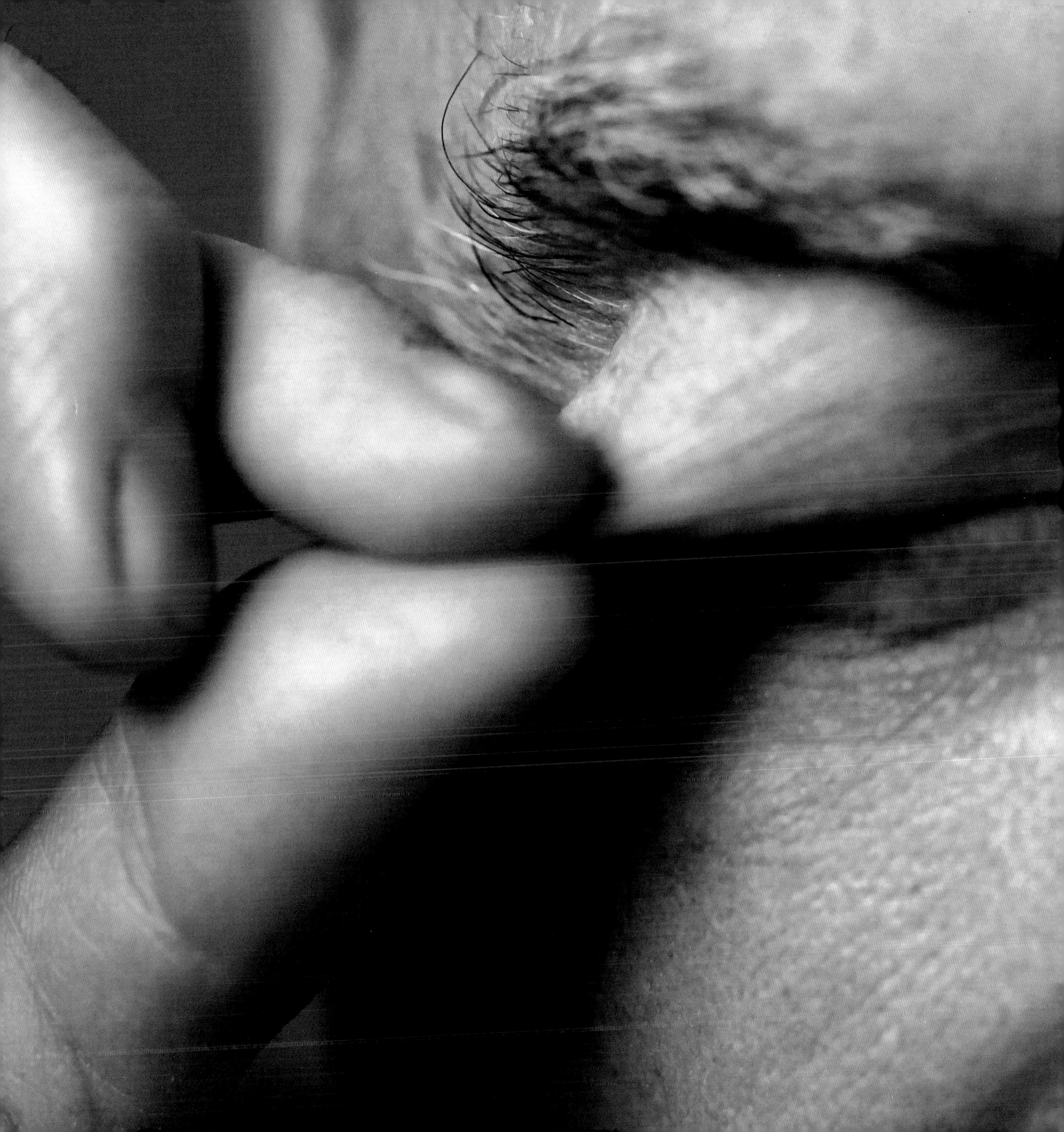

MARIO BATALI

Born in Seattle, Washington; September 19, 1960
Eyes: blue

I've known Mario for several years, and have been invited to a few wonderful dinners with him. I have eaten at a few of his restaurants and always loved each experience. Food is an art form for the senses. As photography is for the eyes, music is for the ears, food is for the mouth. Mario is one of the greats when it comes to the art of creating dishes.

I took this photograph outside Otto, his pizza restaurant in New York's West Village. There's a quaint little street around the corner called Washington Mews, and Mario sat outside one of the houses as we did this shoot. I did the photo of him peeking through his fingers as I wanted to have his hands in the shot; they are the instrument of his creativity.

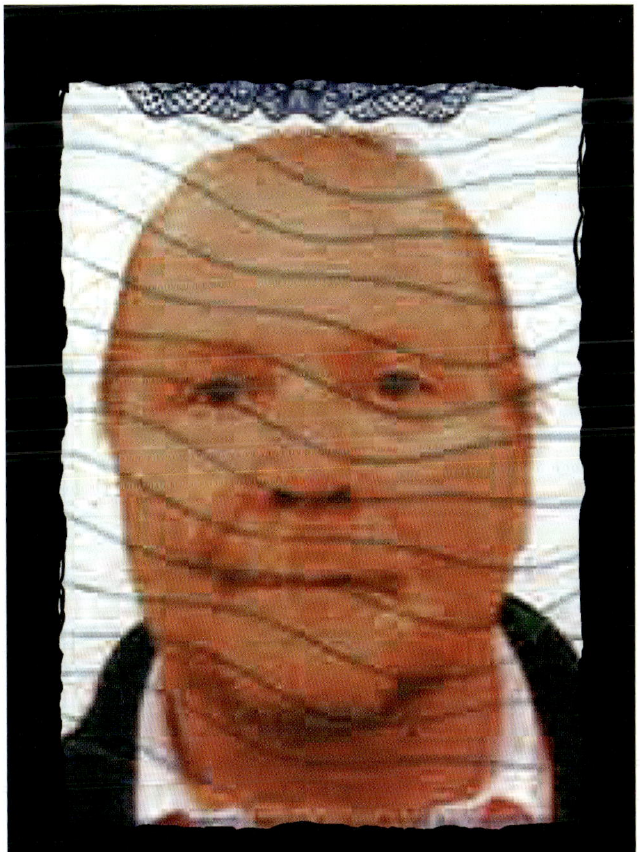

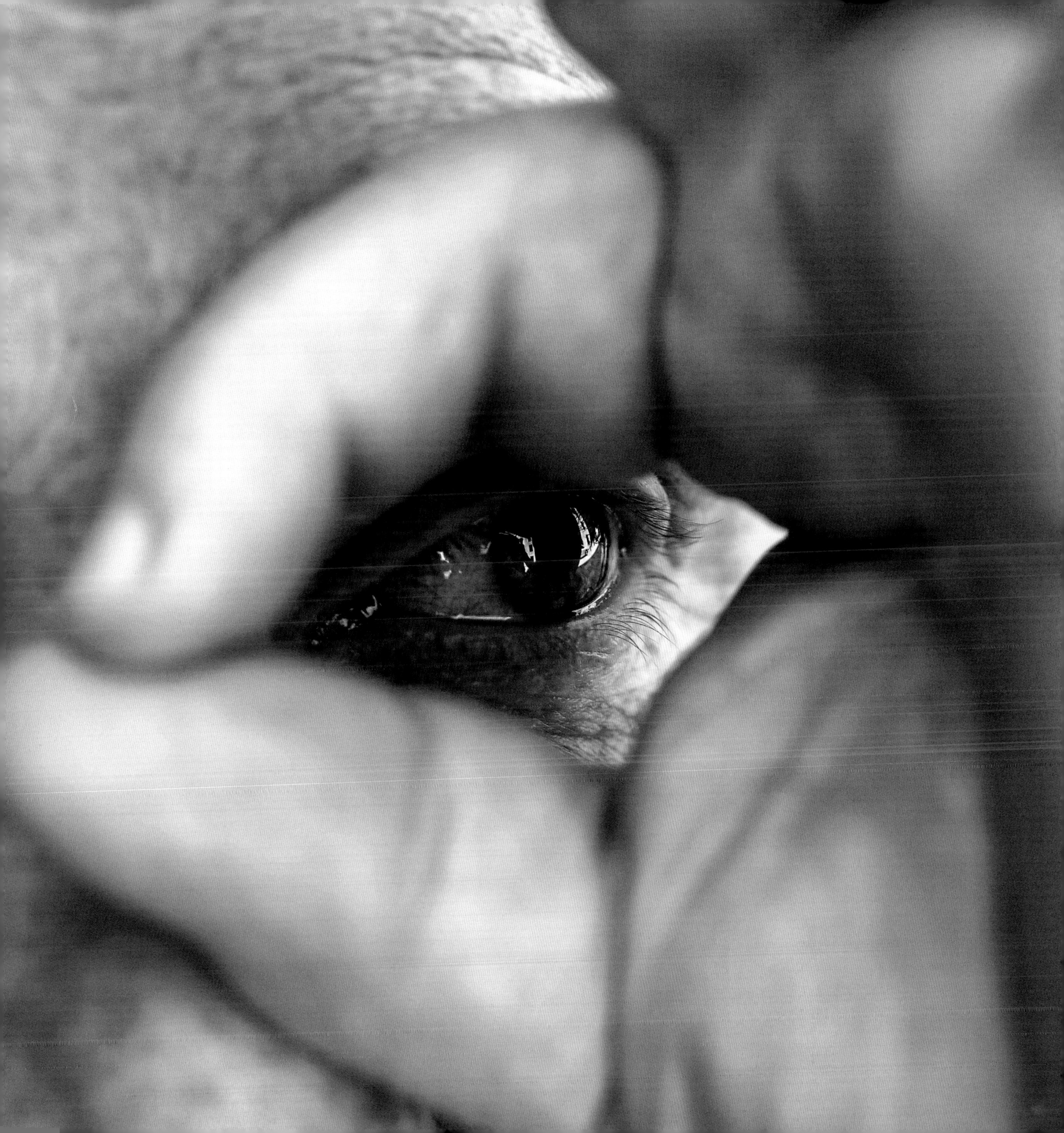

DEBBIE HARRY

Born in Miami, Florida; July 1, 1945
Eyes: blue

Just meeting Debbie Harry in person was a real thrill for me. I have loved her for many years and her music was the soundtrack to so many teenage adventures. I tried lots of different avenues of connections to reach Debbie that all drew a blank so I was delighted when her manager confirmed the shoot and after 5 years she became the last photo I took for this book. I photographed her in a small recording studio in midtown, New York. There were a few ideas I wanted to try with Debbie but I found this shaft of light coming through a small window in the back of the studio and thought this was a perfect place. Her eyes are so striking and iconic that, to me, this shot beautifully represents her.

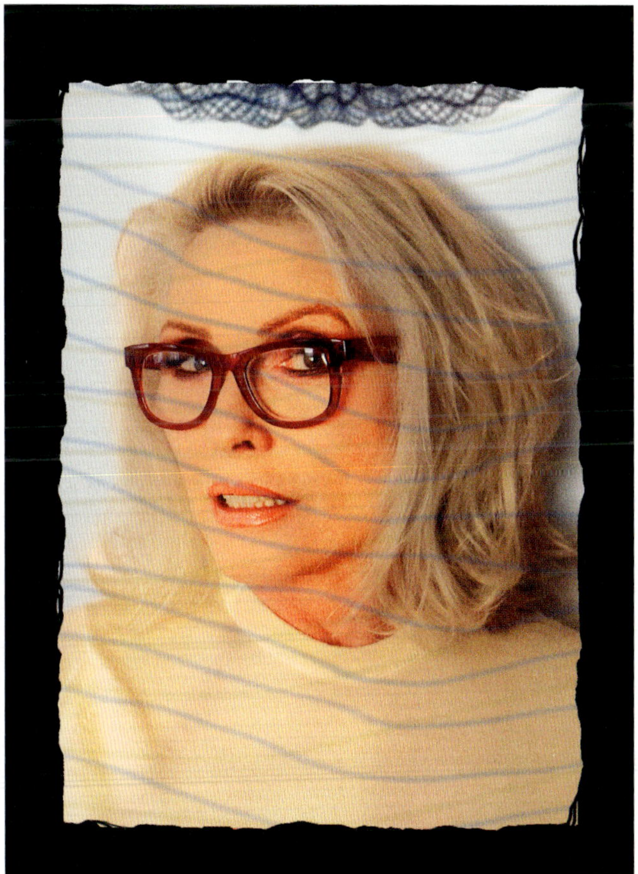

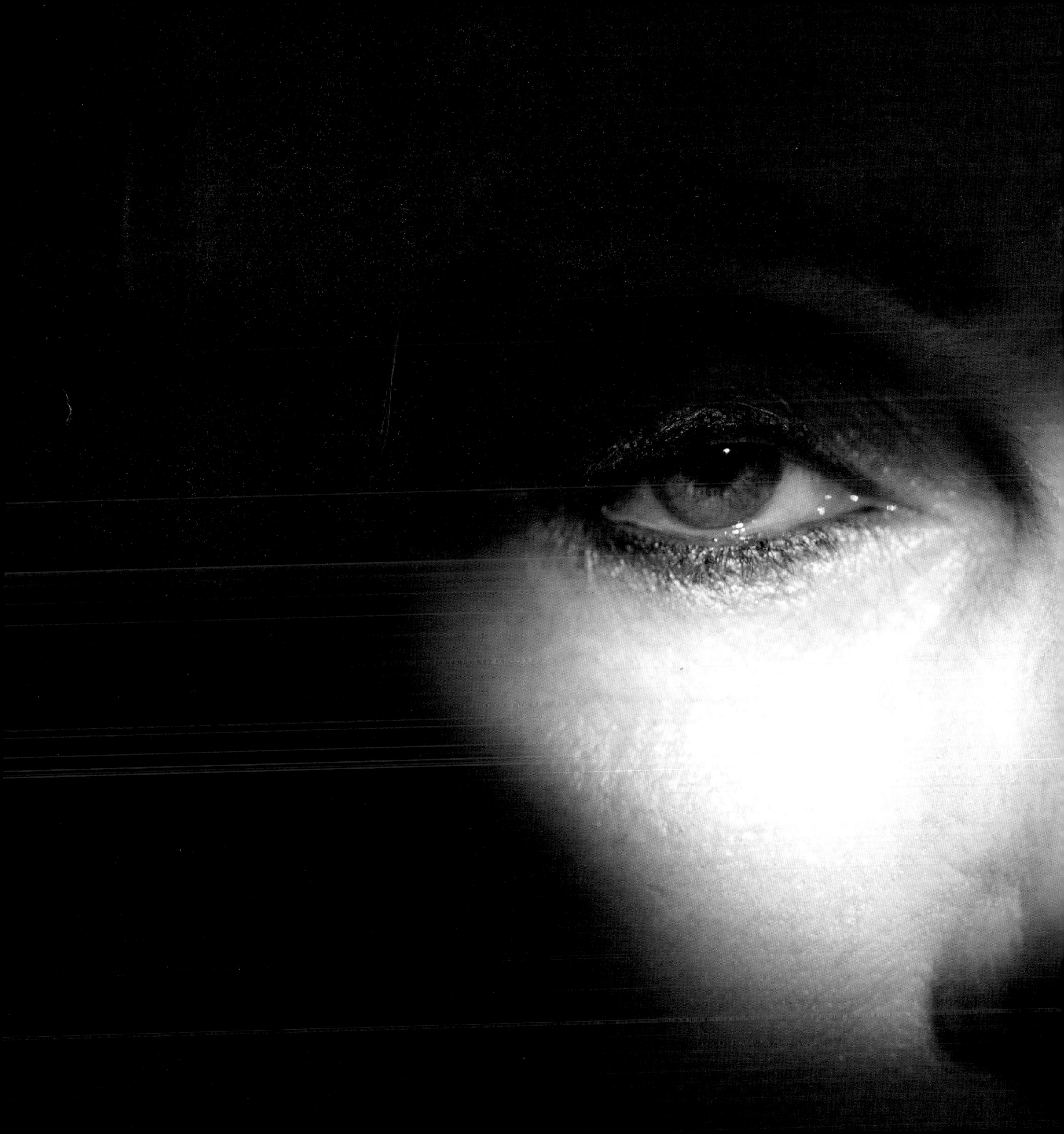

MAYNARD JAMES KEENAN

Born in Ravenna, Ohio; April 17, 1964
Eyes: green

In addition to being the lead singer for Tool, Maynard is also an author, and at the time I did this shoot, he was on a book tour for *A Perfect Union of Contrary Things*. He was giving a talk at a theater on the Upper West Side of Manhattan, I sat in this beautiful auditorium, and when Maynard arrived I got the impression he was quite shy and that his time was limited. There were hardly any words exchanged between us: sometimes the normal kinds of human chemistry and communication are less important than what happens between a photographer and the subject. I believe that photography can be a kind of unspoken language, and in this case, I felt we got a great image and the photograph I wanted.

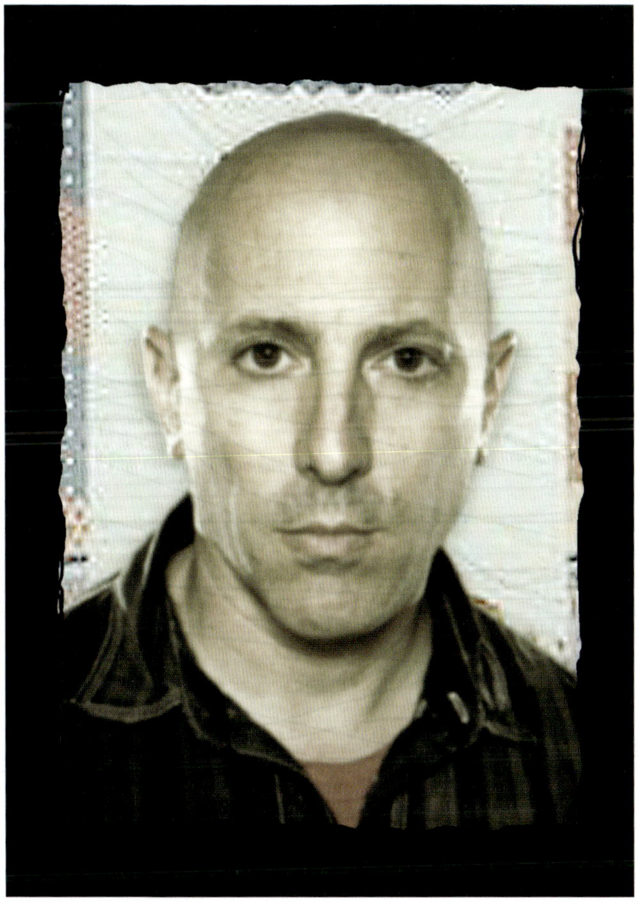

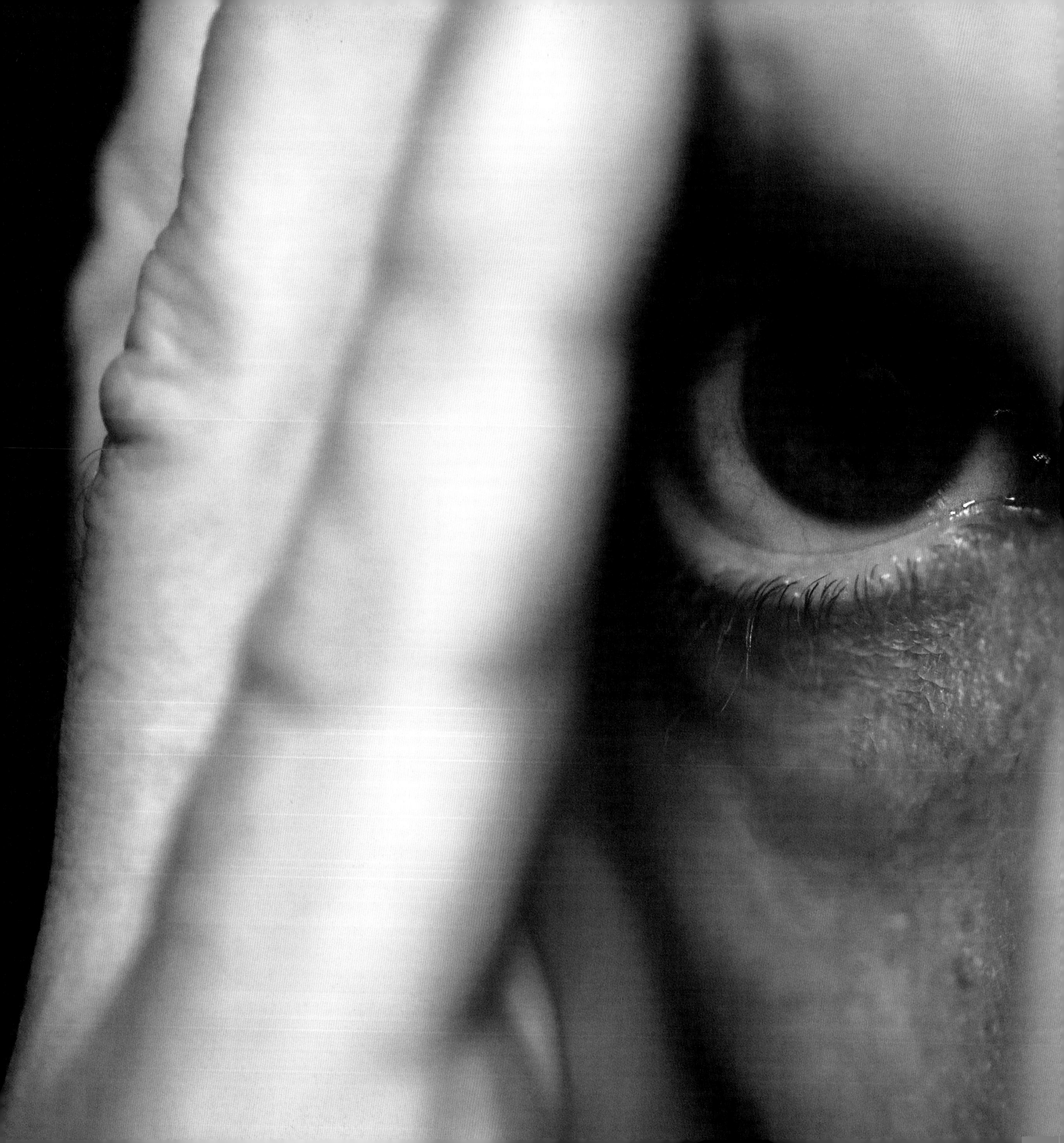

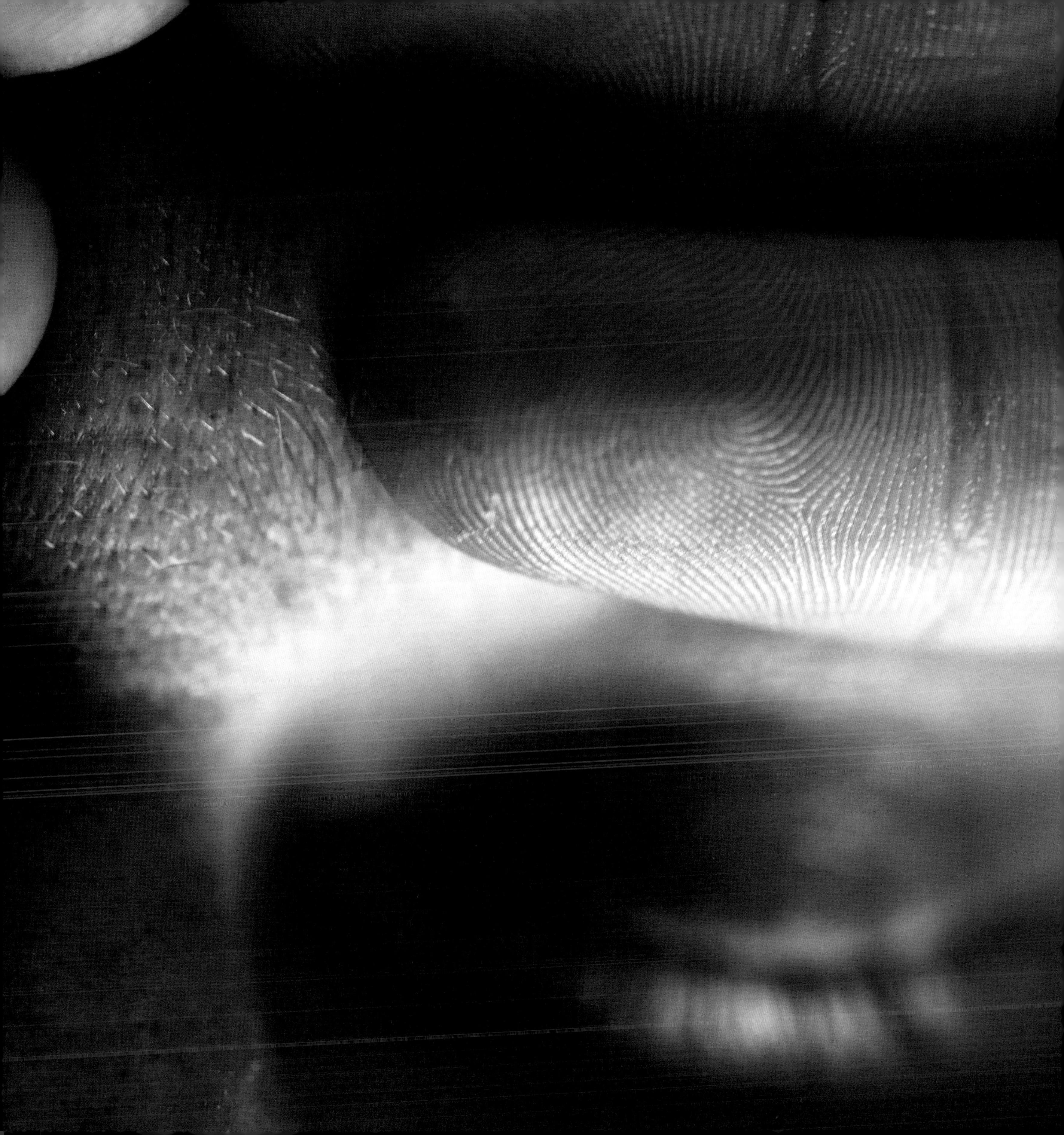

JUSTIN VERNON

Born in Eau Claire, Wisconsin; April 30, 1981
Eyes: brown

Bon Iver seems to thrive on ambiguity. The Wisconsin band is led by the creative vision of Justin Vernon, an enigmatic artist who makes achingly beautiful music. He's cryptic, playful and impossible to pin down. I'm a big fan.

Vernon lives in the woods outside of Eau Claire, Wisconsin, about one hundred miles from Minneapolis. His manager Kyle picked me up from the airport and drove me to his house. The scenery was stunning, snow-covered and vast. Justin greeted me at the house. He was immediately kind and outgoing. We shot the photos 10 minutes after I arrived. I had him lie on his living room floor and I stood above him to take the shot with his hands framing his eyes.

In spite of Justin's reputation for being reclusive, the atmosphere was very convivial and social. Several of his friends were there hanging out. Justin invited me to dinner and I just fell into his social world. His manager kindly drove me back to the airport and I flew home. It was a brief but unforgettable experience of being invited into this extraordinary artistic cocoon.

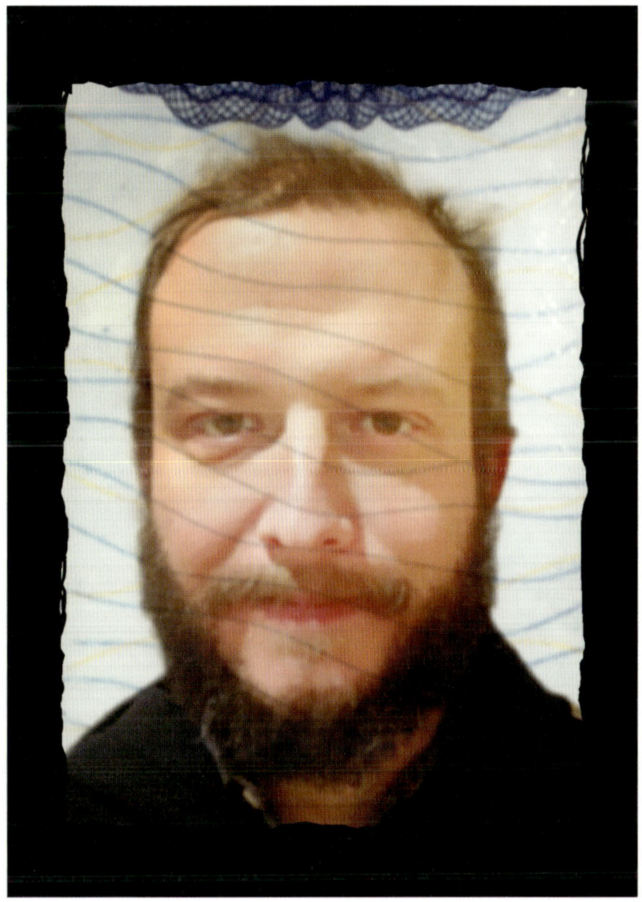

TÉA LEONI

Born in New York City, New York; February 25, 1966
Eyes: blue

Looking out over the Hudson River with the sun streaming into her apartment, Téa sat in her favorite spot. This was the perfect place to take a photograph. Téa exudes a naturalness and grace that matched the setting.

You never know what you are going to find when you are photographing someone in their home. Sometimes I am led by the scene or the subject and in this case it was both.

She had an adorable dog who wanted to be a part of the photograph and was more interested in my camera lens than anyone I've shot!

Between the kind invite into her home, her sweet dog and the warm sunshine, it made for a very relaxing shoot and allowed me to capture a side to Téa that felt honest to both of us.

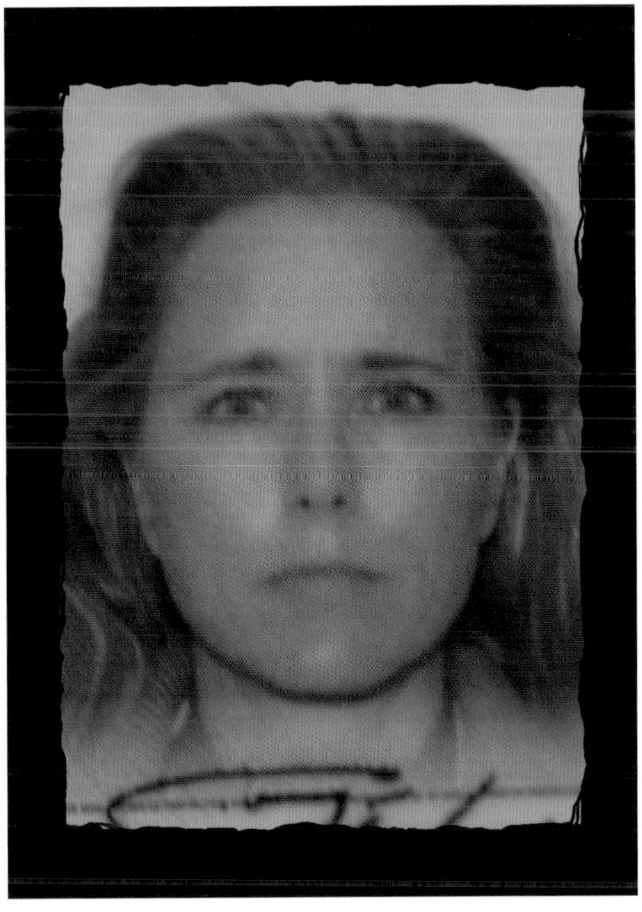

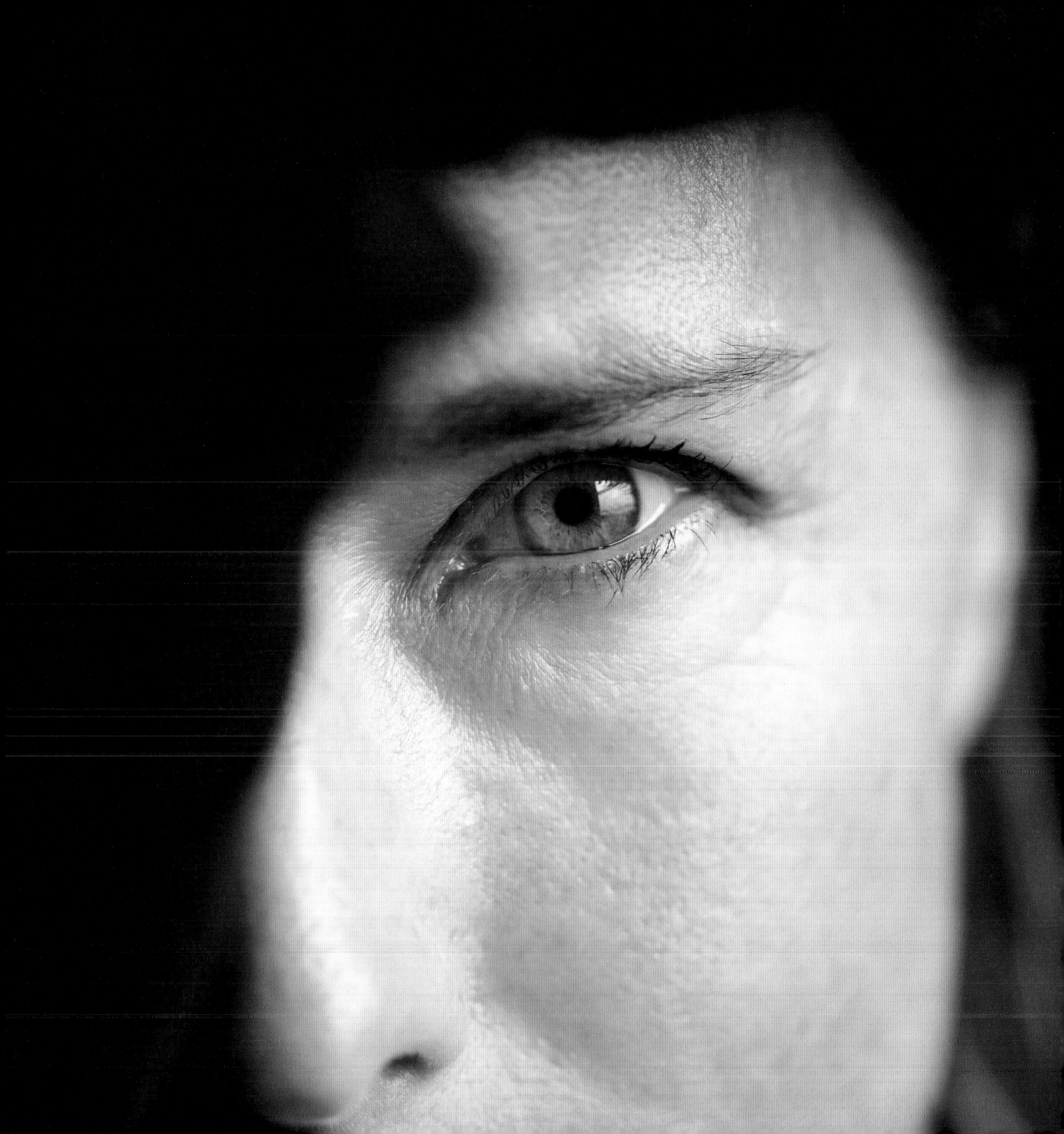

THE EDGE

Born in Barking, England; August 8, 1961
Eyes: blue

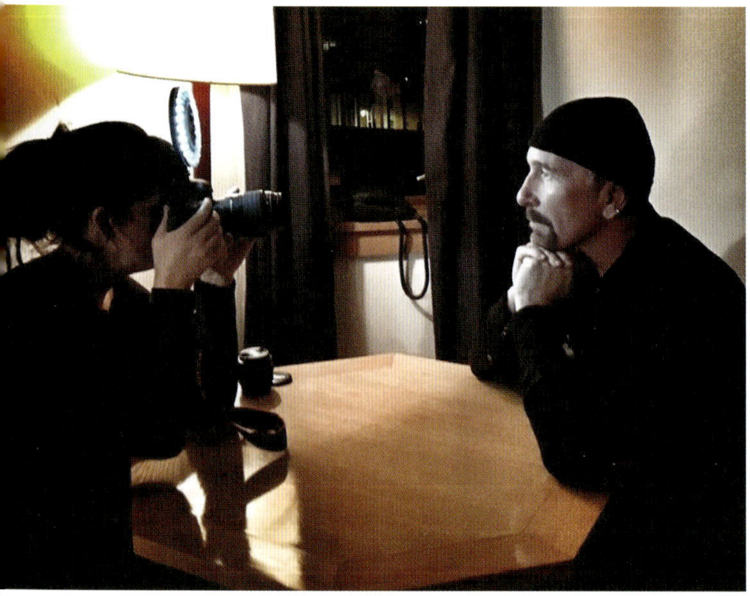

I shot The Edge on the same trip to Dublin as the shoot with Shane MacGowan, so it was a whirlwind of the best of Ireland at Christmas.

I had met The Edge's good friend Chanty O'Sullivan in New York and she introduced us and arranged the shoot. We met up at the Clarence hotel in which Bono and The Edge are part owners. It's a beautiful old hotel on the River Liffey and we went up to one of the penthouse suites. He's known my dad for a while and I've always heard nice things about him, which are all true. The Edge was very friendly and extremely professional. He had everything ready to go.

Of course, he was wearing one of his signature beanie hats and I wanted to get a little of that in the shot because it's so iconic. I did a few photos where his eyes were closed that I liked, but I ended up choosing one with his eyes open and the corner of the hat showing.

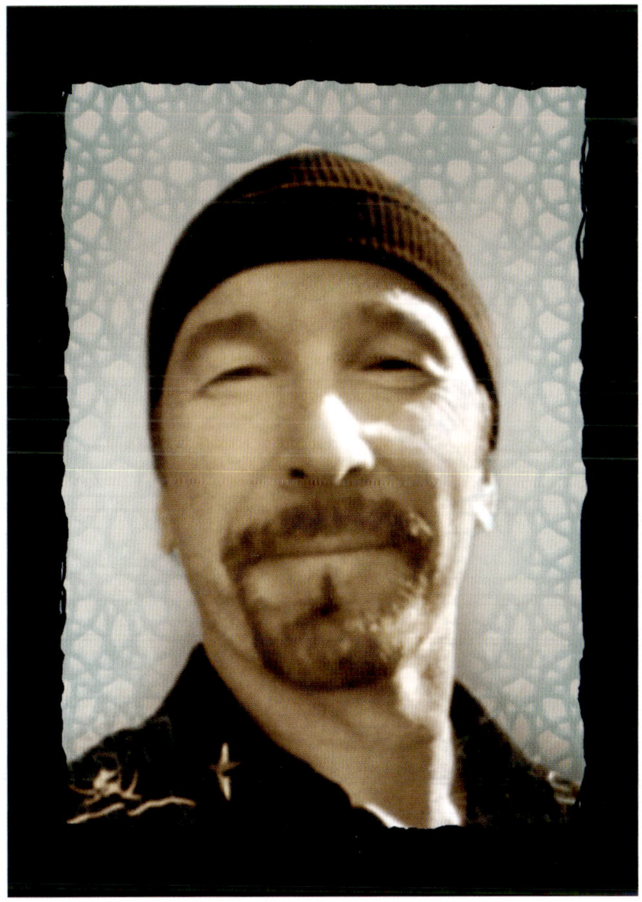

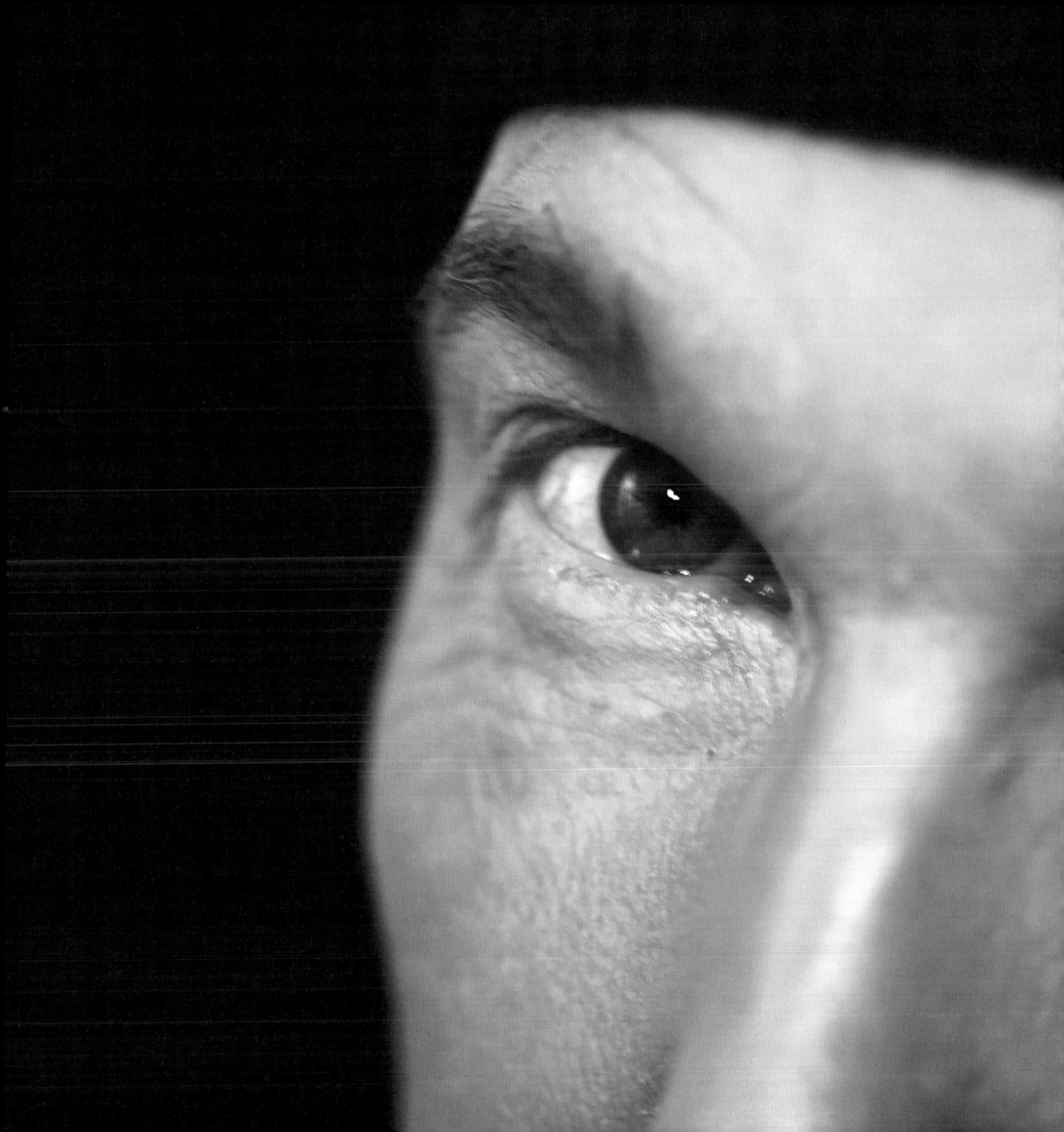

BENJAMIN ZEPHANIAH

Born in Birmingham, England; April 15, 1958
Eyes: dark brown

"This planet is for everyone. Borders are for no one."

That's a quote from a novel called *Refugee Boy* by British Rastafarian poet Benjamin Zephaniah. My dad suggested I shoot Benjamin as he and I have long been fans of his writing. As well as a powerful writer, he's an accomplished musician.

He grew up in the English city of Birmingham but moved to London to pursue his career. Today, he is a teacher at Brunel University. His writing fearlessly tackles issues of race and injustice.

Benjamin has a definite air of wisdom and a natural gravitas about him that makes you want to just sit at his feet and listen to him. I found myself thinking, maybe I should go back to school!

For Benjamin, I wanted to do something different. His office was small and quite dark and I positioned him with the window behind him, so this image is quite blown out. I shot him from the side looking into the camera. There's something intriguing about his eyes, a hint of something unspoken.

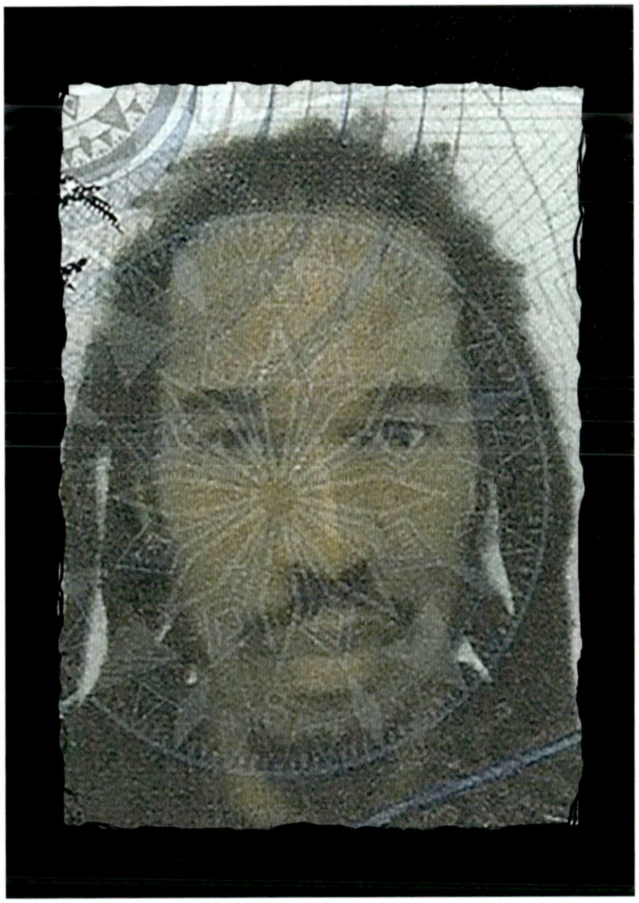

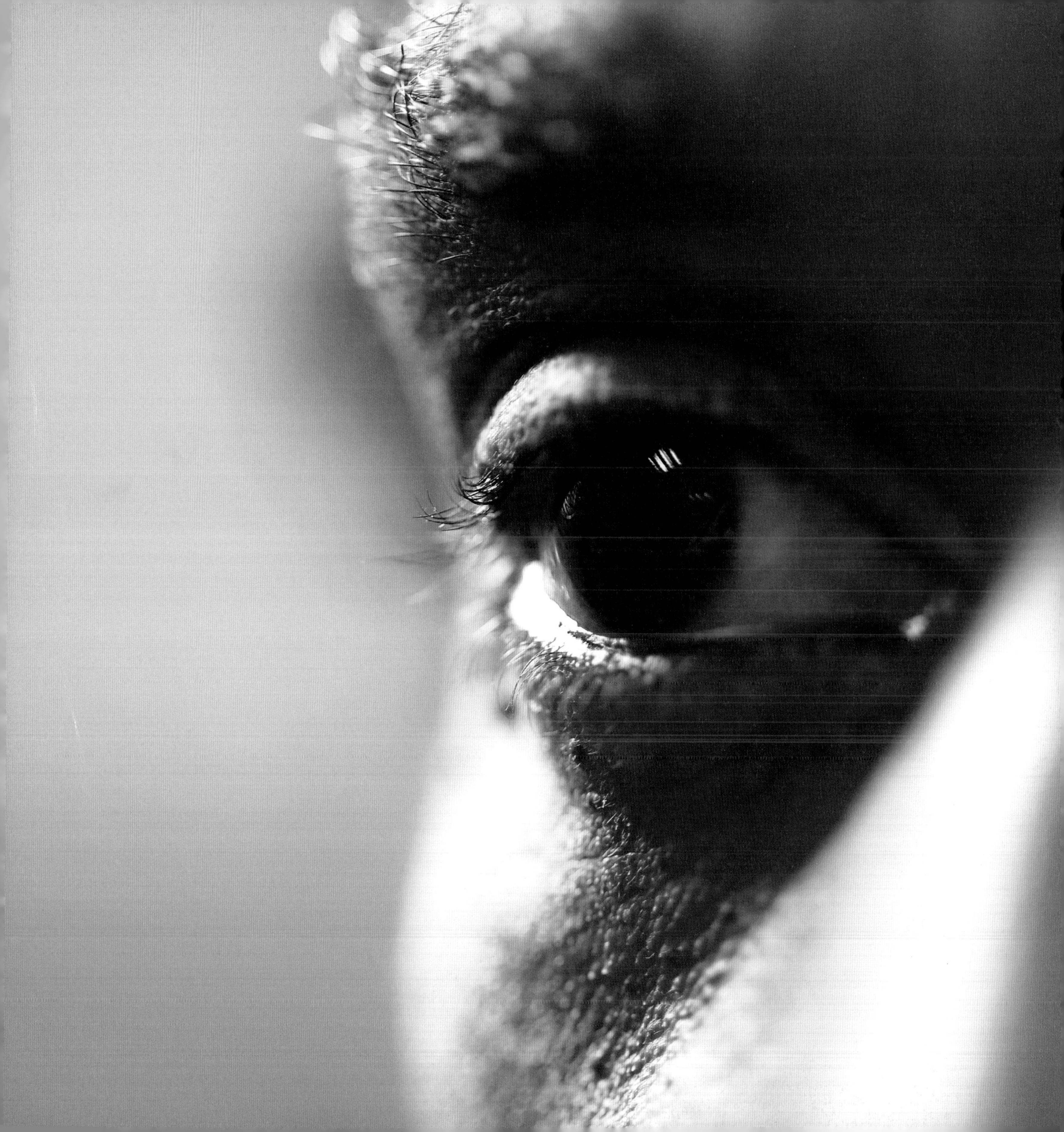

CHRIS BLACKWELL

Born in London, England; June 22, 1937
Eyes: blue

Island Records founder Chris Blackwell is the embodiment of an entrepreneur. He has that kind of singular, restless curiosity and maverick spirit, and an ability to see one step ahead of the culture that's allowed him to discover artists including Bob Marley and U2.

I first met him at GoldenEye in Jamaica at a food and music festival called Nyamjam curated by my friend Reyna Mastrosimone. Chris was calm, quiet and operating on Jamaican time. He was talking passionately about the fact that while Jamaica has been known for its music and sports, the island's food hasn't yet received its due.

Though he was born and raised in Jamaica, Chris is also quite English in a lot of ways: in his properness, his manners, and a certain effortless elegance.

Although he has a place not far from Bath, we took the photo at his home in New York. His apartment was full of large, amazing paintings and my first impulse was to get a shot of him in front of a painting, but I ended up framing his eye without a background. It worked because he has such an interesting face.

His face is a testament to a life lived to the fullest, and you know there are some great stories behind it. The simplicity of his expressions, his gentleness and his easy-going manner are what I hoped to capture in this photograph.

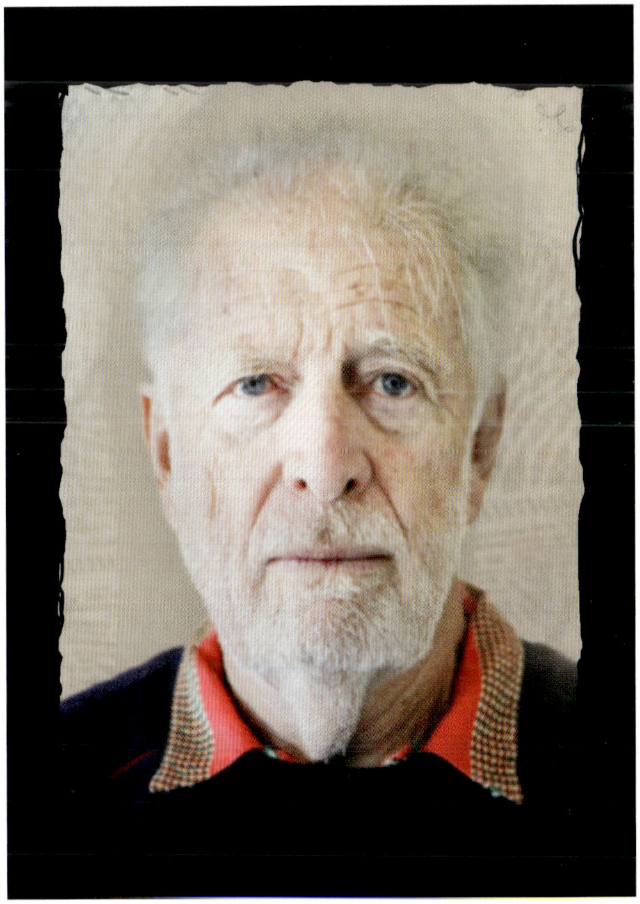

His face is
a testament to a life
lived to the fullest,
and you know there are
some great stories
behind it.

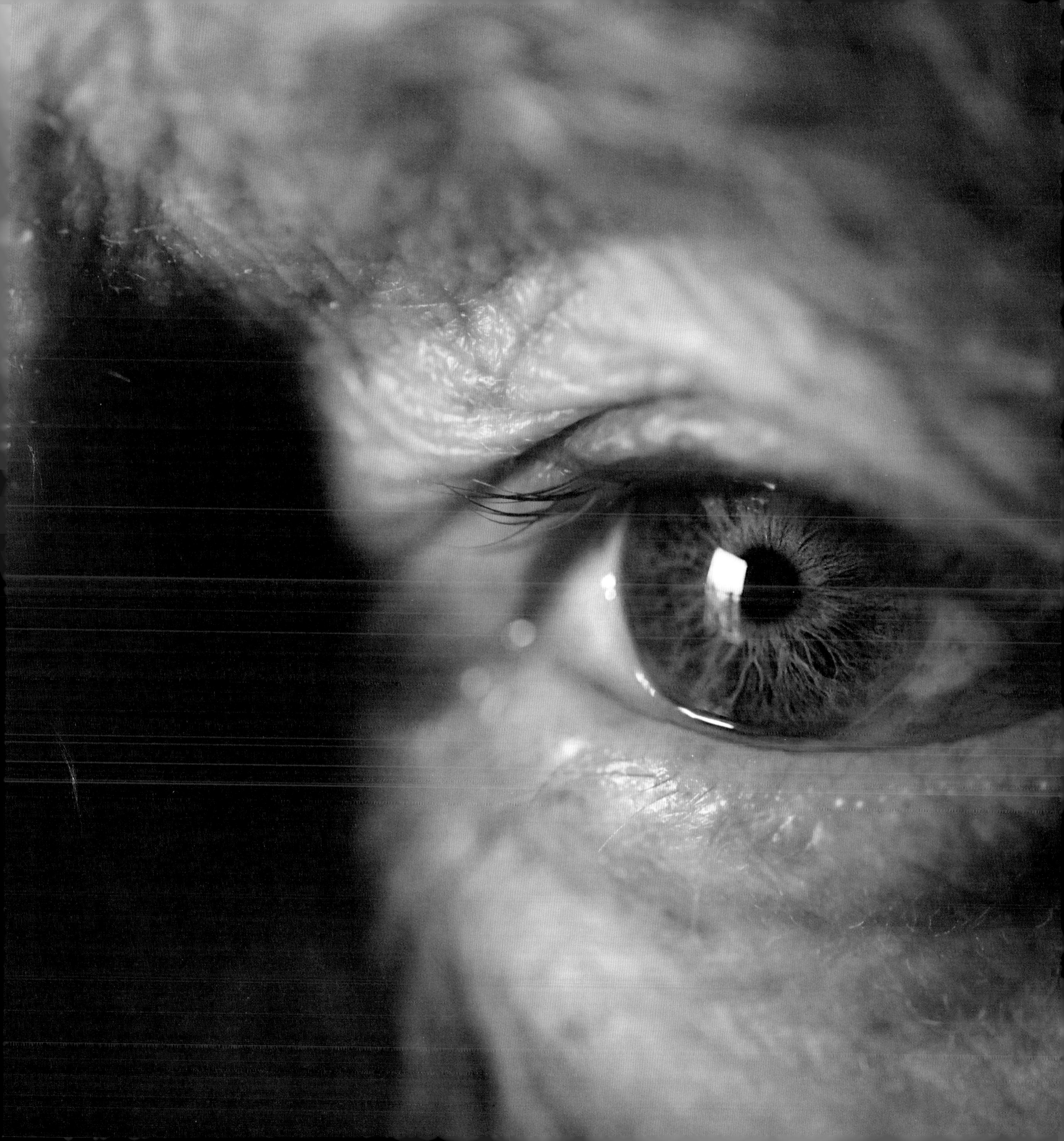

TOM PETTY

Born in Gainesville, Florida; October 20, 1950
Eyes: blue

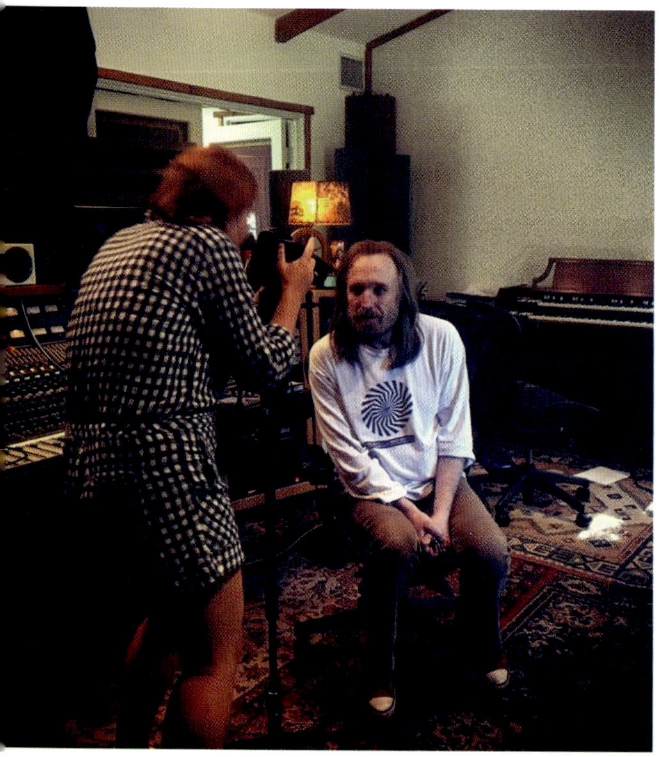

I met Tom's daughter, Adria, in my second year of college when we were nineteen and we've been close friends ever since. I have fond memories of spending time with the Pettys. When I was new to America and feeling homesick, Adria invited me into their home. I was always made to feel part of the family and they will forever have a warm place in my heart.

Tom was a special person with a great sense of humour, and a wonderful storyteller.

When I took this photo, Tom was doing his radio show for Sirius XM. He had a beautiful place up in Malibu with a small studio in the back of his house. I ended up taking these blurry photos as well as some more straightforward shots. I love this image of him as although it's an abstract one, you can see his smile lines and the humorous side of him.

For Tom, his family and playing music was everything, and whenever I think of him, I can see the smile he had in his eyes when he was performing or hanging out with Adria and his family.

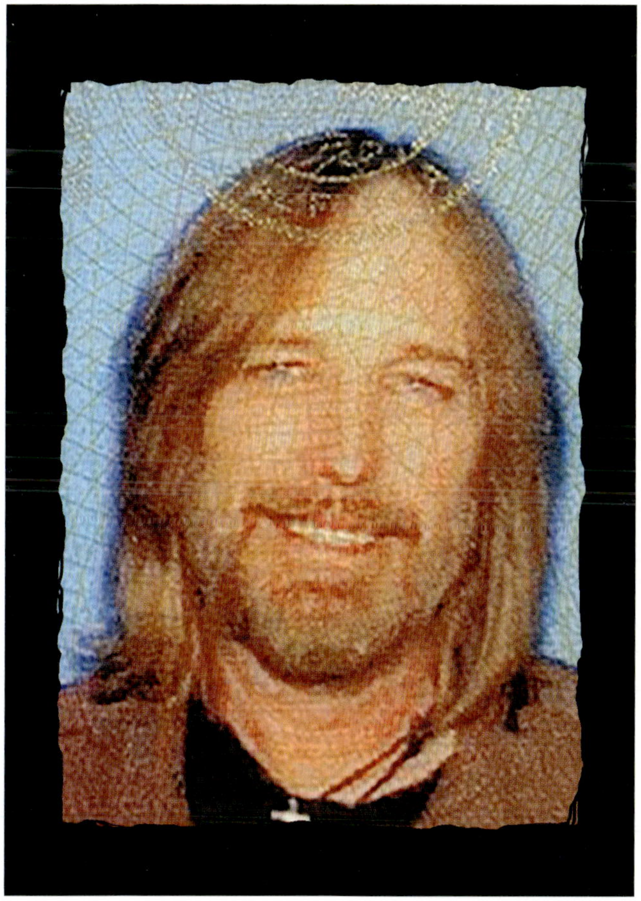

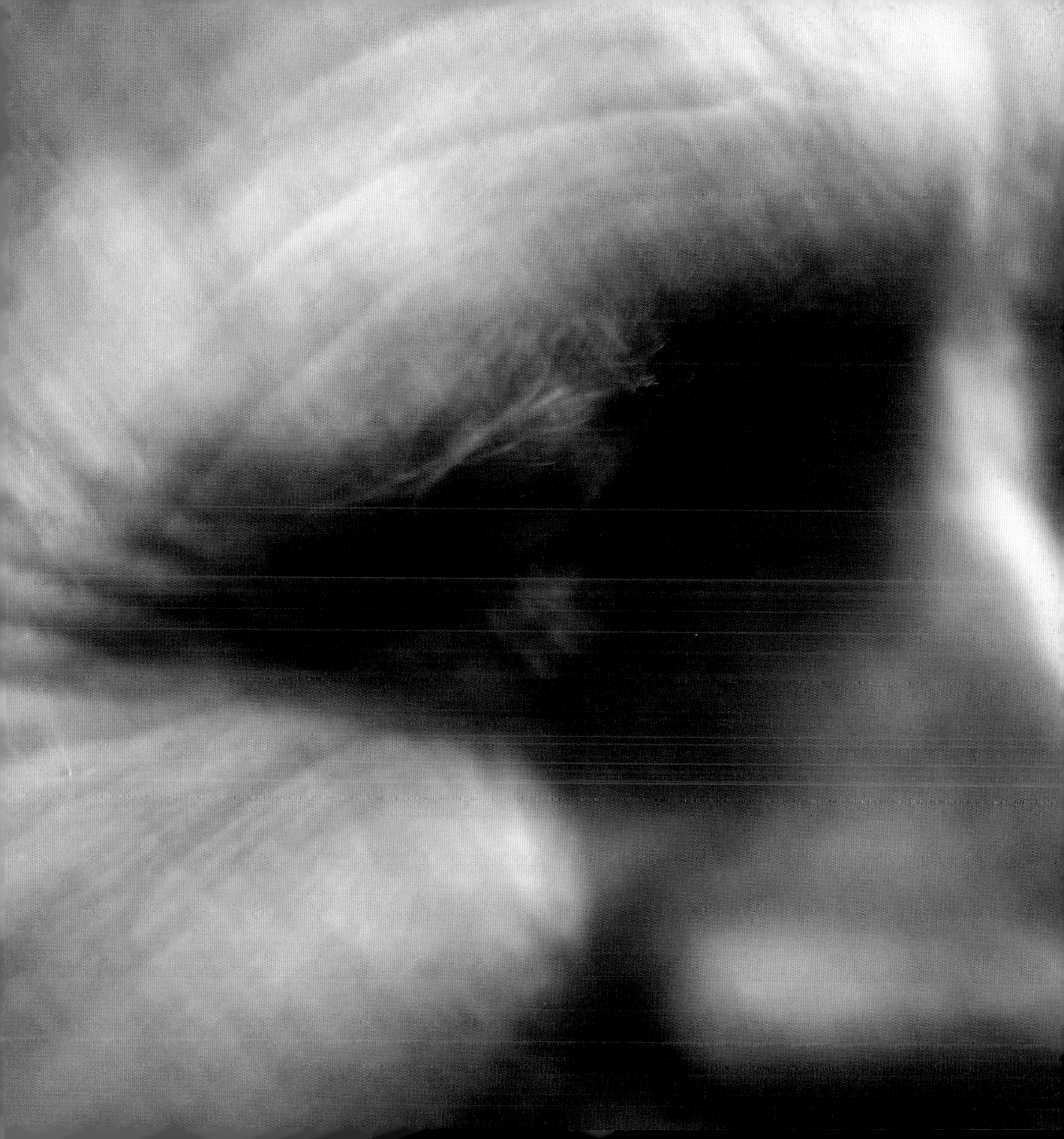

MICK FLEETWOOD

Born in Redruth, England; June 24, 1947
Eyes: blue

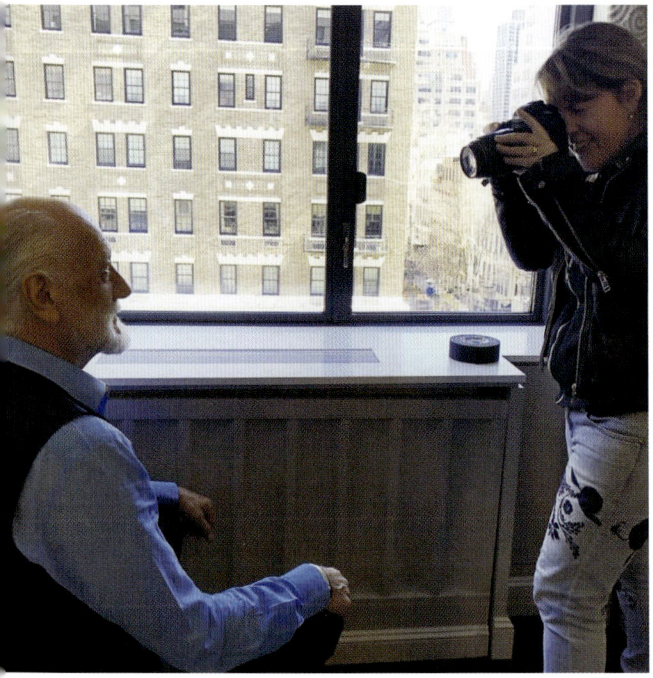

As the drummer and founder of one of rock's most iconic bands, and being well over six feet tall, Mick Fleetwood is literally larger than life. While he might appear intimidating, in person he is the loveliest man.

I've always loved Fleetwood Mac and saw that they were playing at Madison Square Garden so I emailed my father to reach out to Mick. He got back right away and said: "Come to the hotel and do the shoot, and please come see the gig as well."

I went to see him at his hotel suite. He and his wife were getting breakfast. I wanted to get his wrists with the sweatbands in the shot, and I had him cross his arms in front of his face. I was very excited when he got me tickets for the show and the day turned into an unforgettable night.

I like the graphic of this image. For me it represents the power of Mick's onstage persona. When you meet Mick he has a regal and commanding presence and I think this comes through in the shot too.

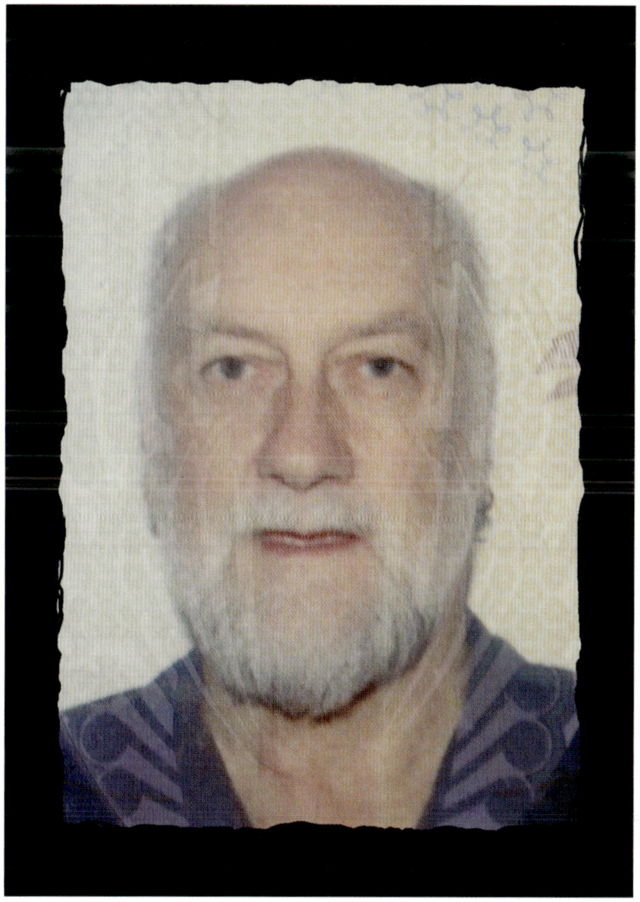

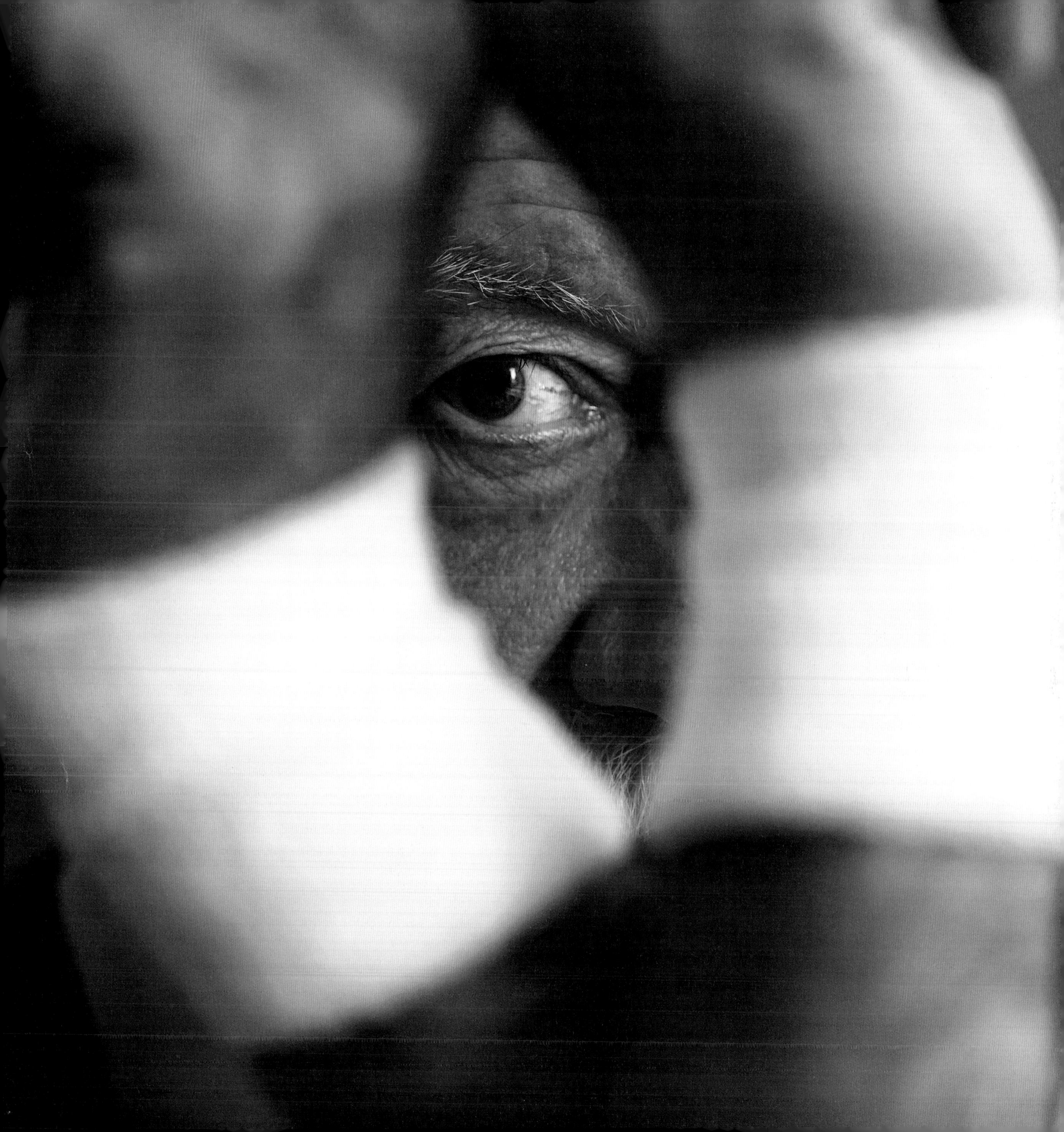

TV ON THE RADIO

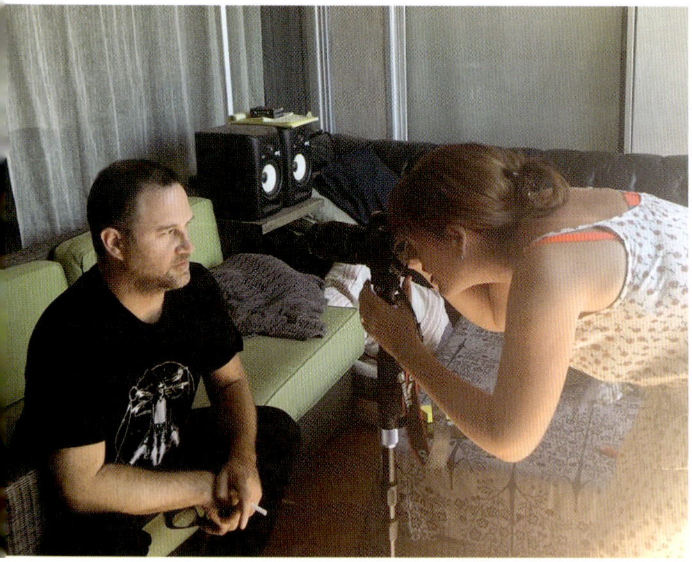

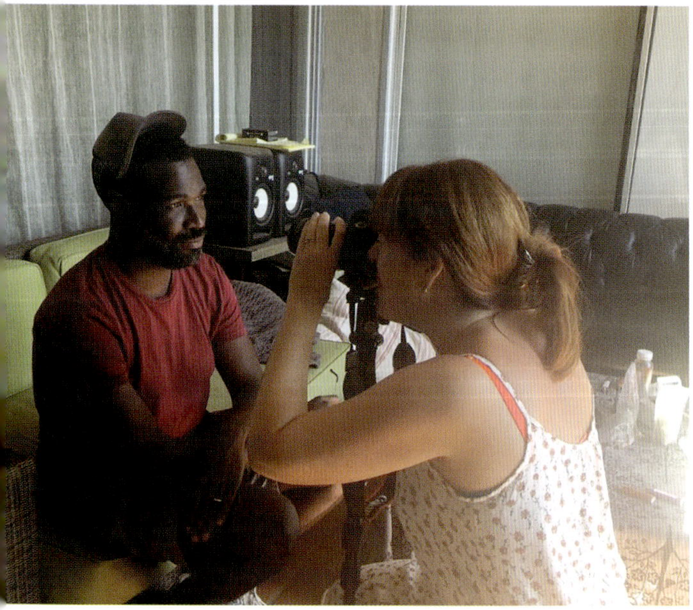

The soulful quartet TV on the Radio started in Williamsburg, Brooklyn, the place I now call home. I first heard about them because many early reviewers talked about how their music was reminiscent of my dad. Like him, they're also committed to social activism.

What makes this photo different from all the others in this book is the fact that there are four guys in the band, and I include all of them. The challenge was by the time I photographed them, two were living in LA and two were in New York. I wanted to capture the band with everyone looking at each other, sort of like a Brady Bunch grid. I shot Jaleel Bunton and Kyp Malone in Williamsburg, Brooklyn and then went to LA to shoot singer Tunde Adebimpe and guitarist Dave Sitek. The image is obviously not as intimate as one person. But I like the visual variation this brings to the book.

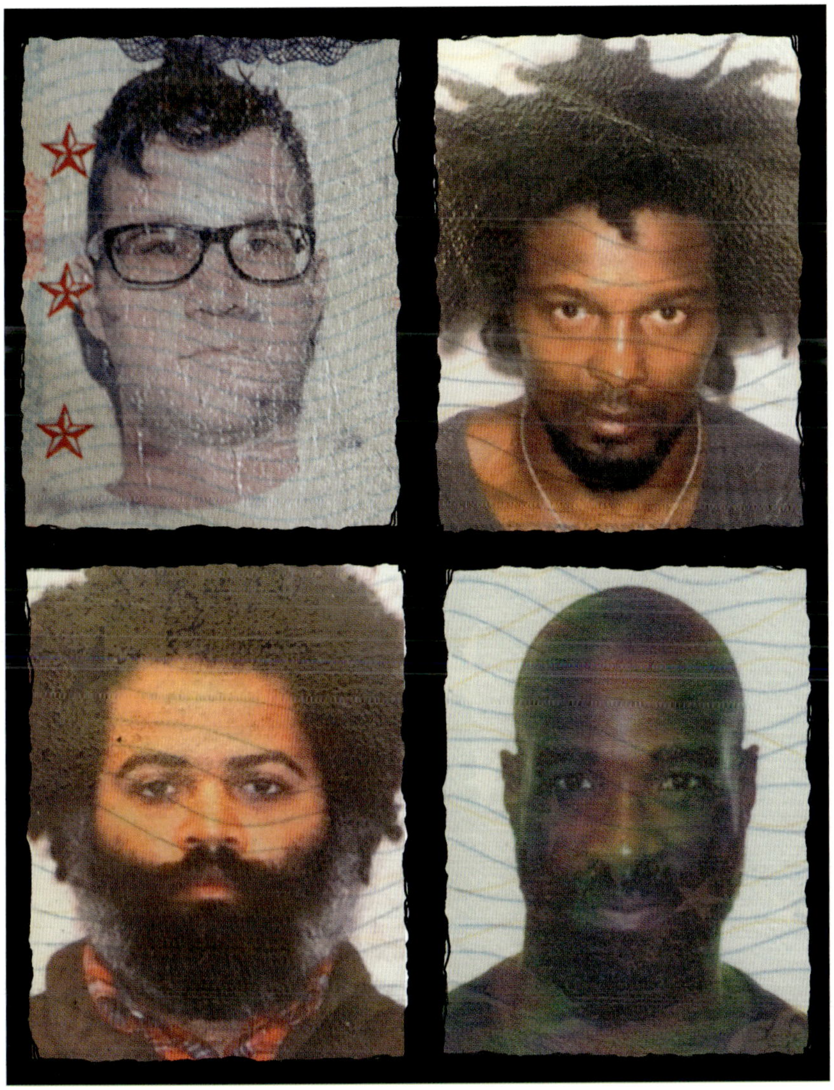

Dave Sitek

Born in Columbia,
Maryland
September 6, 1972
Eyes: brown

Jaleel Bunton

Born in California,
United States
October 24, 1974
Eyes: brown

Kyp Malone

Born in Moon Township,
Pennsylvania
February 27, 1973
Eyes: brown

Tunde Adebimpe

Born in St. Louis,
Missouri
February 26, 1975
Eyes: brown

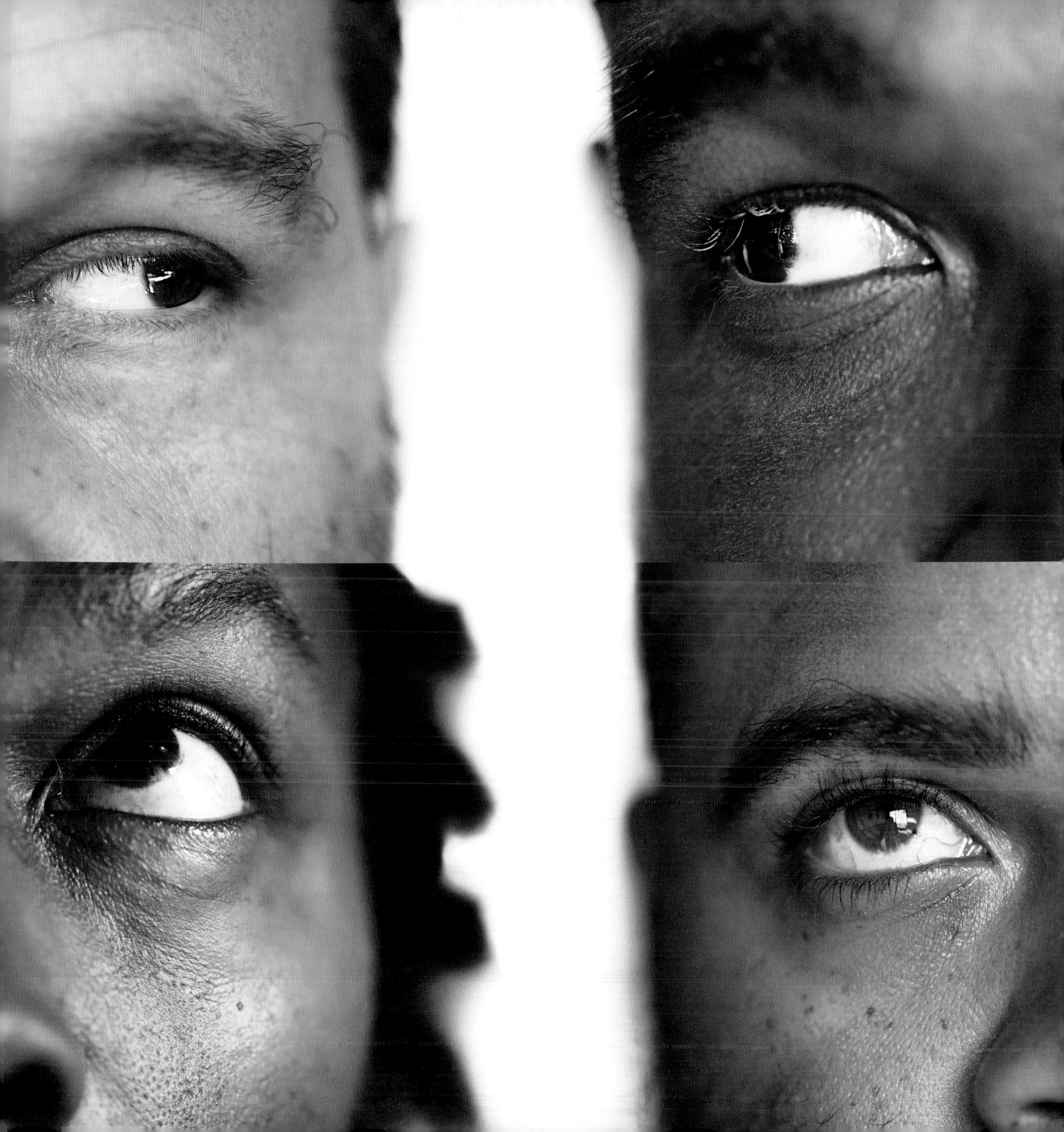

EDDIE VEDDER

Born in Evanston, Illinois; December 23, 1964
Eyes: blue

Eddie Vedder is literally one of the nicest people I've ever met.

I asked my dad if he could reach out to Eddie and a few days later I received a lovely email from him saying he'd love to be part of the project and when could we do it?

A few weeks later, Pearl Jam were playing at the O2 arena in London. Eddie sent me a couple of texts personally making sure I could find my way backstage. There was no manager or publicist interceding on his behalf. I was immediately taken care off and offered some food while Eddie was doing his pre-show routine.

We did the shoot in his dressing room. I asked him to hold some small lights in his hands to light his face. The glowing light looked amazing, which doesn't really come through in black and white; however, we both got excited about the raw colour images on the camera.

He was so complimentary, and after the shoot he gave me parting gifts from the tour swag. He's a great and talented musician but even more than that he is a truly lovely human being.

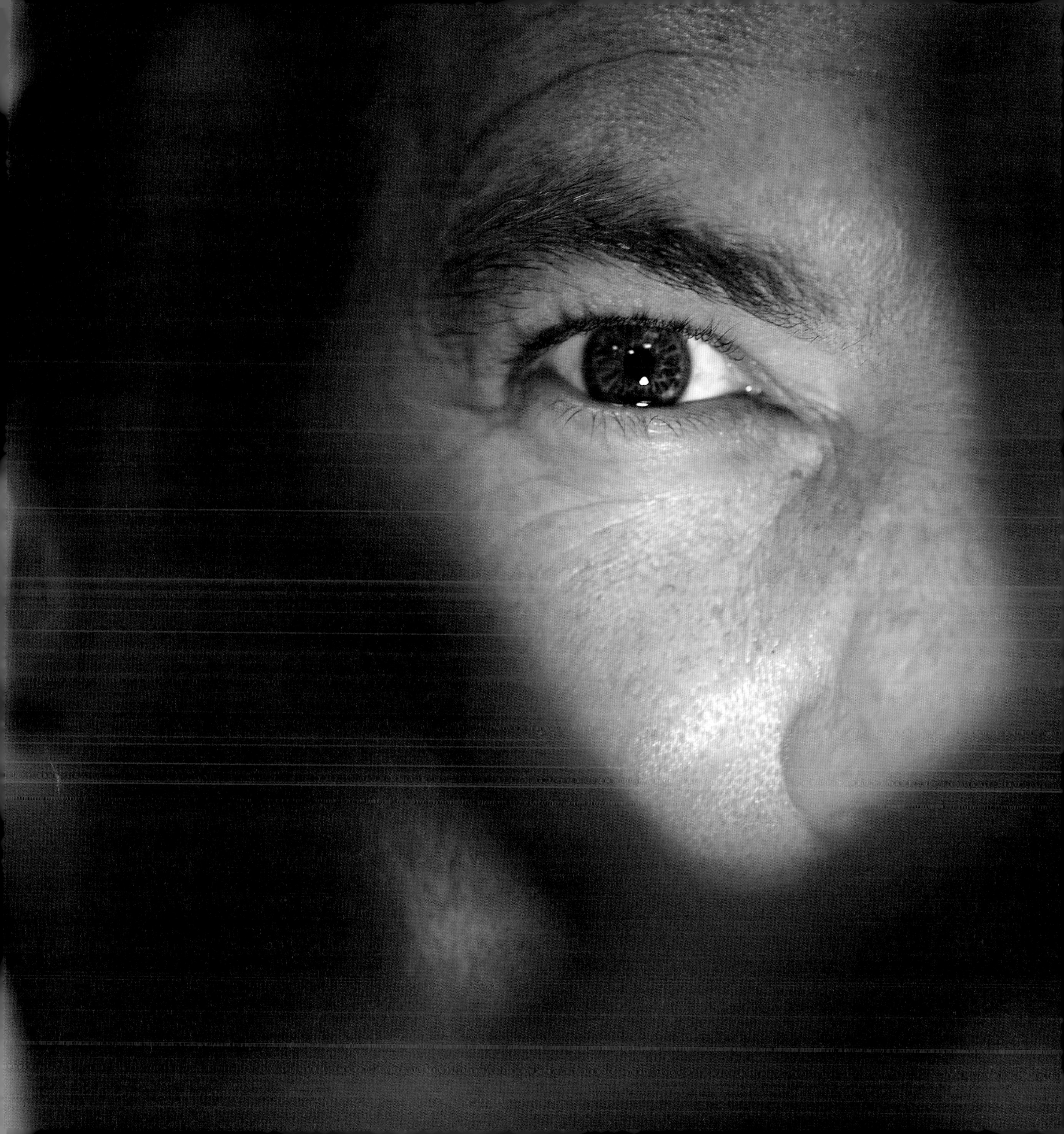

JOSEPH ARTHUR

Born in Akron, Ohio; September 28, 1971
Eyes: blue

I've known Joe for many years; he's an old friend. We met through a mutual friend who had given his demo tape to my dad. He thought Joe was very talented and signed him to his label, Real World Records.

Joe basically became part of the family. We hung out a lot. His lyric writing was what got dad immediately, but he is a talented musician all around. Joe is also an incredible painter and both my father and I love his work.

Joe eventually moved on from Real World but we remained friends. He came to live with me for a few months at a place my dad had in Chelsea.

It was like having the Warhol Factory in my house: musicians, filmmakers, painters, all coming in and out at all times of day. It was a big loft space. Joe covered the floor with a drop cloth and made the whole place an art project. It was fun. He's a creative force that inspires me to create when I'm around him. I made a couple of music videos for him while he was staying with me.

When I shot him, he came to my house. It was in the beginning of the project and I was like: "Let's do something different." So I just grabbed a pen, and he started drawing around his face and his eye. It ended up being different from any of the other portraits in this book. I'm always inspired by Joe.

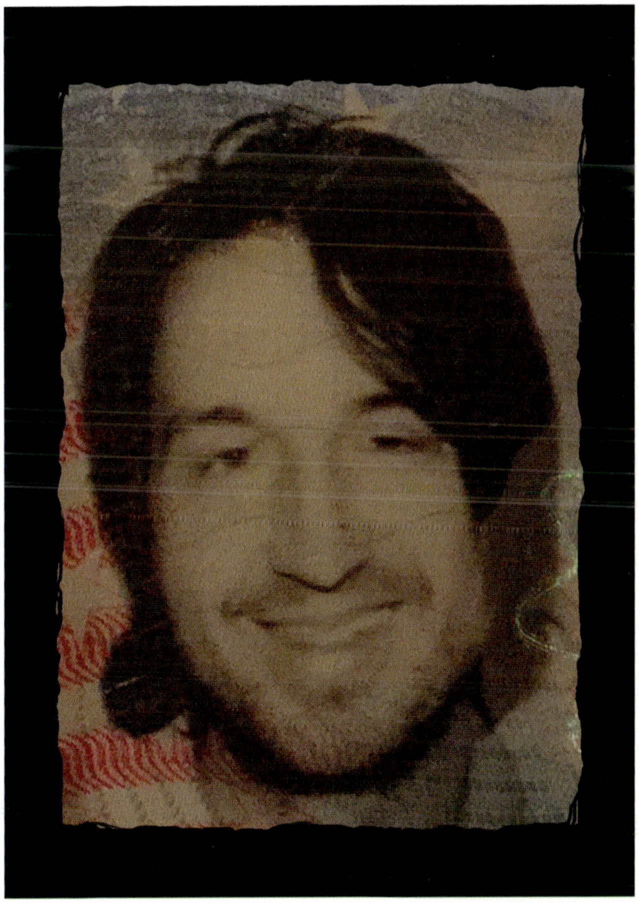

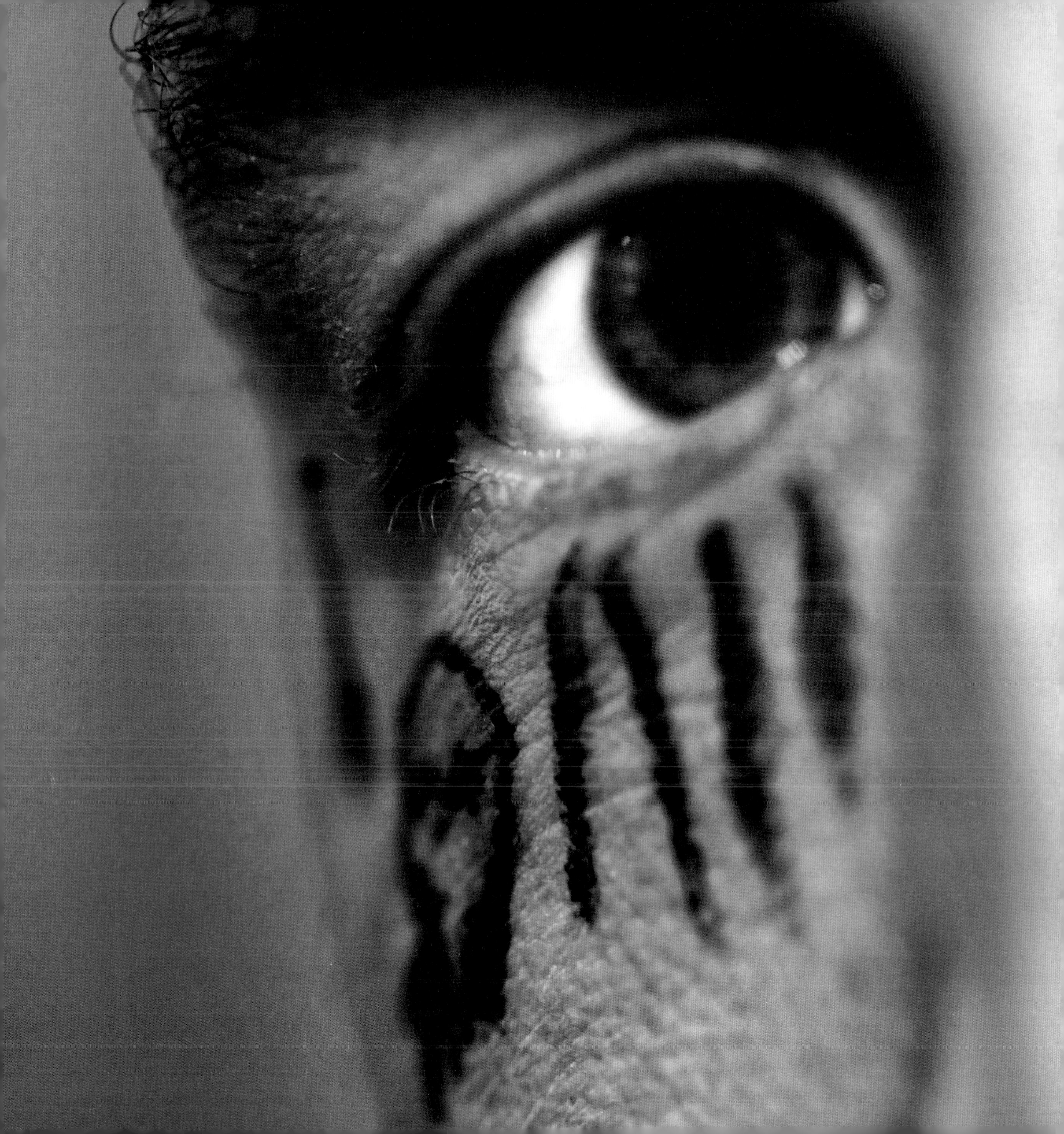

SUSAN SARANDON

Born in New York City, New York; October 4, 1946
Eyes: brown

I first met Susan at a Witness Gala. She is someone who takes her politics seriously, and I admire that about her. Of course, she is also an amazing actress. I got to see her on the film set of *Dead Man Walking*, when she was shooting in New York. I arrived just before they filmed the scene with Sean Penn, right before he gets executed. There's a moment where she sings to him, right before his last call. It's the climactic scene in the movie. Of course, both of them are extremely talented actors. Before the scene they greeted me in a completely relaxed, casual way: "Hi! Nice to meet you!" And then in an instant, they delivered this emotionally wrenching scene. I remember being mesmerised.

For years, she also lived two blocks away from my dad in New York. I went to shoot at her place, and it's a beautiful apartment. You walk into this massive loft space – an incredible room full of windows. She was extremely curious about this book and asked me about the basis of my interest in eyes. She was the only person in this book who actually wanted to discuss the project.

She also has amazing eyes, with wonderful long lashes. Really unusual and stunning. I wanted to do a simple shot, using daylight from one of her windows. I love this photo. It's simple but just shows how beautiful she is.

During the shoot I went to the bathroom and the floor is just covered in awards. You have to make a pathway through about 30 or 40 awards. I felt it was a testament to how she doesn't need to show off her accomplishments.

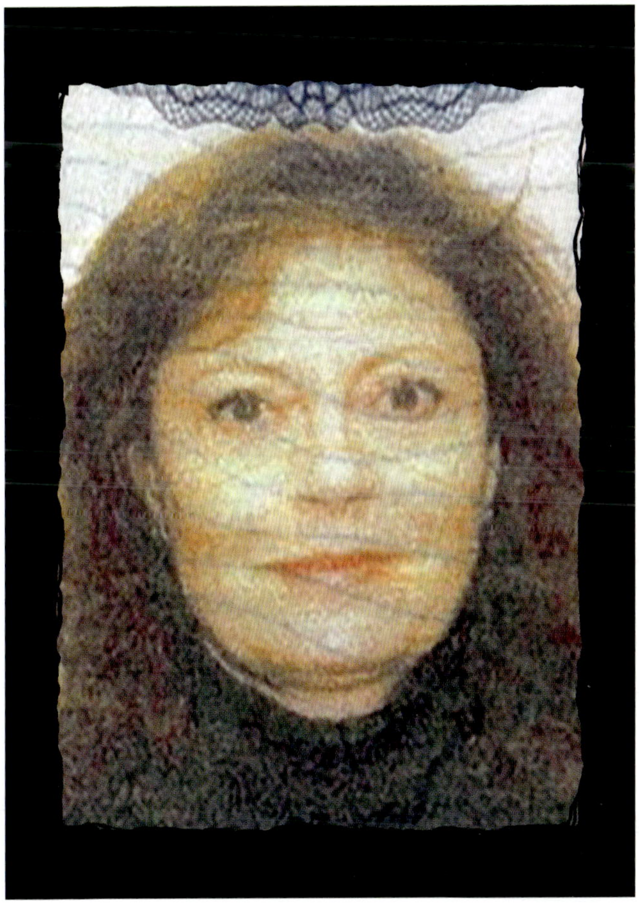

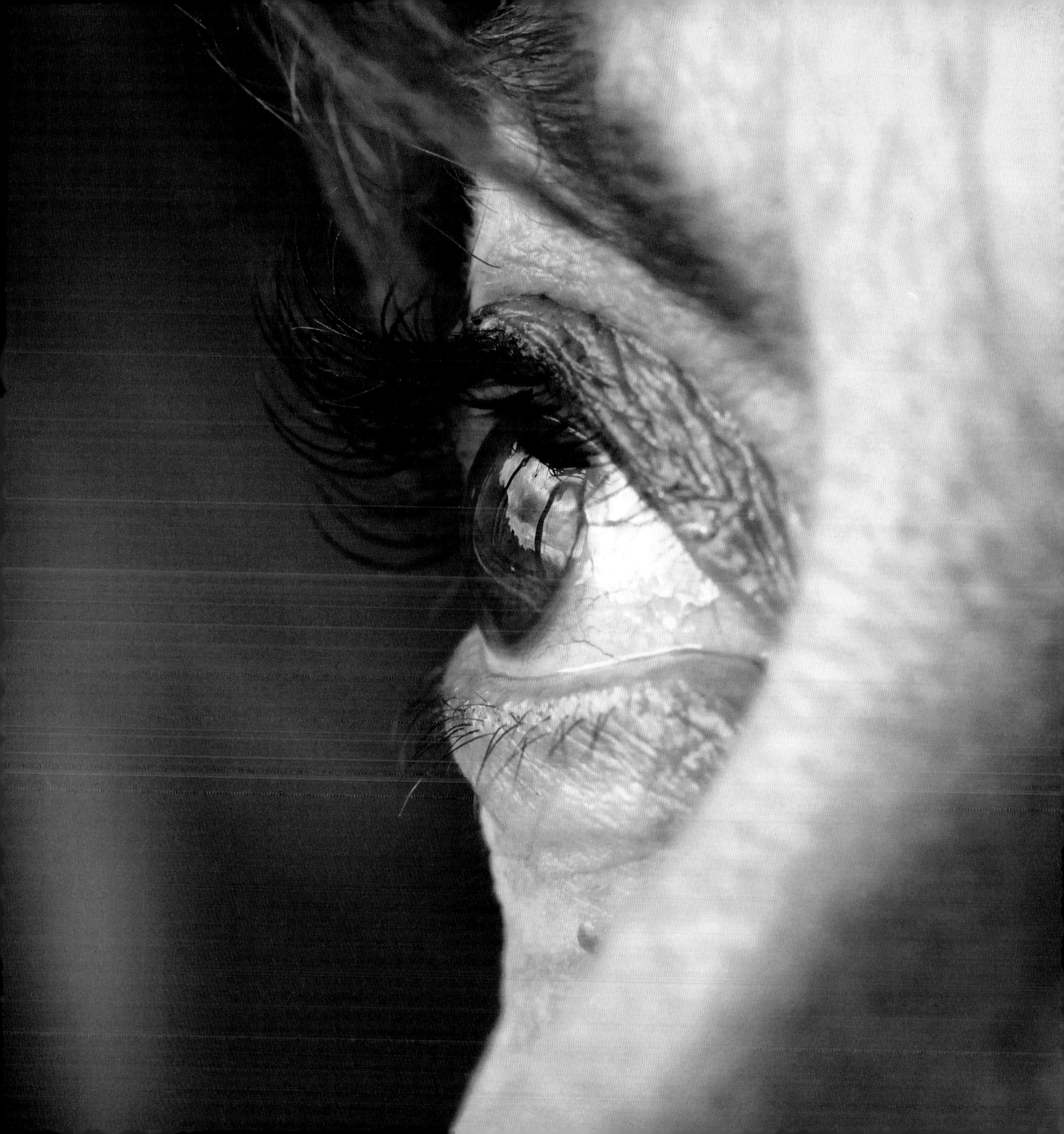

ROBERT PLANT

Born in West Bromwich, England; August 20, 1948
Eyes: blue

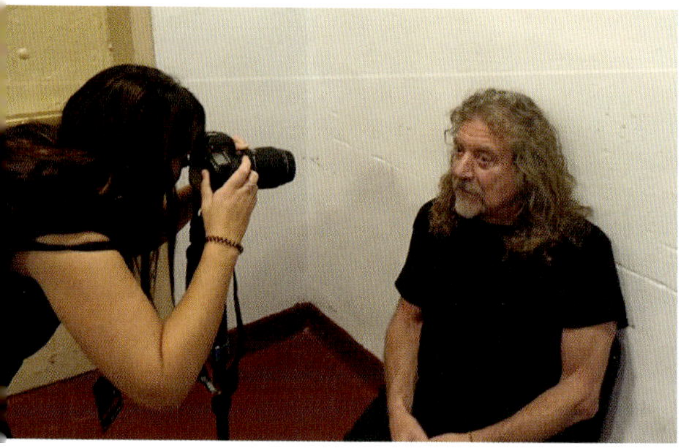

This was another shoot I really enjoyed. I shot Robert at The Town Hall in New York City. He was performing with Emmylou Harris, Steve Earle, Buddy Miller and The Milk Carton Kids. It was a great show programed as songwriters in the round.

The organisers of the show asked me to shoot some pictures of the performance so I spent much of the night in the photographers' pit. One of the highlights for me was Joan Baez joining Emmylou Harris at the finale. They are two women I have always admired. It was my first time meeting Robert and he couldn't have been more welcoming. He teased me about my dad being a cheat on the tennis court; they are great friends and have an admiration for each other's music.

We chatted backstage and Robert enthused about the American performers he was singing with that night and his love of their authentic roots music. He struck a self-deprecating tone which I found typically English, eschewing his Led Zeppelin back catalogue as "Hobbit songs" before performing an empathetic set of Americana. However, I am sure the American performers were just as in awe to share the stage with a bona fide British legend.

I shot Robert in a bright, unforgiving hallway backstage. We were standing at the bottom of a busy stairwell with people bustling around us. I quickly grabbed a shot and in spite of the pre-show chaos, I felt it captured something tender in his eye. A stillness in a man who, while being a relentless force onstage, has in these last few years evolved into a more wizened presence.

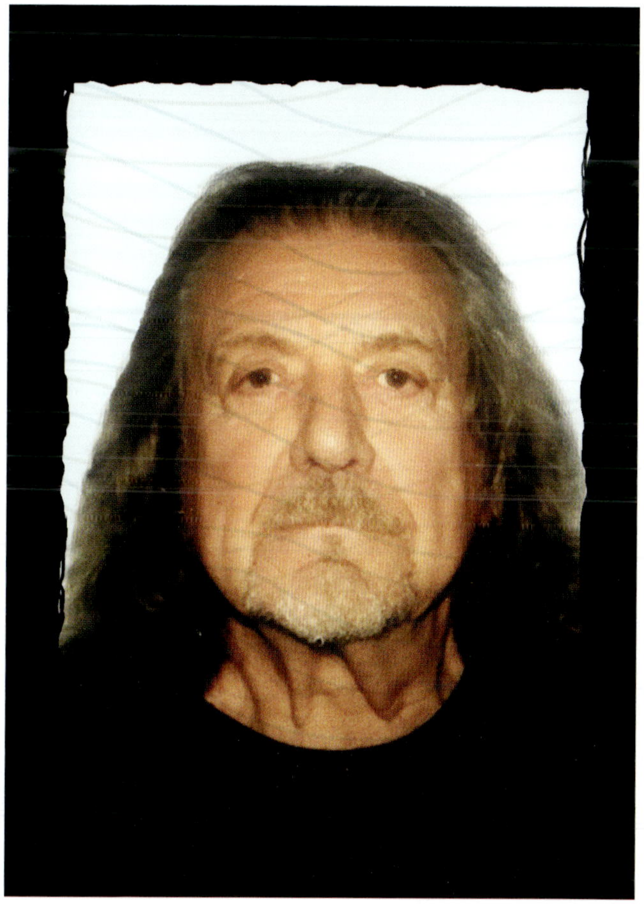

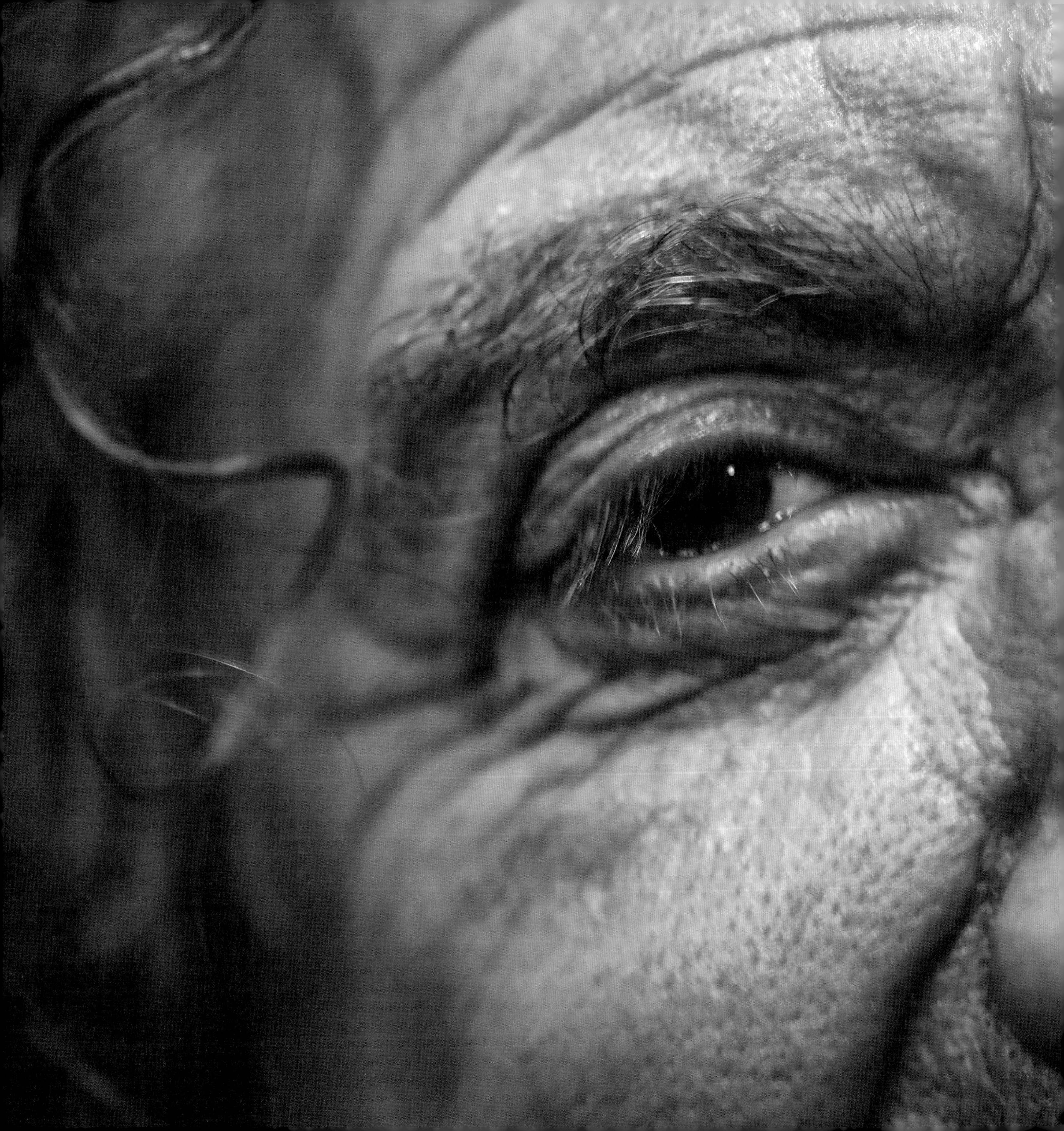

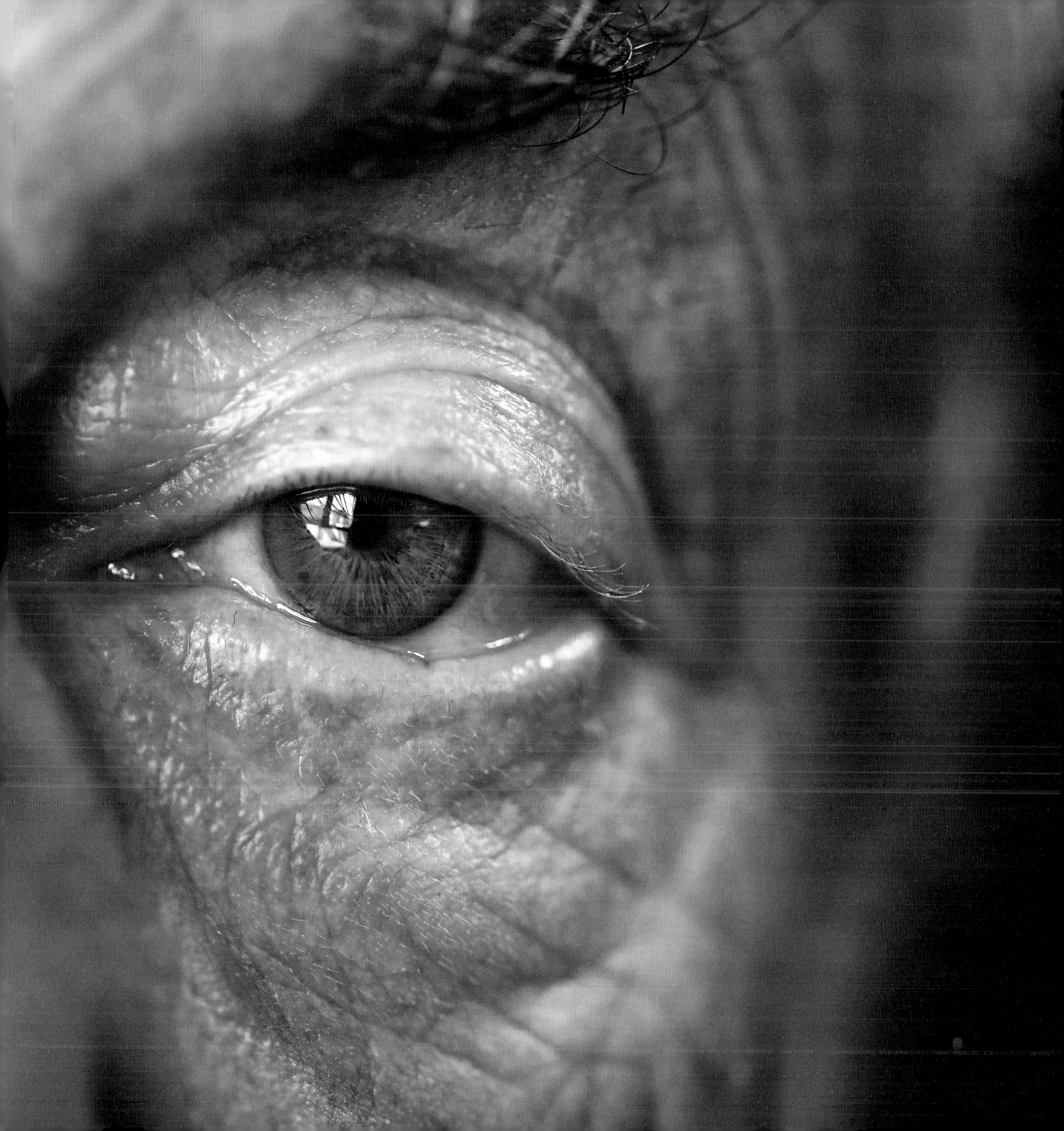

NICK MASON

Born in Birmingham, England; January 27, 1944
Eyes: blue

Nick is one of the founding members of Pink Floyd. I have a fond memory of seeing Pink Floyd at Wembley as a teenager. I watched the show from the mixing desk and a huge disco ball rose out from beneath us and lit up the stadium. The visual aspects of their shows, much like dad's, always appealed to me and left an impression.

Nick lives near my dad in the West Country; they have been good friends for years. I photographed Nick at his office and was completely taken aback by a massive vintage Ferrari race car parked in the center of the room. It was impressive. As someone who doesn't know much about cars this was clearly an undeniably beautiful piece of machinery. I've since found out Nick is a race car driver himself.

The shoot was quick, as usual, but I really like this photo. Nick was unconcerned about how he looked in the photo, and I found the lines on his face compelling and quite beautiful. The shape of his eyes and the lines around them created something graphically interesting. In addition to being a driver, he's also a mechanic, so there's something meticulous and precise about him that I think comes through in the image.

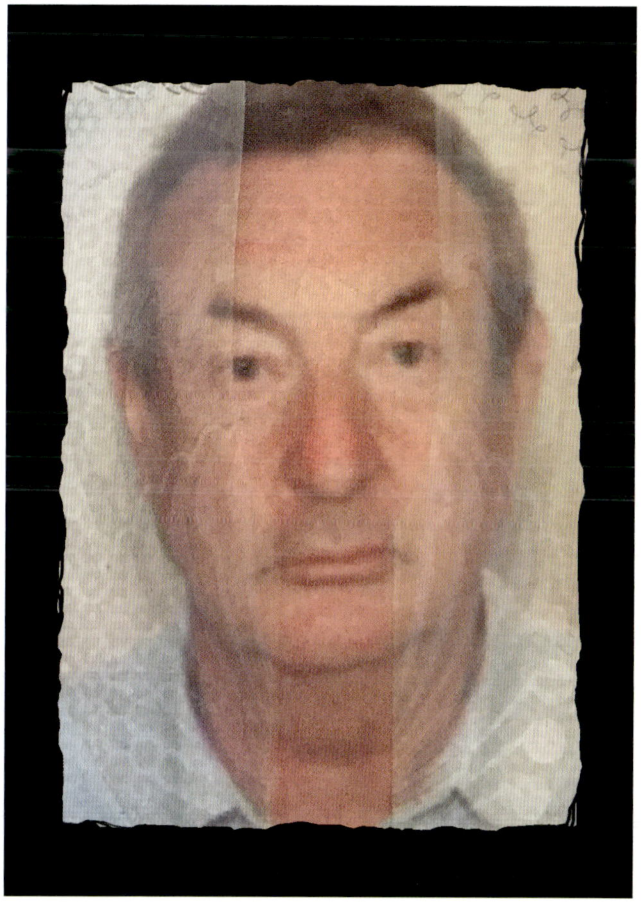

3D from MASSIVE ATTACK

Born in Bristol, England; January 21, 1965
Eyes: blue

Trip-hop pioneers Massive Attack are from Bristol, which is not far from Bath, where my dad's Real World Studios are located. Though geographically nearby, Bristol has a distinct culture, with more of an industrial, working class history that's morphed into a hip, vibrant art and music scene. Massive Attack have recorded at Real World Studios before, but if we met back then, it was too long ago for me to remember.

3D, in addition to being a part of Massive Attack, is also a notable artist. He invited me to come by his office, which is half recording studio and half art studio. His art is incredible and just after I shot him there were rumors swirling in the press that he is Banksy (a claim he denies).

He showed me around the studio and inspired by his own creativity, I wanted to do something a bit out of the ordinary. So I used a hand mirror next to his eyes to create a strange abstract image. He was quite open to the idea. We started playing around with the mirror. As he put it up to his eye, it began making interesting reflections.

Since Massive Attack made the music I grew up with, I was a little intimidated at first. When you get right up against someone's face with a camera, you're really entering their personal space. But 3D didn't have a problem with it. I always send a photo after each shoot to get each person's approval. 3D came back with great enthusiasm for the photo, which was exciting for me as a fan of his art.

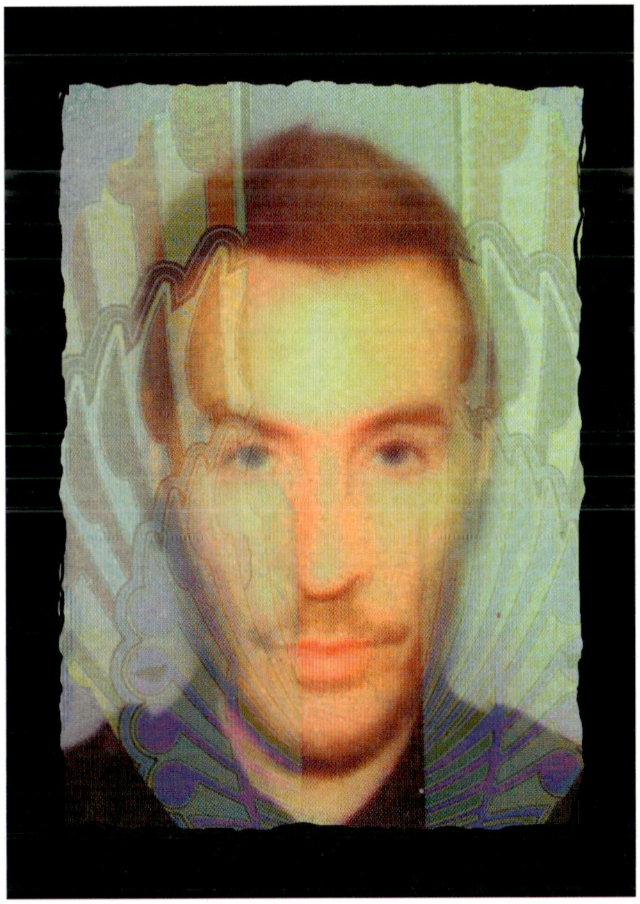

When you get right up
against someone's
face with a camera,
you're really entering
their personal
space.

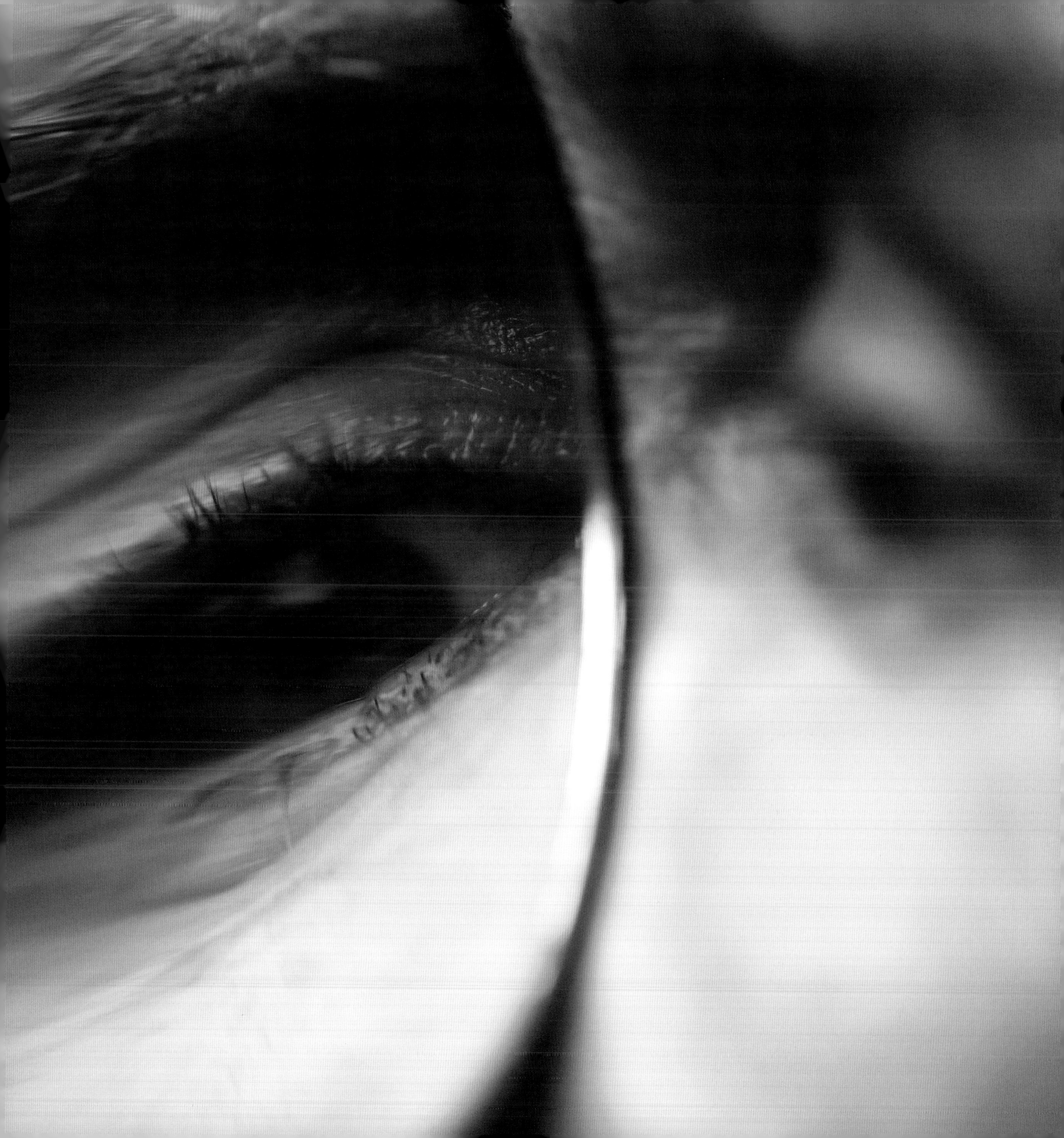

MICHAEL STIPE

Born in Decatur, Georgia; January 4, 1960
Eyes: blue

I've known Michael for years. We both often attended an annual event called the Amnesty International Human Rights Awards, with which my dad was involved. In fact, it was because of these events that the idea for Witness was born. Witness began as a way to help people document human rights abuses, and it's evolved over time as video cameras have become ubiquitous, but Michael was there at the inception and involved in the early days of Witness.

It made sense that Michael was one of the first people we approached for this book. He's interesting to me because he's a private man with many layers. I was curious as to which aspect he would reveal when we took his photo.

I went to Michael's apartment in New York and he came up with a great idea. We were sitting by the window in his bedroom, and were about to take the photo when he said: "Hang on a second," and went to the bathroom. He came back wearing the most amazing gold eyeliner. This photograph is really best in colour to see the gold but it still captures a side to Michael I hadn't seen before.

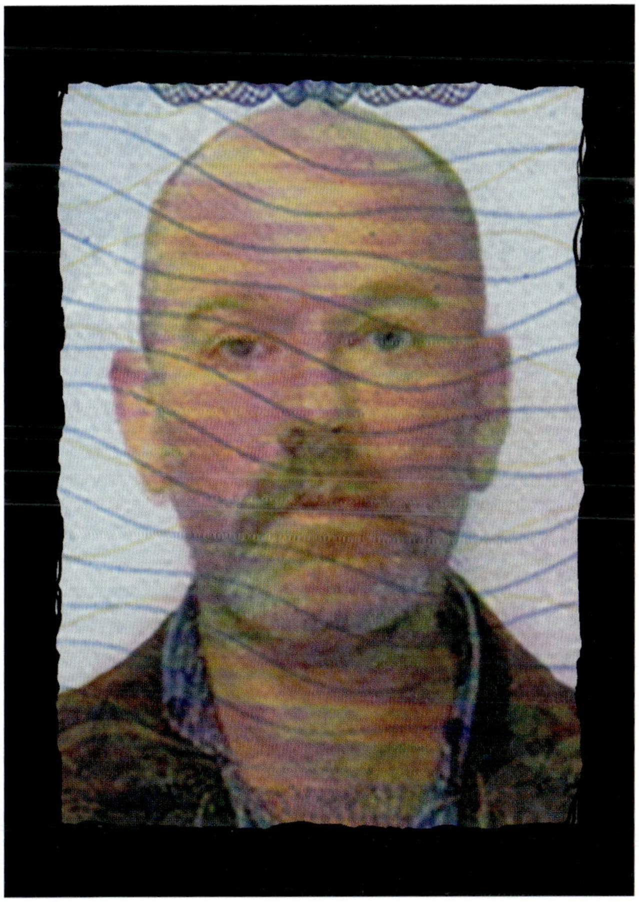

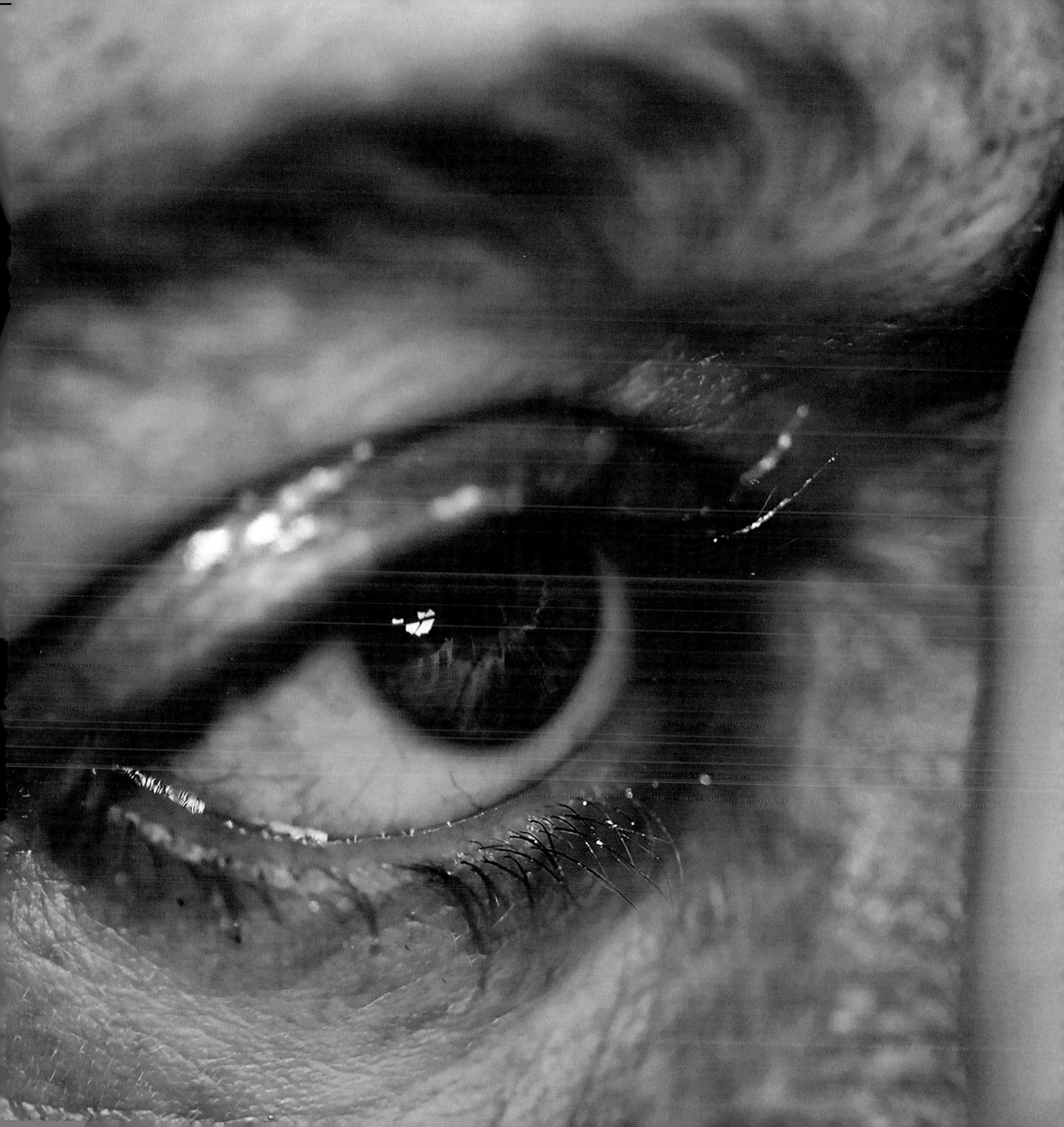

RICHARD BRANSON

Born in London, England; July 18, 1950
Eyes: blue

Richard is a real prankster. A bit like dad, he's very shy at first but can get very playful and funny. He and dad play off each other; they get very competitive and have a good time.

I know Richard as a larger-than-life family friend, who's silly, self-deprecating and willing to do anything to get a laugh. When I was younger we went on several family vacations together and my family has known the Bransons for many years.

However, I hadn't seen Richard for quite some time before this shoot. I shot him at the Virgin office in New York. It was a less than ideal setting, because I was shooting him in the middle of a big office surrounded by Virgin employees and he was under time pressure. This created a strange tension because despite knowing him quite well, there was no intimacy to the shoot.

I wanted to capture the cheeky prankster element that I remembered so well, so I tried to manipulate the photo so it looks like he was holding his eyeball at a distance from his face. He then started playing around and pulling on his eye, and I immediately knew this was the Richard I was trying to capture.

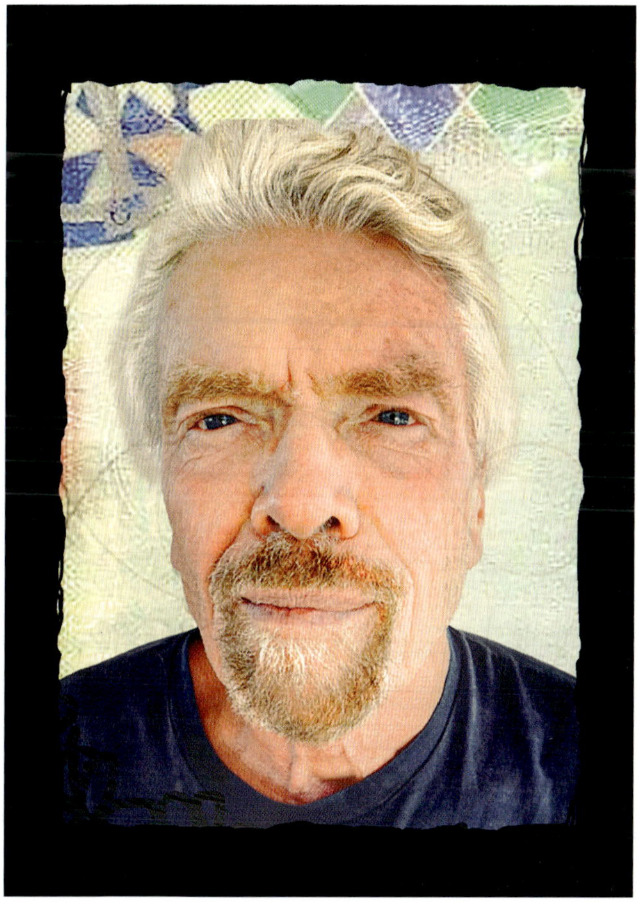

I wanted to capture the
cheeky prankster element
that I remembered
so well...

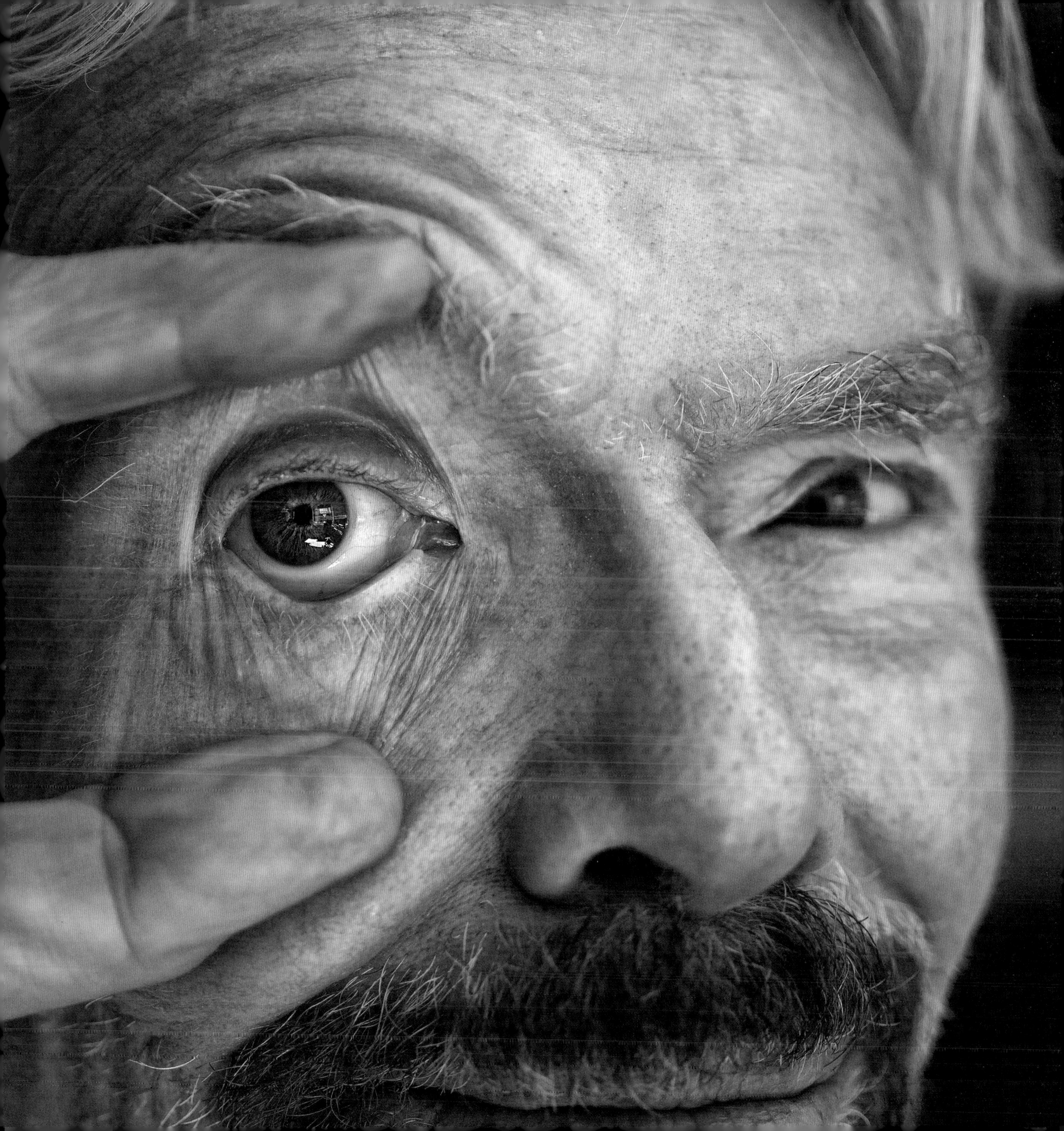

AMADOU & MARIAM

Bagayoko

Born in Bamako, Mali; October 24, 1954
Eyes: dark brown

Doumbia

Born in Bamako, Mali; April 25, 1958
Eyes: dark brown

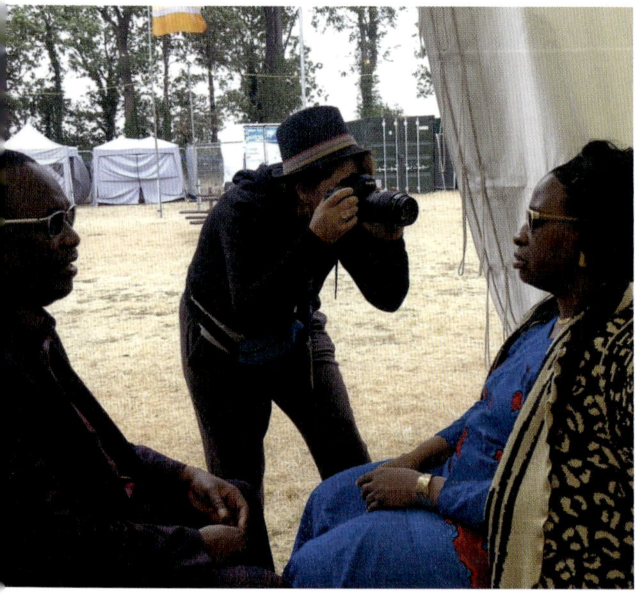

Growing up, my sister and I were exposed to world music through the WOMAD festival, which my dad co-founded. This gave us an appreciation for music from different cultures, specifically Africa.

Amadou and Miriam are a husband and wife duo from Mali, which is next door to Senegal where my father had a house when we were younger. They're both blind, and met when they were students at a school for the visually impaired. My dad has loved their music for a long time and asked them to perform at his wedding in Sardinia. It was a magical night and we all had fun dancing the night away to their incredible music.

When I photographed them, they were performing at WOMAD festival in the southwest of England. I wasn't quite sure how to do this shoot since they are both blind, and they don't like to take their sunglasses off. I decided to shoot them sitting opposite each other. I wanted to capture their reflection in the sunglasses. It was tricky especially at a festival in a tent because reflections are hard to get if you don't have the right lighting.

Even though this photo doesn't reveal their eyes, I feel it says something about who they are and their intense closeness to one another.

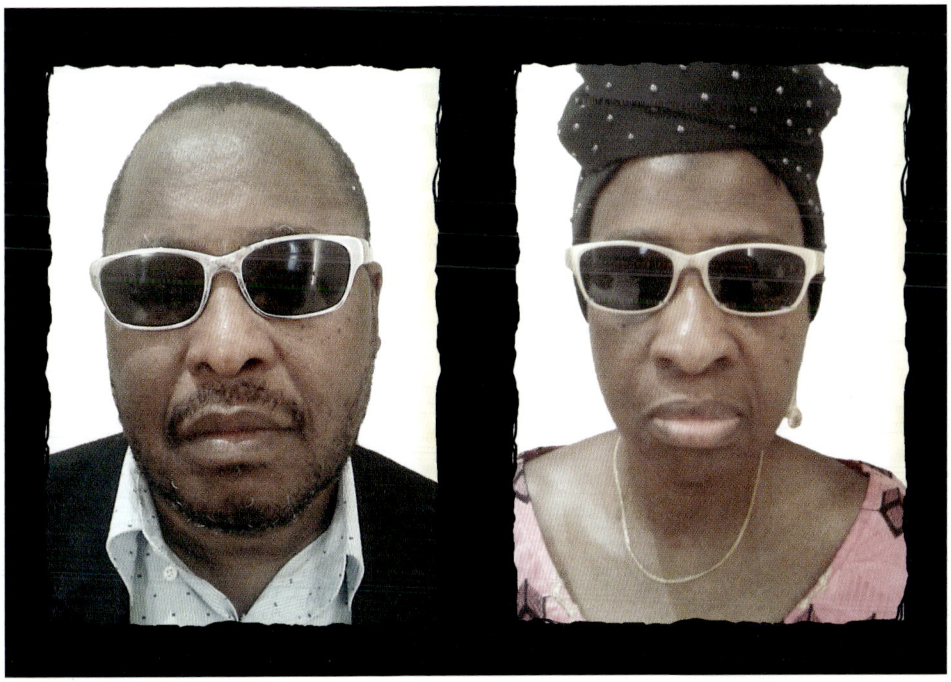

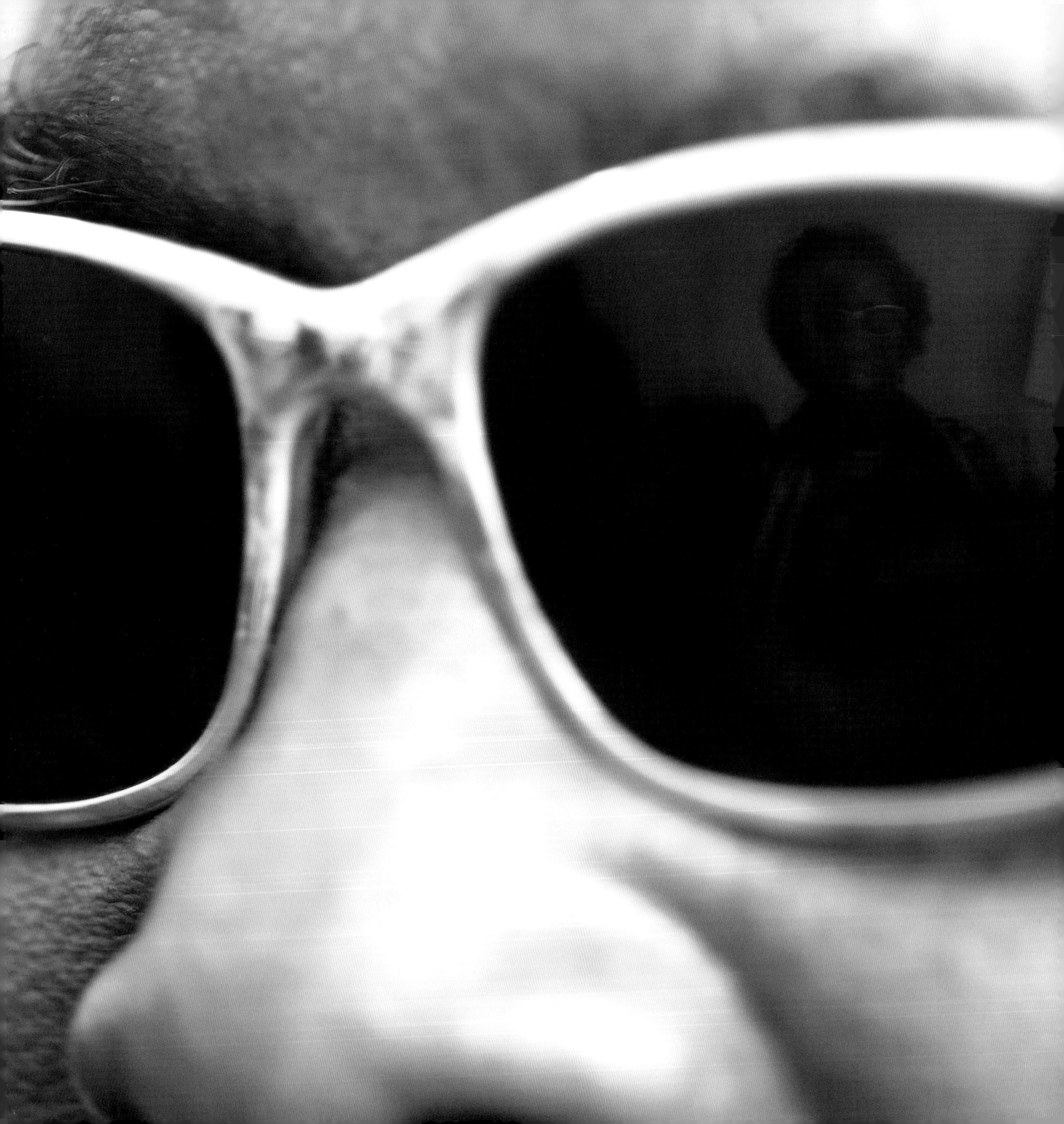

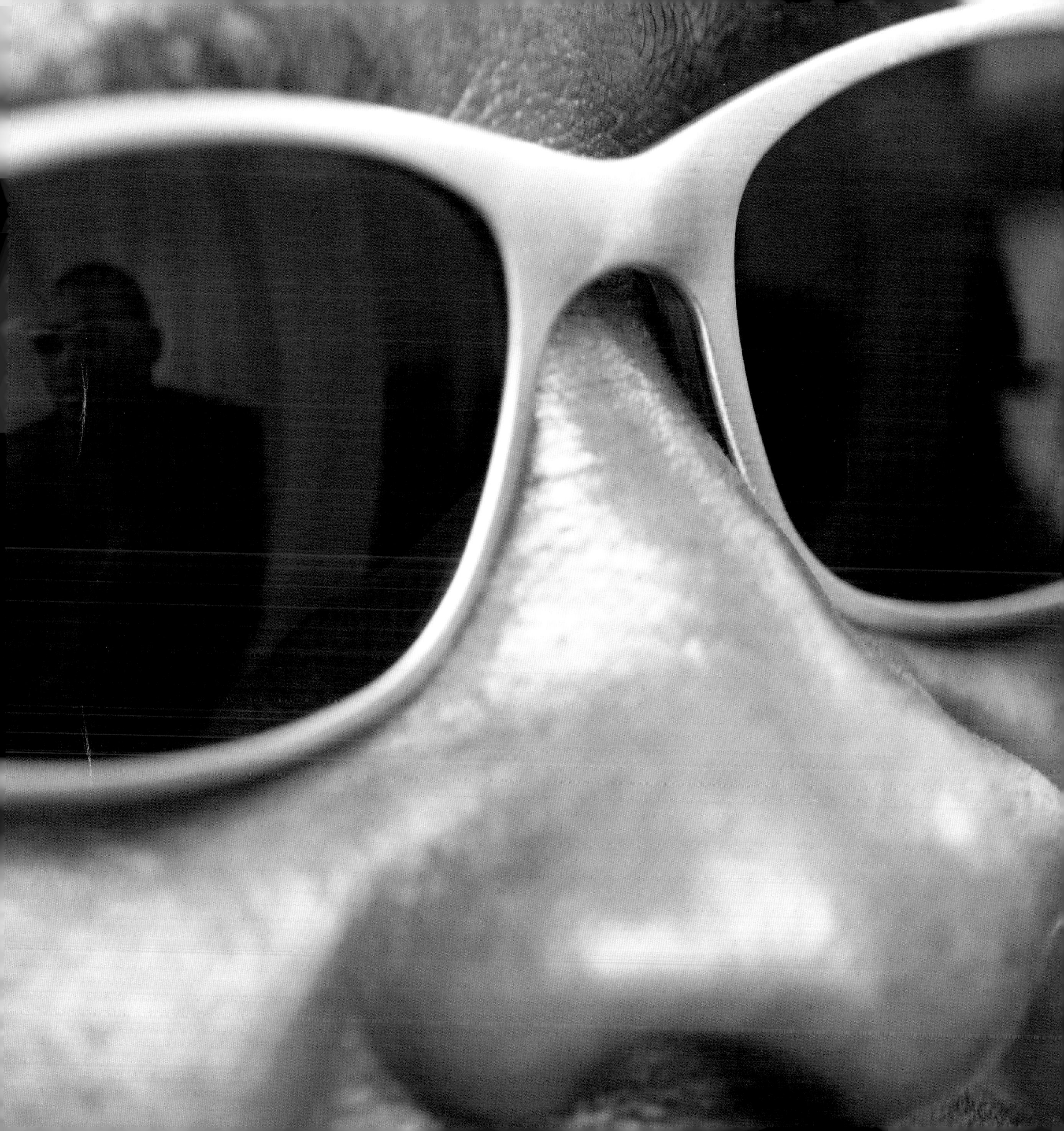

LOU REED

Born in New York City, New York; March 2, 1942
Eyes: brown

Lou Reed had been friends with my dad for many years. They had a wonderful and funny rapport together and I have happy memories of dinners with them both making each other laugh. Lou was a part of the covers album; my dad covered a beautiful love song he wrote for Laurie called "Power of the Heart" and Lou did "Solsbury Hill".

When we first reached out to Lou about being part of this book, he was reluctant to commit to it due to time constraints. In any event he offered to take his own photo and send it to me. When the photo arrived, I didn't know what to think of it. The image was one big blur. It took a moment but I came to realise there was something quite beautiful about it.

In college, I took a series of blurry out-of-focus photographs so I have always liked that aesthetic. Still, the decision to include it in the book was a difficult one at first since it's the only photo I didn't take. However, given that Lou is sadly no longer with us, I feel like there's a strange poignancy about this spiritual, blurry, self-portrait. It's an honor to have a piece of Lou's artwork included in this series.

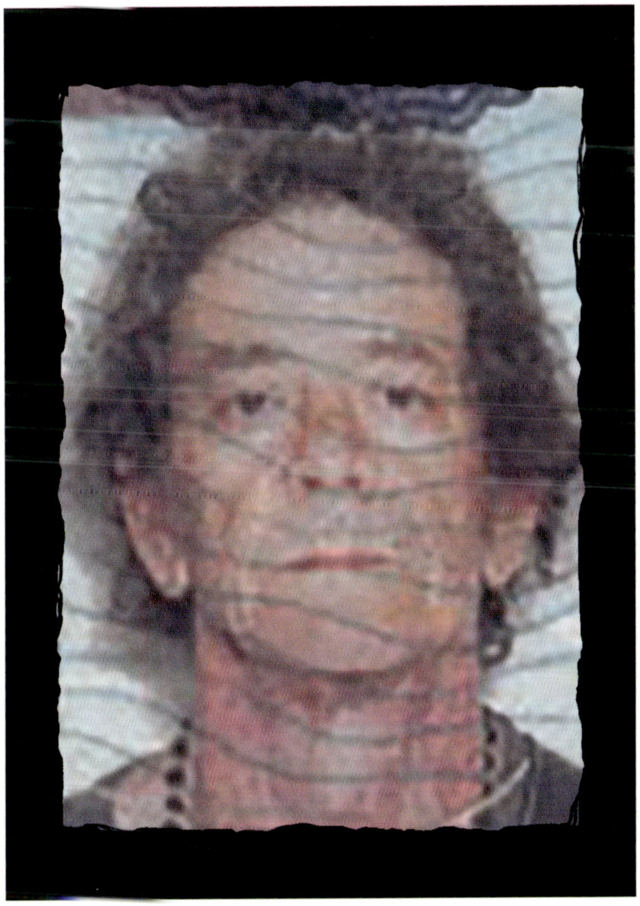

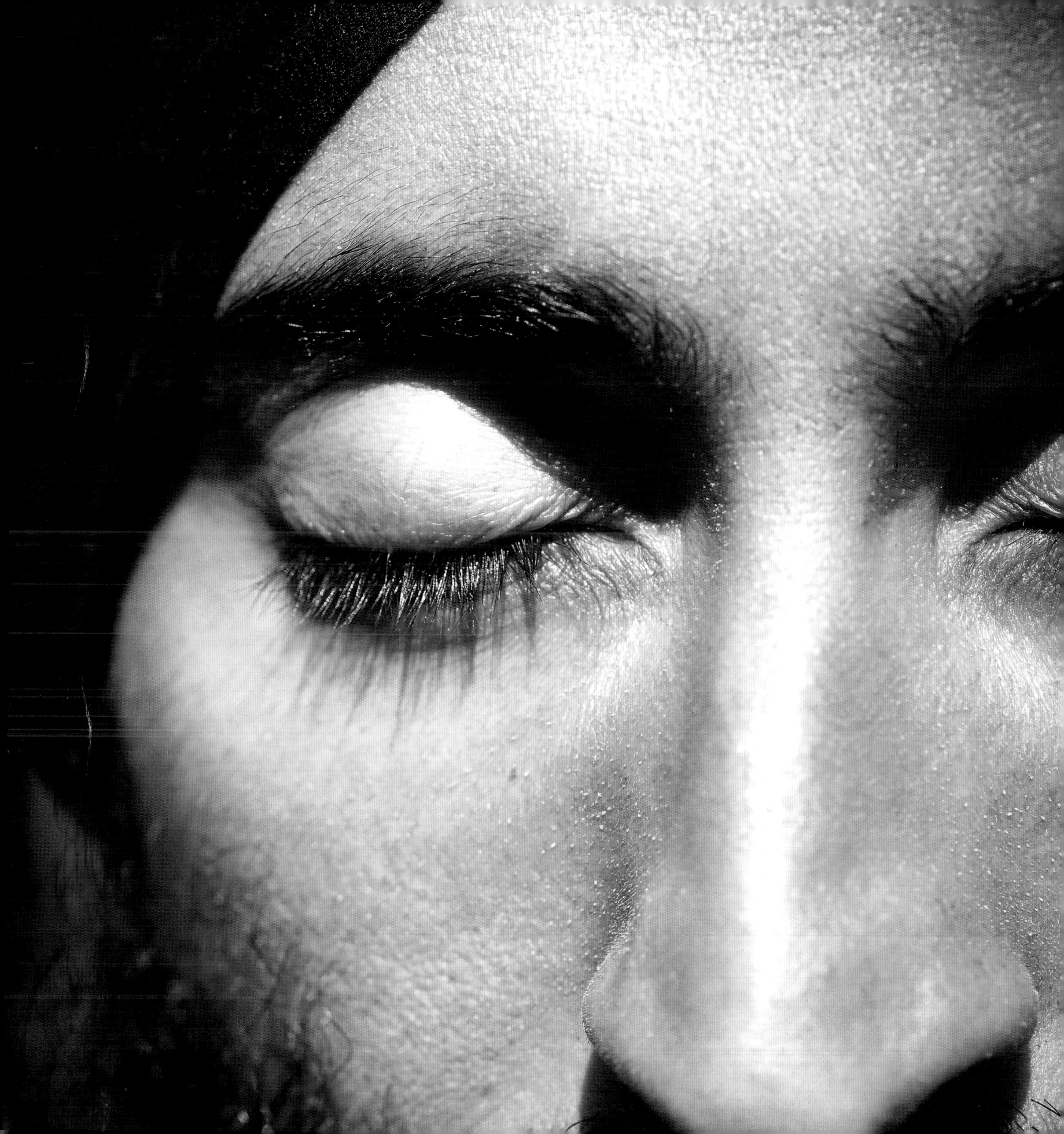

WARIS AHLUWALIA

Born in Amritsar, Punjab, India; 1975
Eyes: dark brown

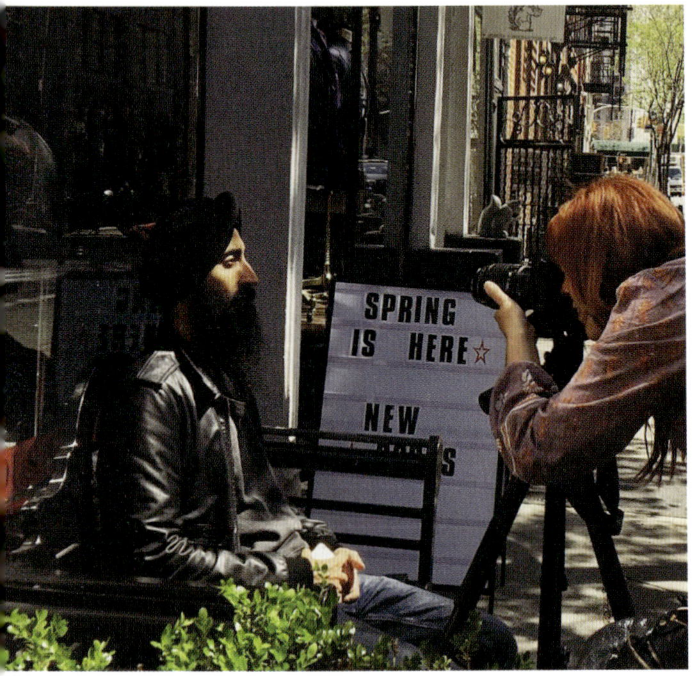

Waris is one of those people who seems to be everywhere, know everyone, and do everything, with style. Waris's talent is difficult to pigeonhole but it begins with fashion and jewelry and extends to film, art, restaurants and philanthropy. The only common link seems to be his unstoppable exuberance, highly-refined aesthetic sensibility, and his effortless cool.

I first met Waris while working with Adria Petty; she and I were co-directing music videos at the time, when Waris got in touch with us. Waris is a bit like *Where's Wally*, in that he constantly pops up in unexpected places. He's always involved in something new and fascinating and he's a great connector of people. He is always exquisitely well dressed and has a terrific sense of humor.

I shot him outside a clothing store in the West Village. We sat on a bench outside. Waris is one of the few people I shot in this book with their eyes closed. He looked so perfect. While we obviously don't see his eyes, I really like how this photo captured the beauty of his face.

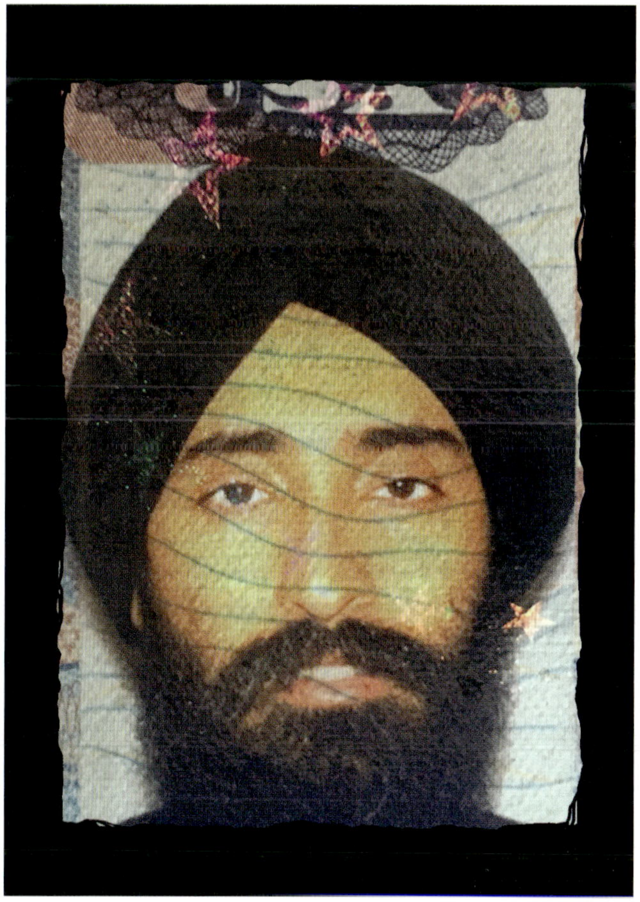

LAURIE ANDERSON

Born in Chicago, Illinois; June 5, 1947
Eyes: green

Laurie Anderson is unlike anyone else on this planet. She is diamond-like: her eyes sparkle with a mischievous, curious, iconoclastic spirit. She has a wizened air about her. Her slightest gesture contains multitudes of meanings.

I had met Laurie a few times because she's an old friend of my dad. When I was growing up she was someone who's always been spoken about in our house with reverence.

They wrote a song together called "This is the Picture", which I have always liked as it melds both their artistic spirits, with each of them releasing their own versions.

When I moved to New York, my first apartment was on Canal Street and the West Side Highway. With a slight envy, I would always notice that the building next door had an incredible roof deck, and think to myself: "Whoever lives there must have an amazing place."

I would occasionally see Laurie wandering around the neighbourhood with Lou Reed, so I figured she lived somewhere nearby. And when I finally went to shoot her for this book, I realised she was the one with the roof deck next door. In addition to being enormously creative, she is also someone who's very open and approachable. We chatted about how the petrol station near our apartment was being turned into condos and how the neighbourhood was changing and rapidly gentrifying.

Inspired by her, I wanted to do something playful and unexpected, and I knew she'd be up for it. I did all these double exposures of her eyes, which I felt represented her, but in the end I decided not to use them because they were too different from the rest of the book.

For some inexplicable reason, nearly every person I photographed for this book has wanted me to shoot their left eye. I keep on trying to get people to allow me to shoot the other eye so that we have a mix. True to her reputation as someone who always zigs when others zag, Laurie Anderson let me shoot her right eye. Perhaps by coincidence, she has a song called "My Right Eye".

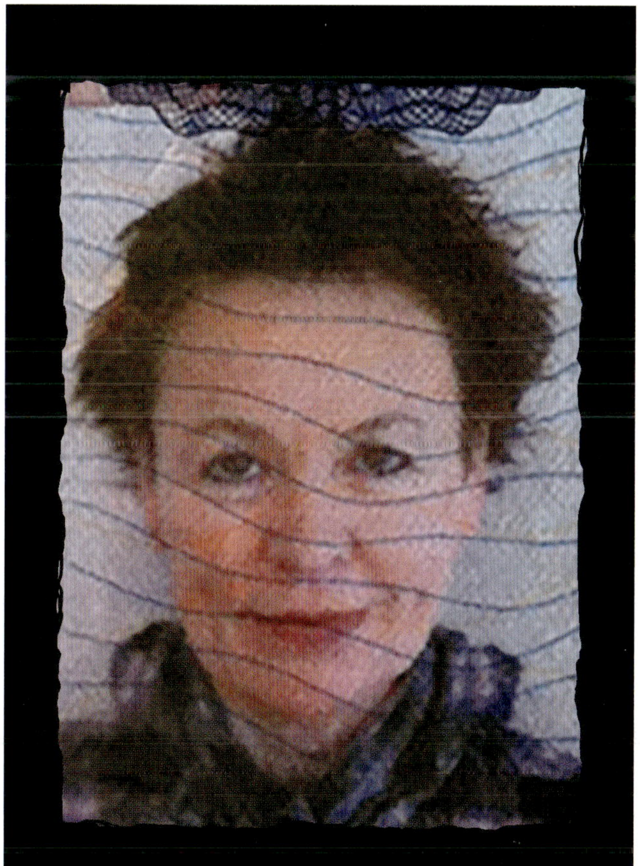

For some
inexplicable reason,
nearly every person
I photographed for this book
has wanted me to shoot
their left eye...

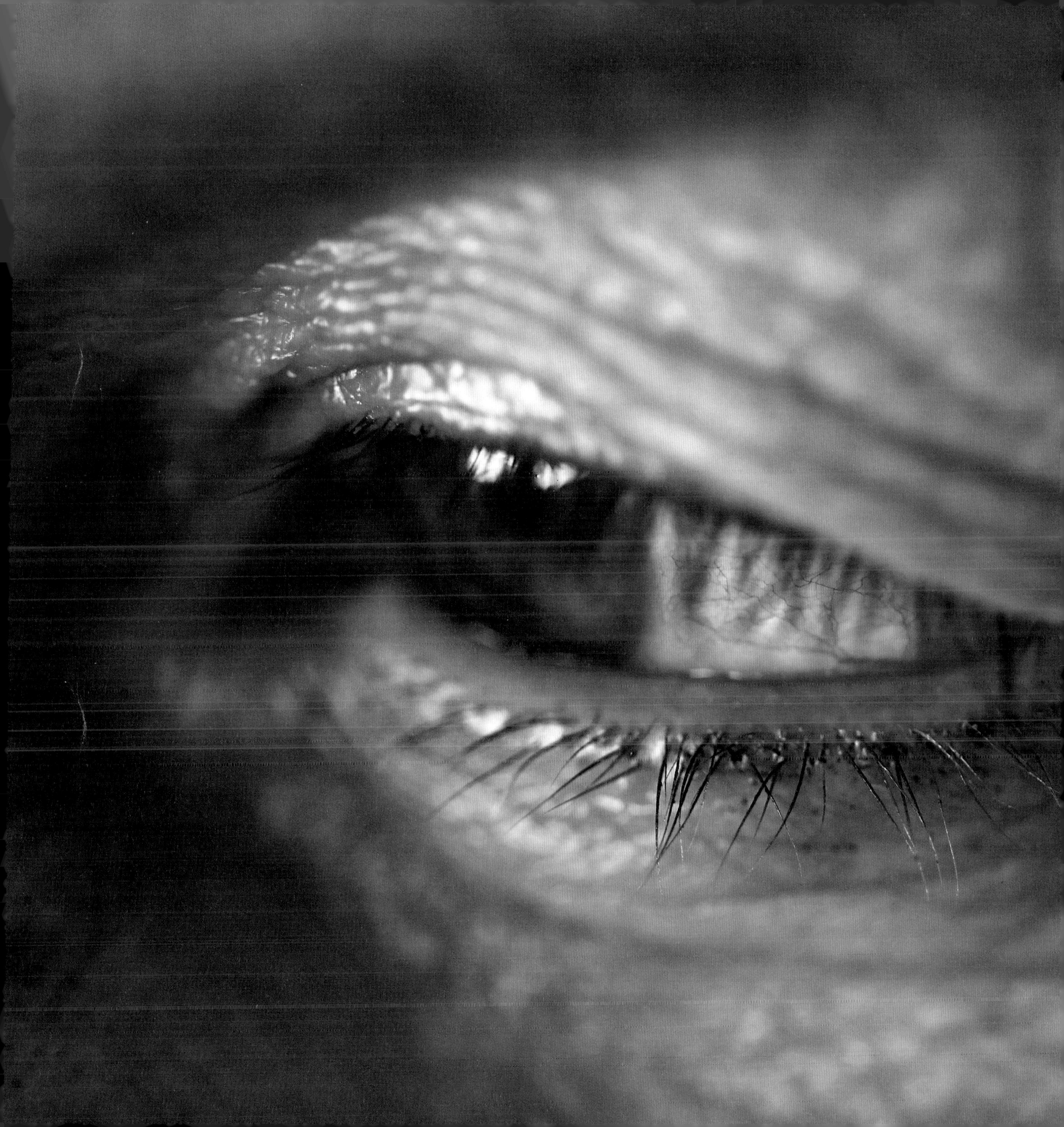

ALEXANDER EBERT

from EDWARD SHARPE and the MAGNETIC ZEROS

Born in Los Angeles, California; May 14, 1978
Eyes: blue

For my shoot with Alexander, I went down to his house in New Orleans. The location by itself instantly made this shoot one of my favorites, because I love the city, and used to go there quite often during my college days.

I would describe Alex as a spiritual person, by which I mean he has a kind of authentic inner gentleness. What makes Alex so rare is that he has a way of being genuinely respectful and present with everyone he meets.

The day of the shoot was one of those perfect spring days in New Orleans. I enjoyed every step as I walked the considerable distance from my hotel to where Alex lives beyond the French Quarter, a warehouse type space with a little backyard.

When I arrived, Alex was hanging out with friends and family, it was a very relaxed vibe. We went out into his back yard and Alex gazed up at the sky. His eyes were shut because it was so bright but there was something beautiful in this moment and I took the shot.

Even though, later I shot more photos inside with his eyes open, I felt I had captured something that represented him. His openness. His vulnerability. It was just a moment of peace.

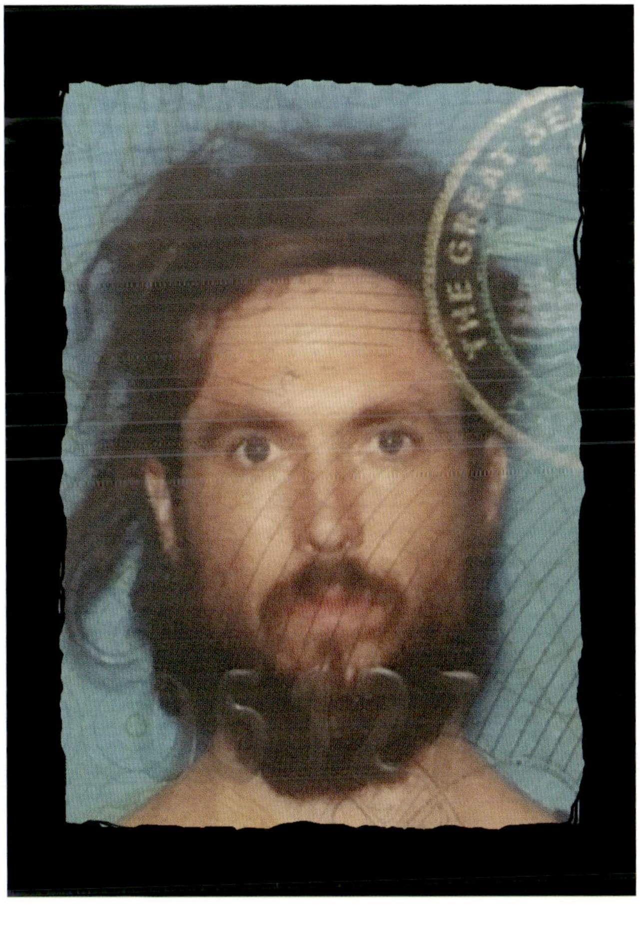
THE GREAT

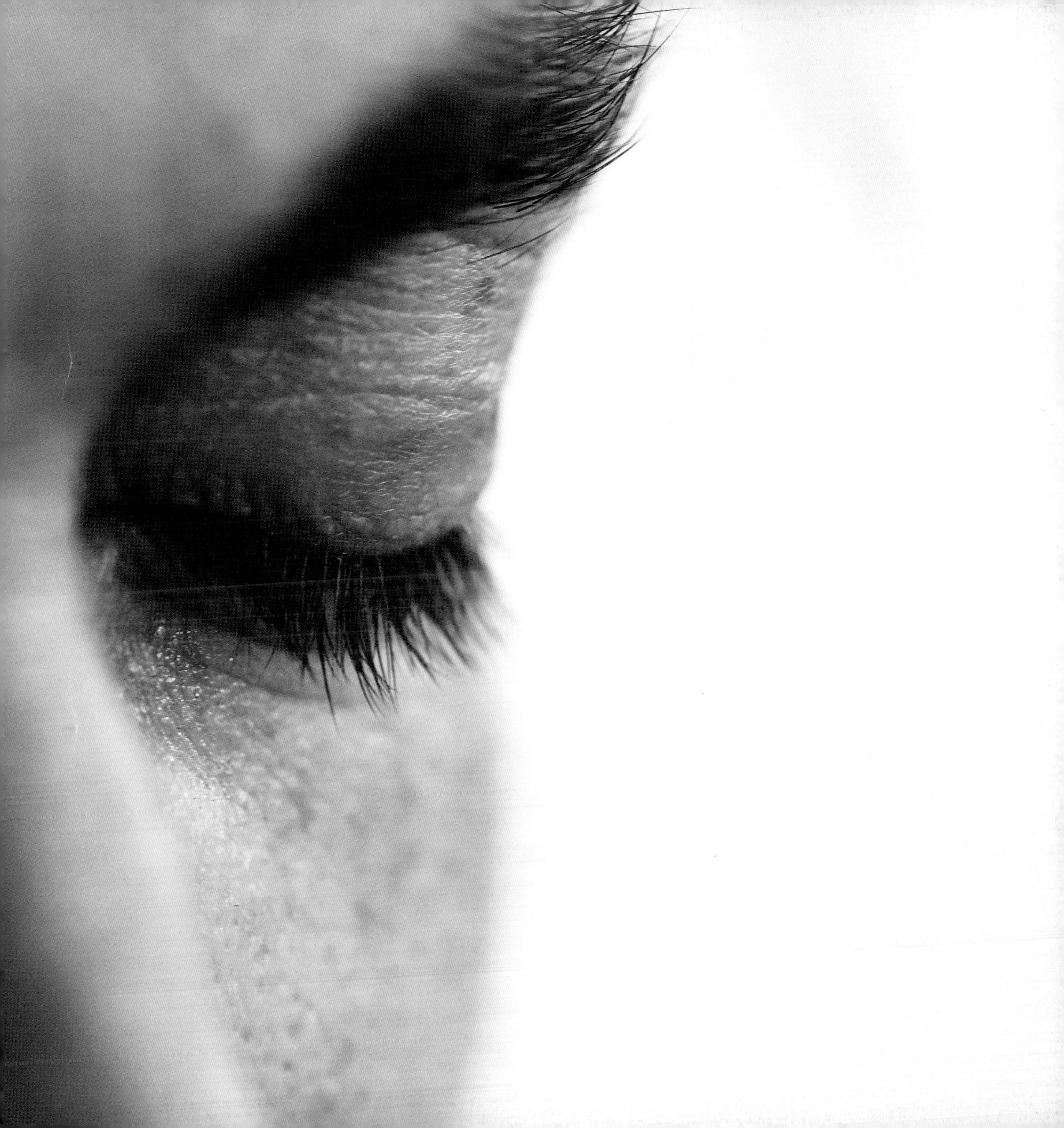

GUY GARVEY

Born in Bury, England; March 6, 1974
Eyes: green

In addition to being a fan of Elbow, I also love Guy Garvey's BBC 6 music show. Although I hadn't met Guy before, Elbow spent a lot of time recording at Real World and my dad covered one of their songs "Mirror Ball".

I photographed him at Real World in my dad's writing room, which is a studio that has incredible skylights so there's beautiful daylight. The room is full of random musical equipment, so I was tempted to use some of the vintage gear as a prop. At first, I was trying to take a photo of his fingers as well as his eyes as this was an early shot in the series, but I felt like that made his eyes look too dark. Personality-wise, there's nothing dark about Guy as he's full of warmth and enthusiasm. I really like the intensity of Guy's stare into the camera. I didn't feel it at the time but when I looked back at the shots I saw a sadness in his eyes that was quite beautiful.

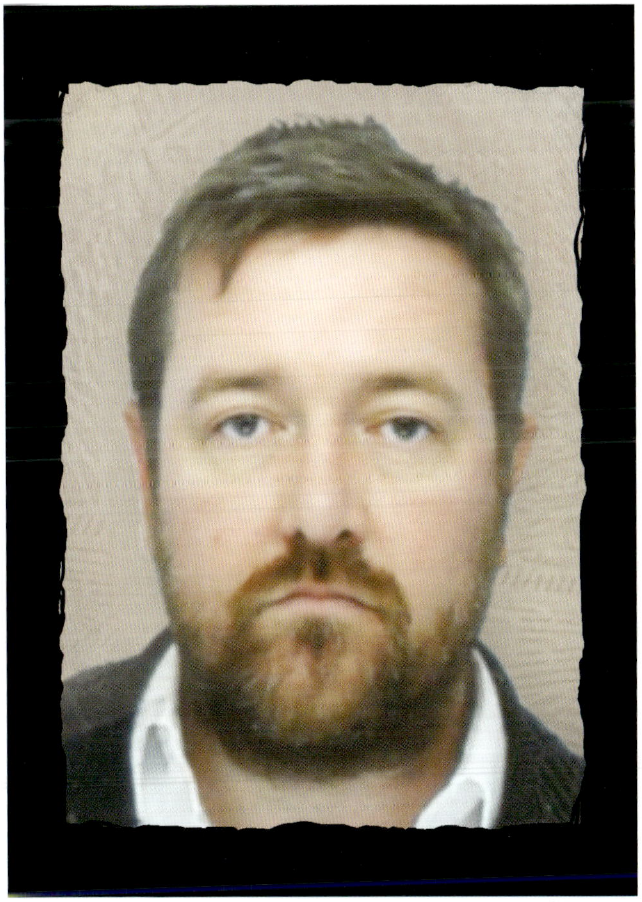

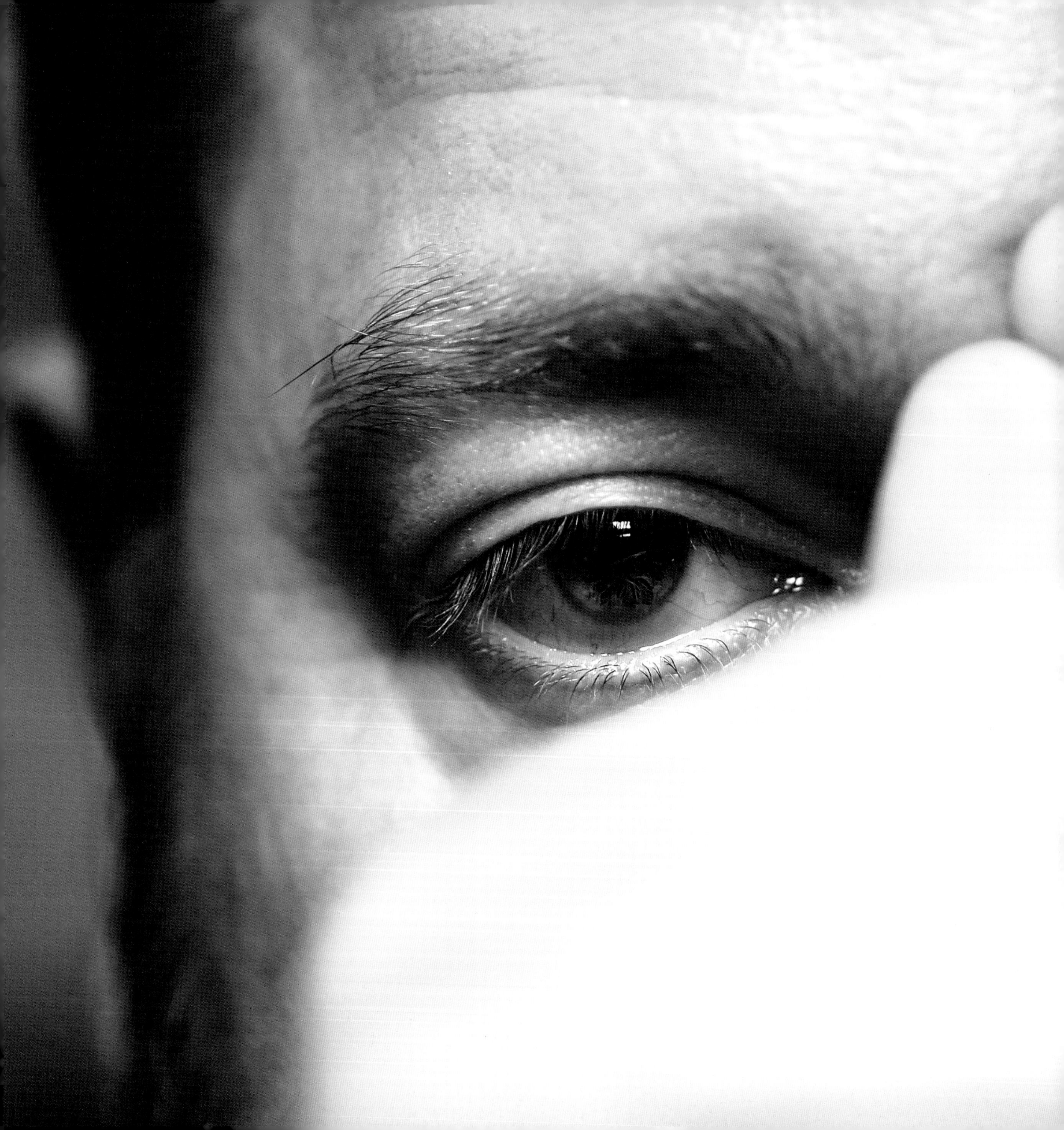

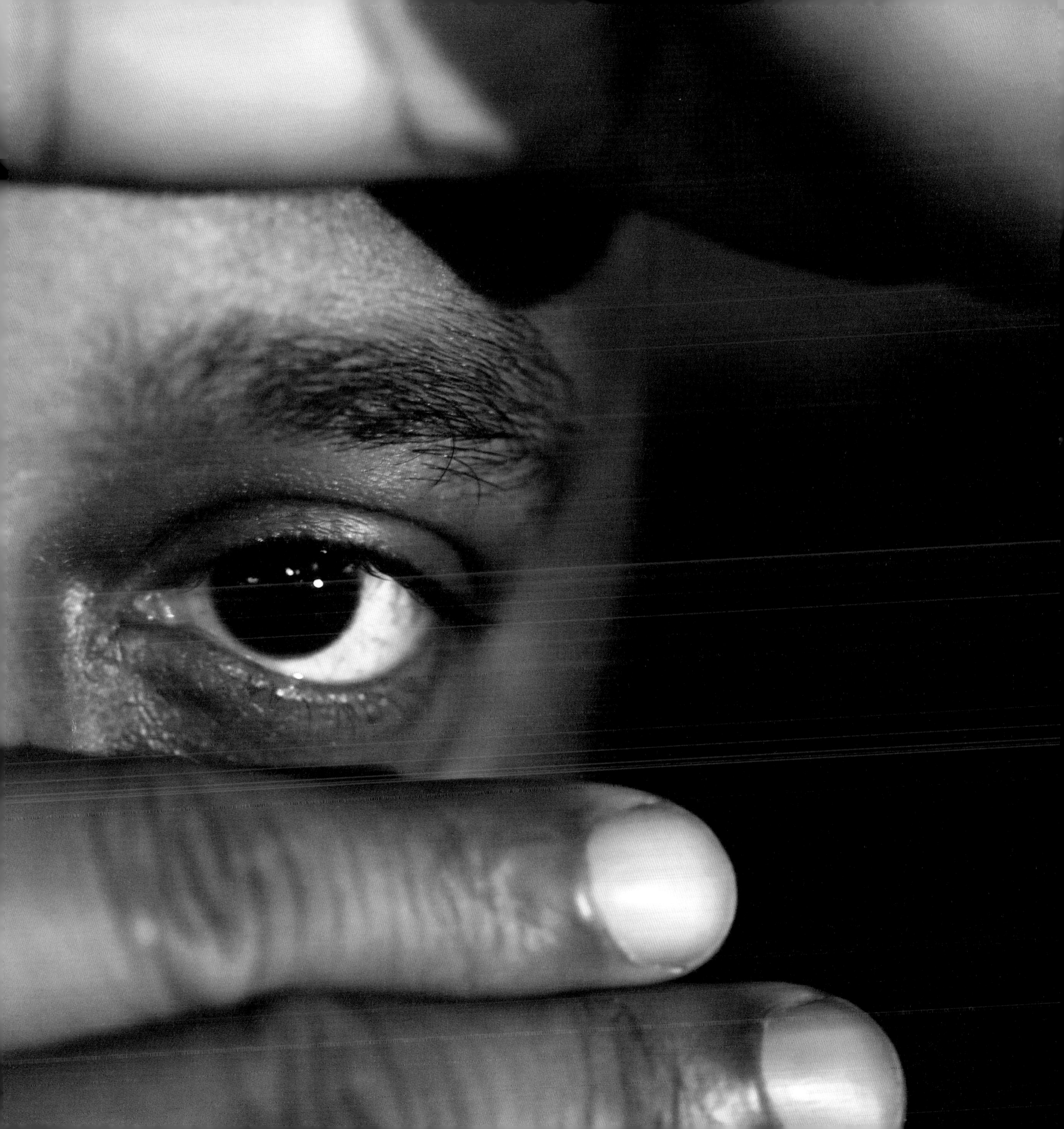

DAYMOND JOHN

Born in New York City, New York; February 23, 1969
Eyes: dark brown

Daymond is best known as the founder of the fashion company FUBU and also well-known to many as a judge on Shark Tank. I shot him while he was filming a panel discussion for Black Entrepreneurs Day, with LL Cool J, Chance the Rapper and Ice-T. They had this beautiful set in the Jane Hotel with a grand velvet chair by a fireplace.

I was running late because I'd recently bought a car and thought I'd chance driving into the city. Of course I couldn't find parking. Finally, I found a space to park but the hotel wouldn't let me in without a Covid test. So that delayed me even further. I can't bear being late for anyone so I was pretty stressed, but it turned out Daymond had luckily been delayed too so by the time we were ready to go it was a quick and simple shoot.

We went to the makeup area where they had a few bright lights as the rest of the set was dark and moody. I wanted to get his hands in this shot. He had been wearing a mask the entire time but he took it off for the photograph. I was tempted to shoot him with his mask on but in the end I didn't want to immortalise the pandemic in this photograph.

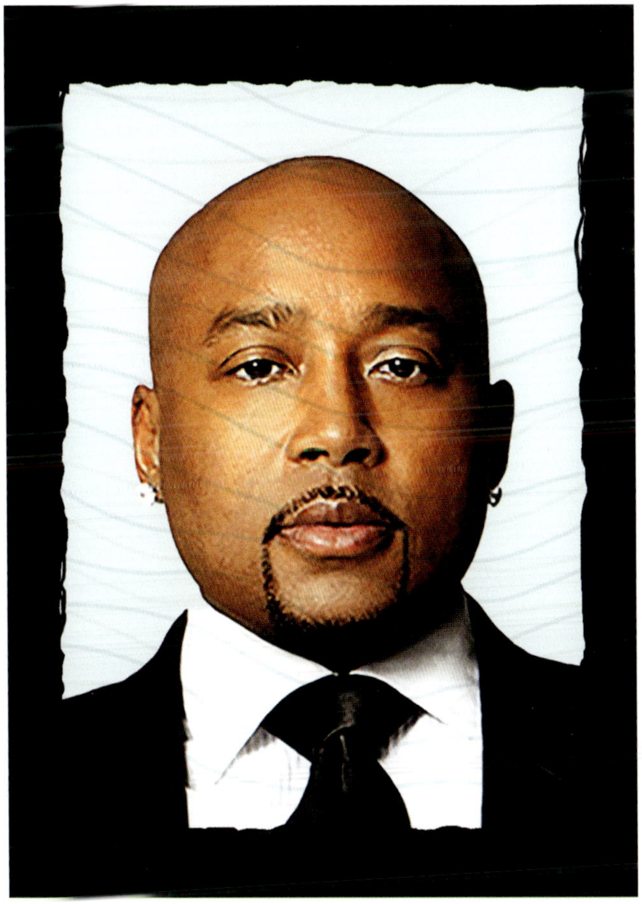

JEAN-MICHEL JARRE

Born in Lyon, France; August 25, 1948
Eyes: brown

Jean-Michel is the consummate showman. His performances are enormous visual spectacles, featuring lasers, gigantic sky projections, and fireworks. In person, he is someone who radiates confidence and Gallic charm.

I met him at his hotel in midtown Manhattan where he was staying for a flying visit. His hotel was one of those tragically hip hotels that's more like a nightclub, with a lot of neon lights and very few windows. So we went outside the front door of the hotel, in search of light.

I tried to find a quiet moment to take this intimate photo while millions of people were streaming past us in the middle of Times Square. The doorman was helpful, and tried to stop people from getting in the way of the shot. Normally with a close up you don't have to worry so much about that, but with Jean-Michel I wanted him to hold his hand in front of his face at arm's length to create some depth of field. Despite the throngs of humanity, we managed to make it work.

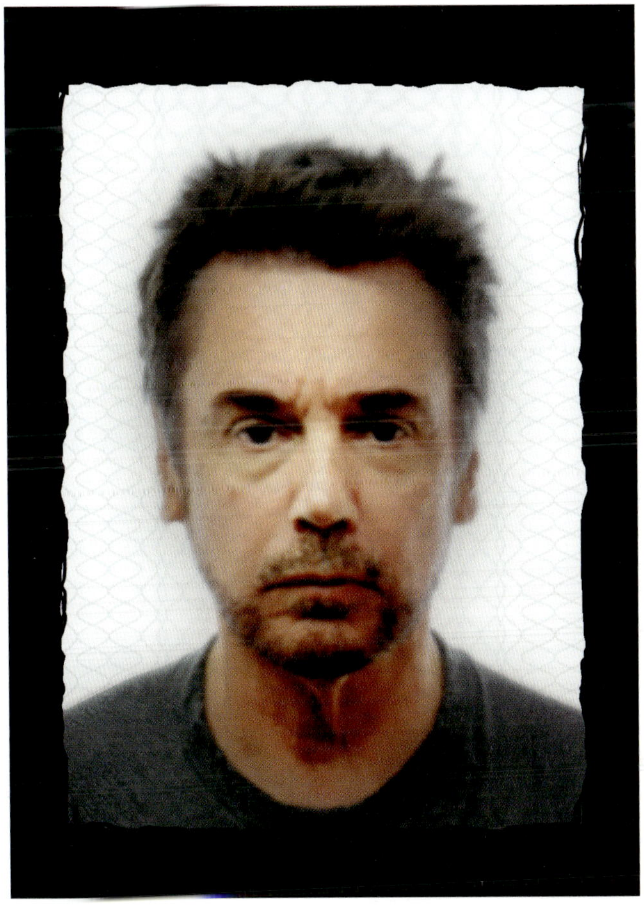

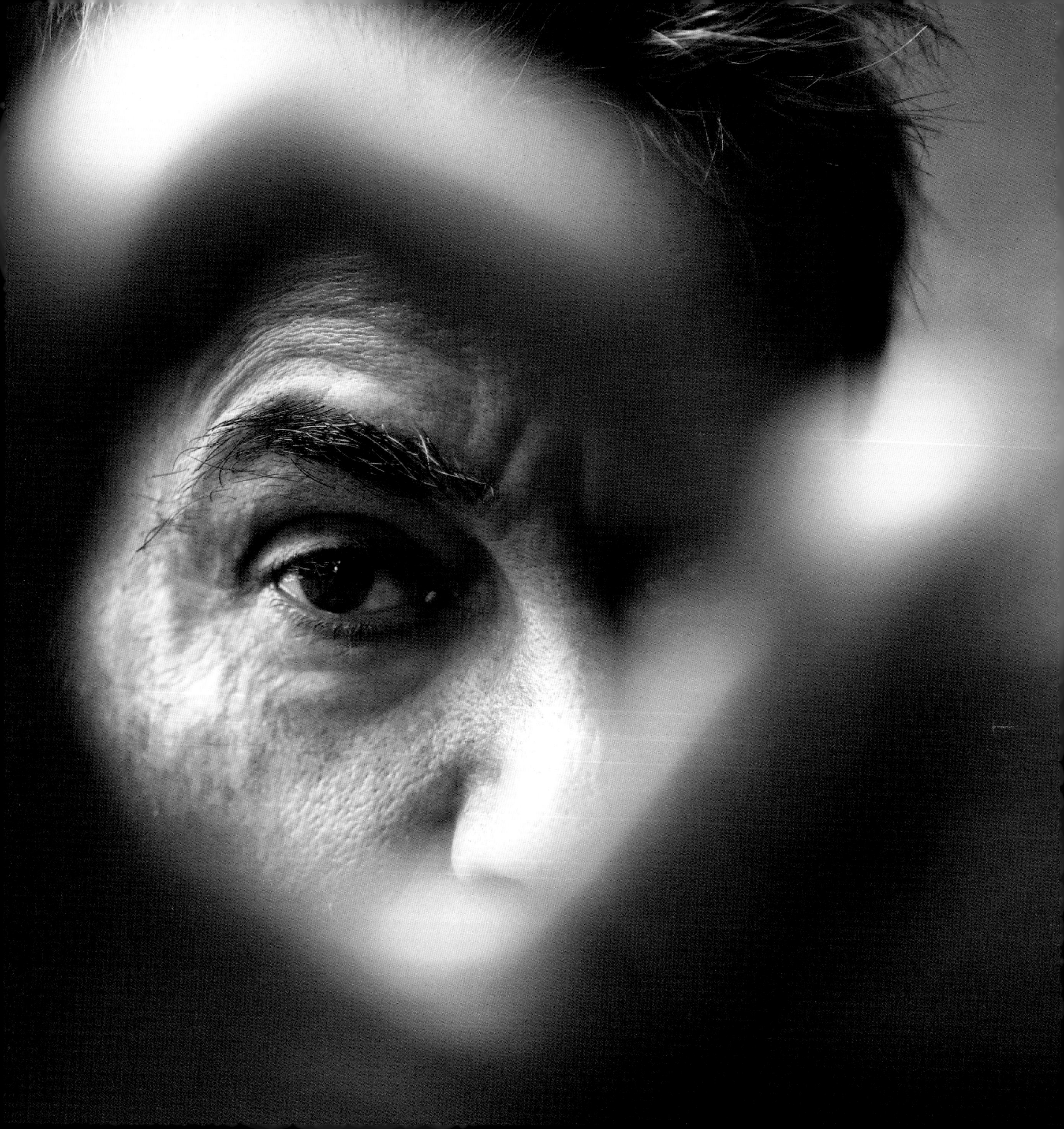

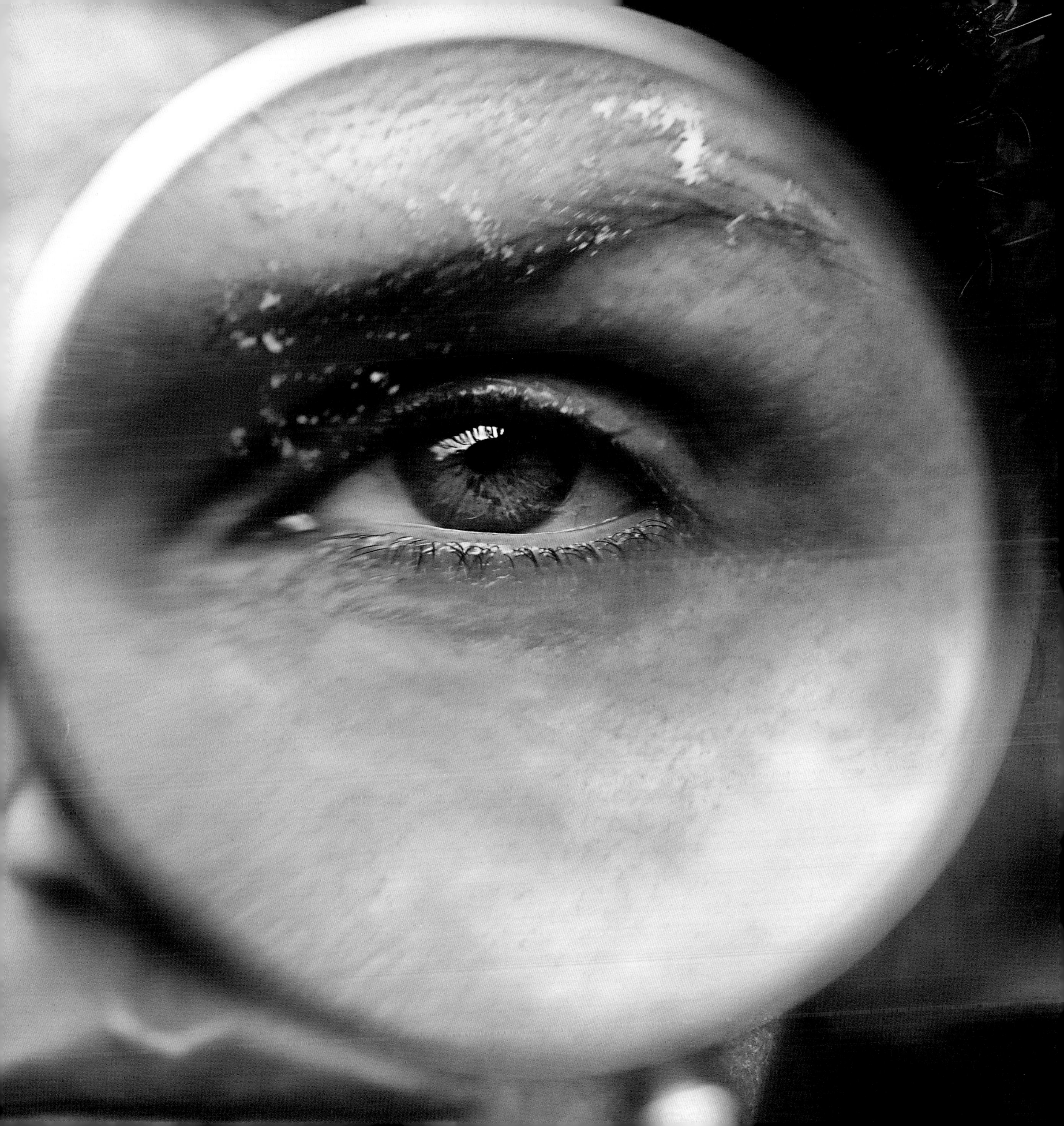

HELENA CHRISTENSEN

Born in Copenhagen, Denmark; December 25, 1968
Eyes: green

Helena lives in the West Village in a large loft space that's beautifully decorated with an extensive array of trees and plants; like a mini paradise. We did the shoot on her deck and I decided to use a magnifying glass. I find with beautiful people, their faces are so symmetrical that it's interesting to explore ways of disrupting that. I put the magnifying glass in front of one of her eyes, and ended up cropping the image so it looks like a circle within a square. She has stunning green eyes. But the magnifying glass kind of distorts her eye which creates some magic in the shot.

Helena is also a photographer herself, and she gave me some great advice on editing the photograph. She suggested lighting an edge. She made some smart suggestions that improved the final image.

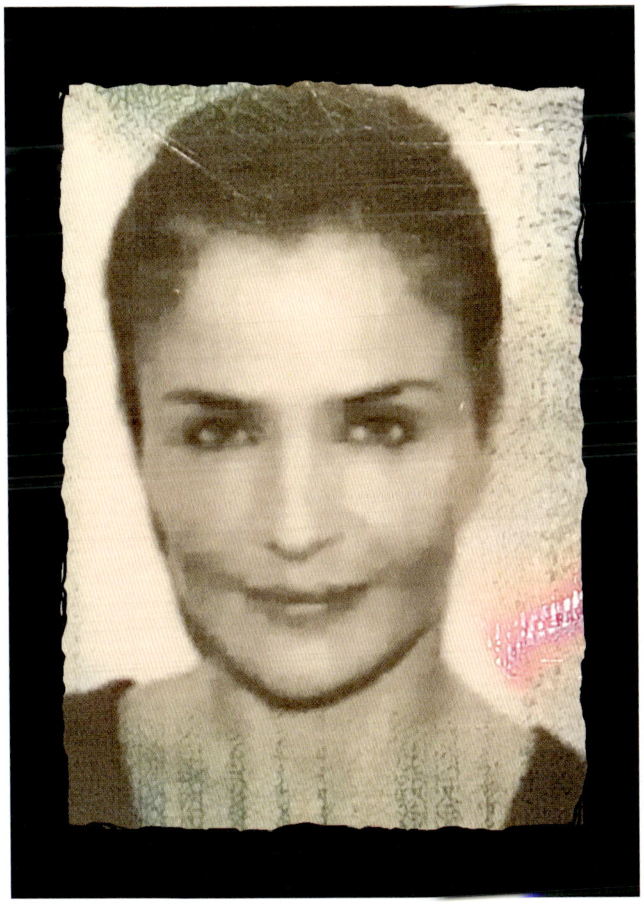

STING

Born in Wallsend, England; October 2, 1951
Eyes: blue

I've known Sting since I was a kid. He and Trudie have a house near where I grew up in Bath, a beautiful home with huge grounds, a pool and a tennis court. I remember going there with my dad when I was young. I watched Sting and my dad play tennis, which was funny because they're both so competitive. They did a tour together a few years ago where they took turns performing songs. I was able to watch the rehearsals and make it to a few of the shows. It was interesting to watch them together. They both egg each other on and play off each other, which heightens the energy of the show.

His son Jake has a daughter who attended the same kindergarten as my son. So we had been chatting as parents at the school for a few months before we realised who our dads were and that they were on tour together at the time. It's a small world!

I took this photograph at Sting's apartment on Central Park West. I shot him in his living room by the window. He was peeking through his arms. He has strong facial features and his eyes can be a little intimidating. His eyes peering through his arms was striking and intense. He's looking directly at the camera. He can be quite forward and directional as a person so this really worked.

I also like this photo as a graphic image. I knew I wanted to get that strong, confident side of him and I think I succeeded.

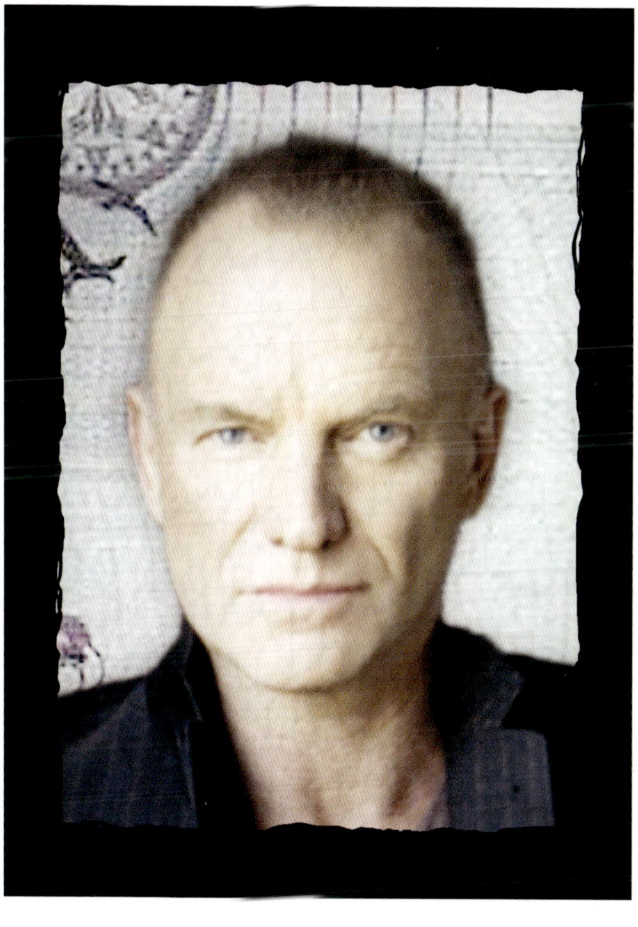

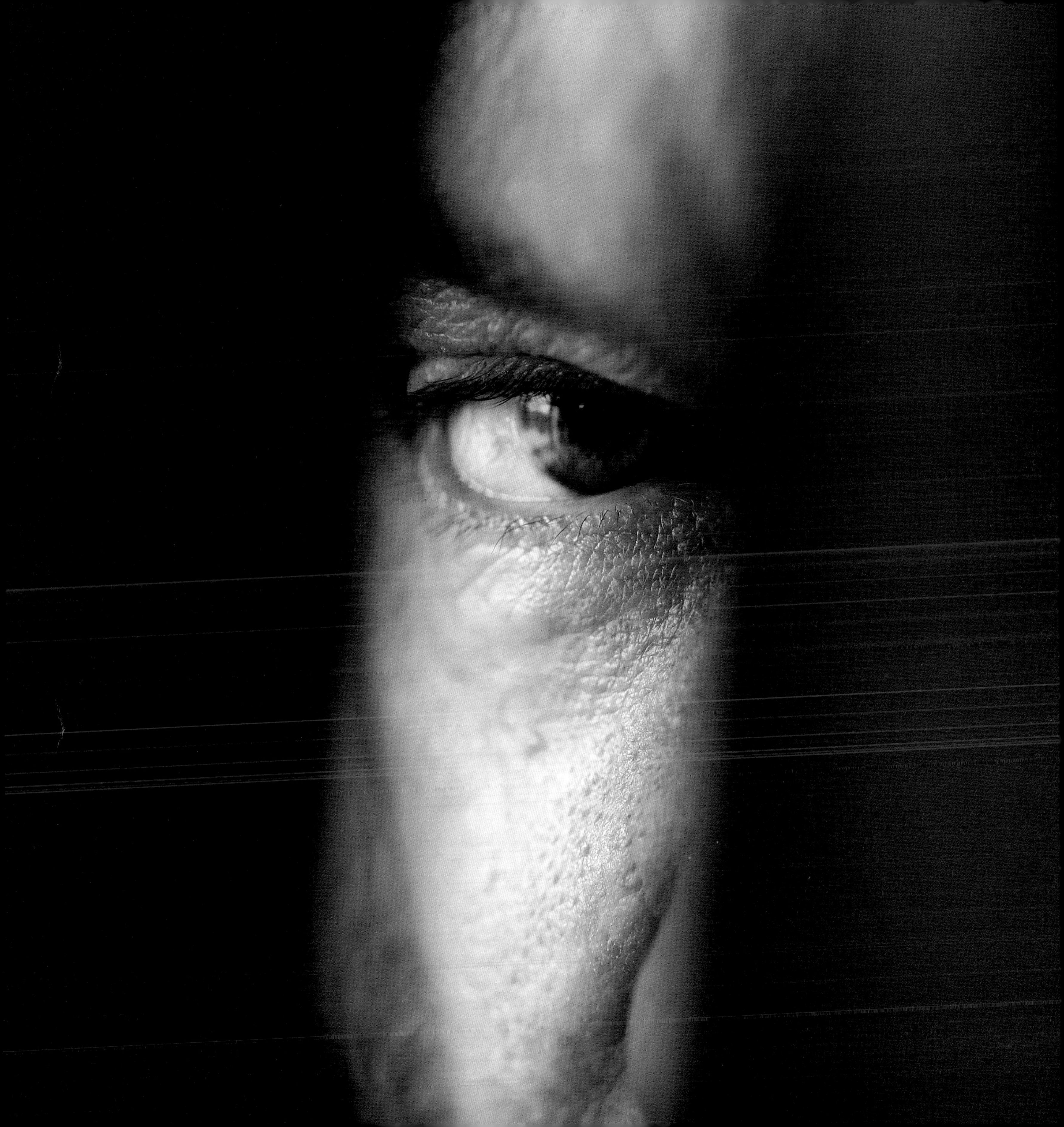

SHANE MACGOWAN

Born in Royal Tunbridge Wells, England; December 25, 1957
Eyes: blue

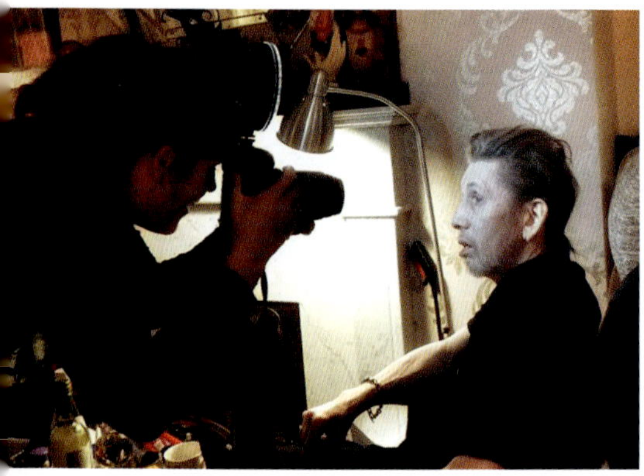

I photographed Shane MacGowan in Dublin the night before Christmas Eve. I left my hotel in the heart of town and could hear his beloved Christmas hit "Fairytale In New York" ringing out from the bars and filling the raucous streets of Dublin. It felt a world away from the quiet living room where I found Shane in an armchair watching TV with his lovely wife Victoria.

I'd met Shane once before at one of my husband's gigs at The Boogaloo in Highgate. We ended up staying for a lock in after the bar had closed. In between long cackles of laughter and a slurred London-Irish delivery, Shane makes for a fascinating and knowledgeable conversationalist. It is then that you remember you are in the company of a poet. I wanted to capture something of this in my photo.

When I saw Shane this time he was recovering from a recent bout of ill health accompanied by a period of sobriety. It created a strangely intimate dynamic. Not only was it the holidays but I was in his home while he was unwell and his wife was caring for him. We sat in his living room sharing Christmas chocolates and watching TV. In fact we were so relaxed and lost in conversation, that after an hour or so I did begin to wonder if we were ever going to take the photograph! I nudged our friend Gerry O'Boyle, who had set up the shoot, to see if Shane was ready to do the shot, to which Shane barked: "What, are you in a rush?" It was very funny so I relaxed and it felt as though we were at a good friends house celebrating the holiday season. At the end of the night, I took the shot of him as he sat near the fireplace and although he wasn't well I felt like the photo showed a softness in his eye which really portrayed the intimate moment we shared at his house that night.

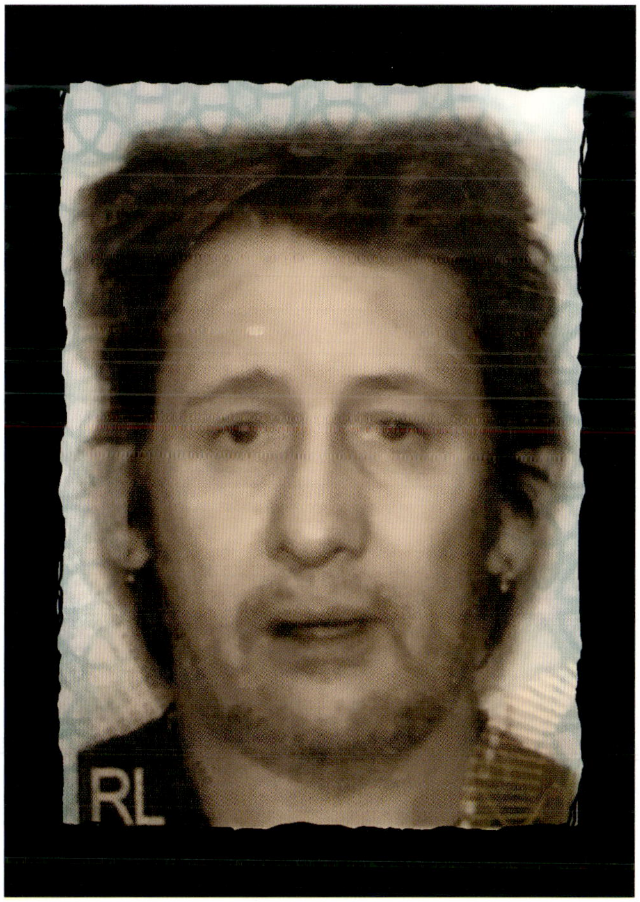
RL

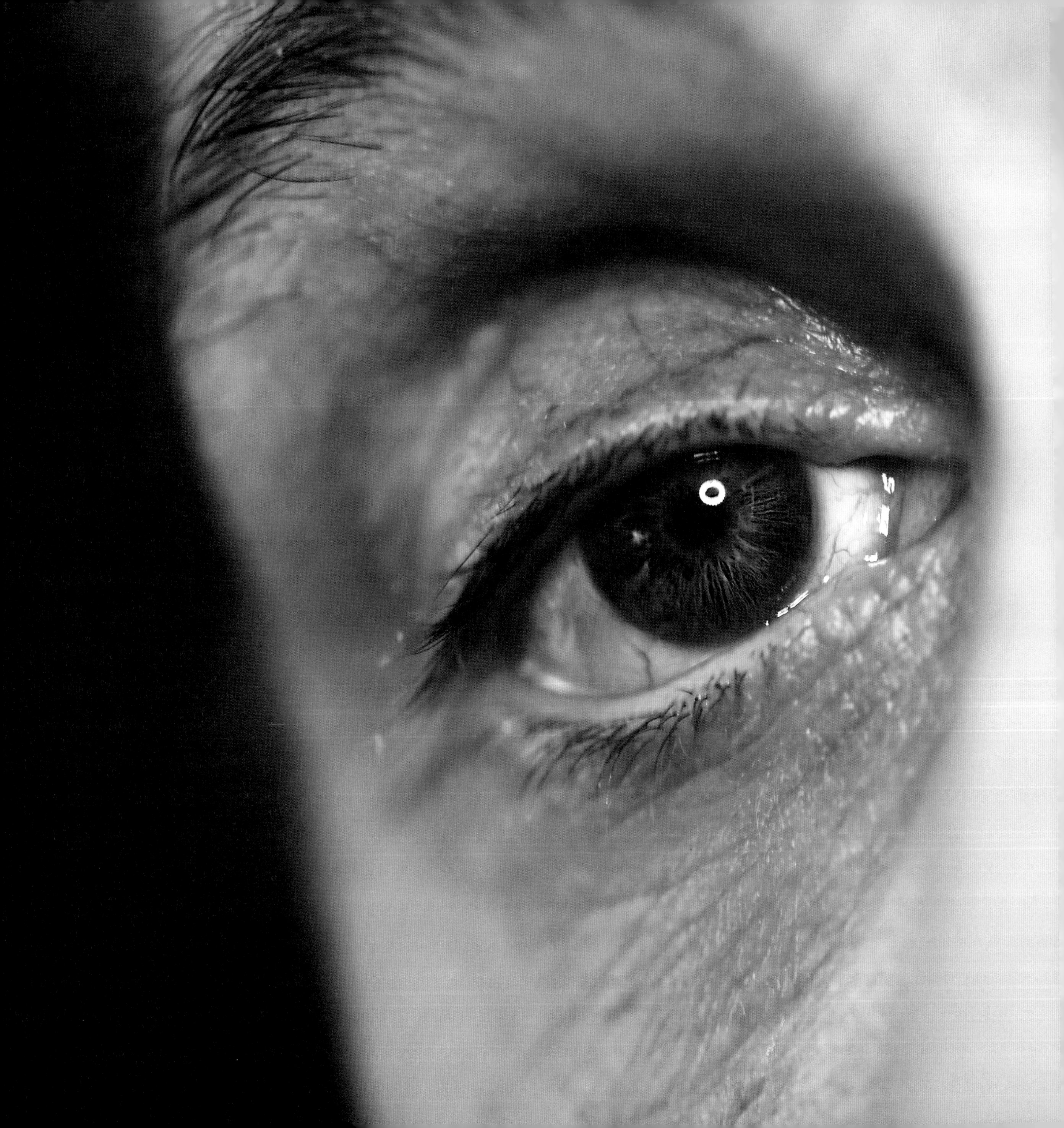

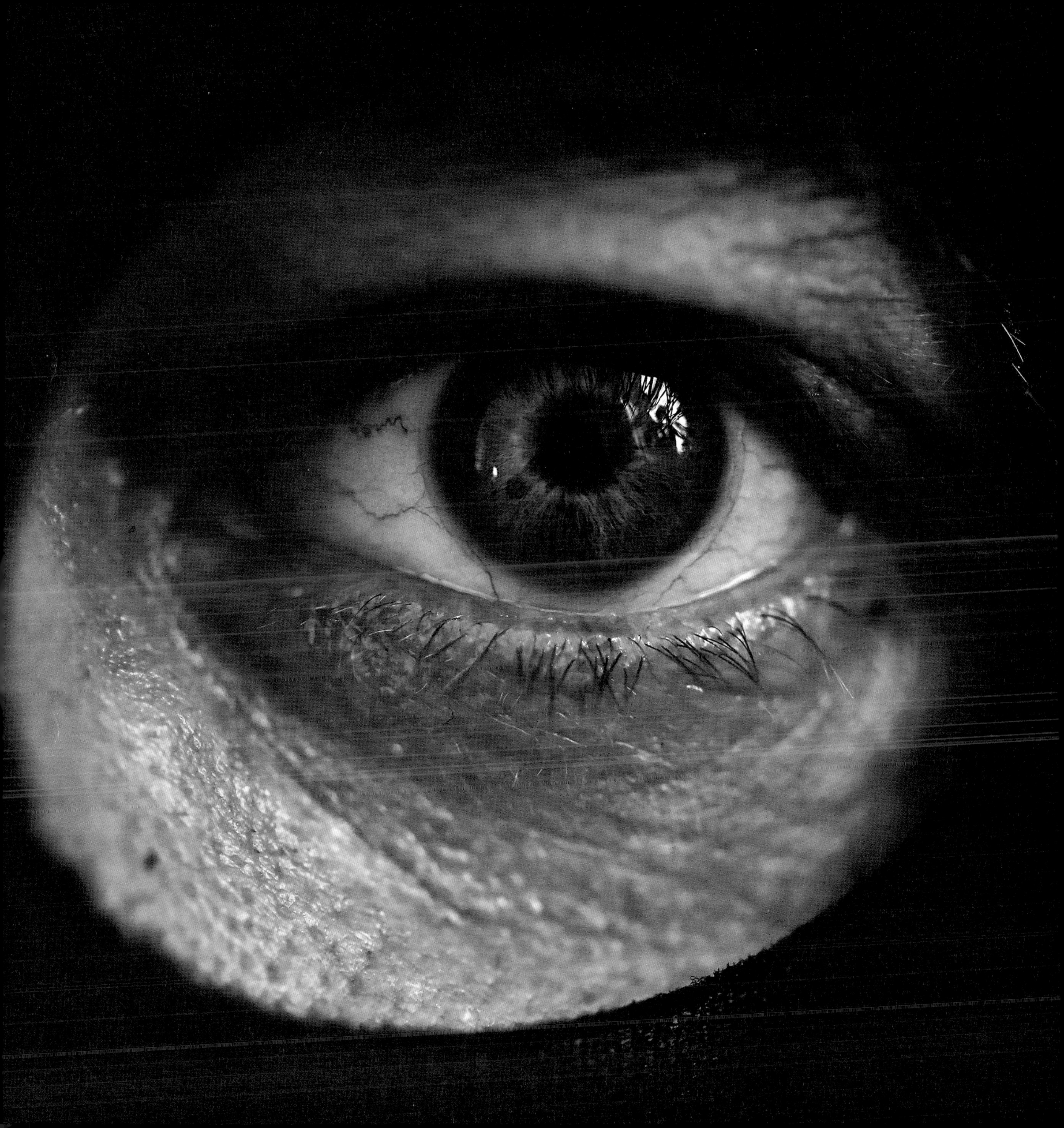

FISHER STEVENS

Born in Chicago, Illinois; November 27, 1963
Eyes: blue

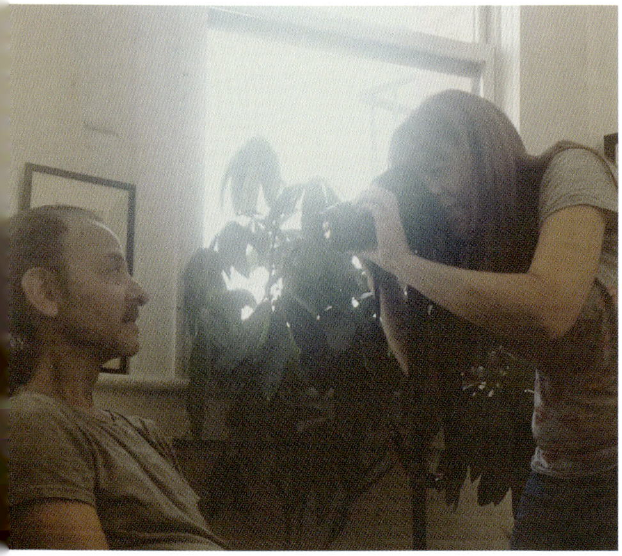

After a long career, having acted in almost 60 films, Fisher Stevens reinvented himself as a documentary director, and has gone on to massive acclaim. I'm a big fan of his documentaries, including his Oscar-winning and hugely influential film about Japanese dolphin hunters, *The Cove*.

At the time I went to shoot him he was producing *Before the Flood*, his climate change documentary with Leonardo DiCaprio. I was hoping to get a sneak peak of it in the edit room but time was short.

We went down to his office in Soho and I wanted to put a pair of tights over his head with holes cut in them, and have him look through it. He was willing to try anything so we had some fun throwing stockings over his head. He's sort of a chameleon personality-wise: a bit hard to pin down. So I like the ambiguity of the image, which I feel is dark and mysterious.

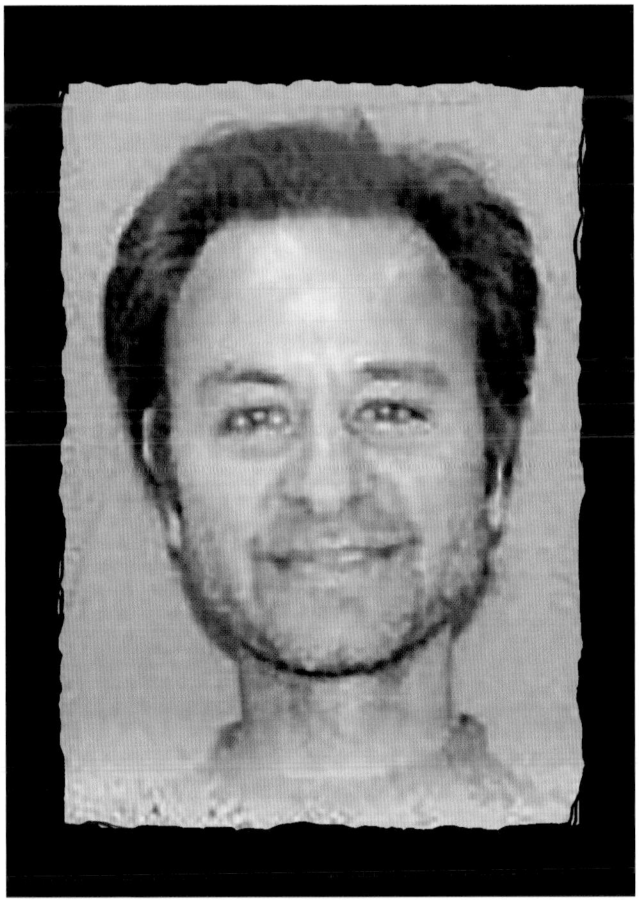

RUFUS WAINWRIGHT

Born in Rhinebeck, New York; July 22, 1973
Eyes: green

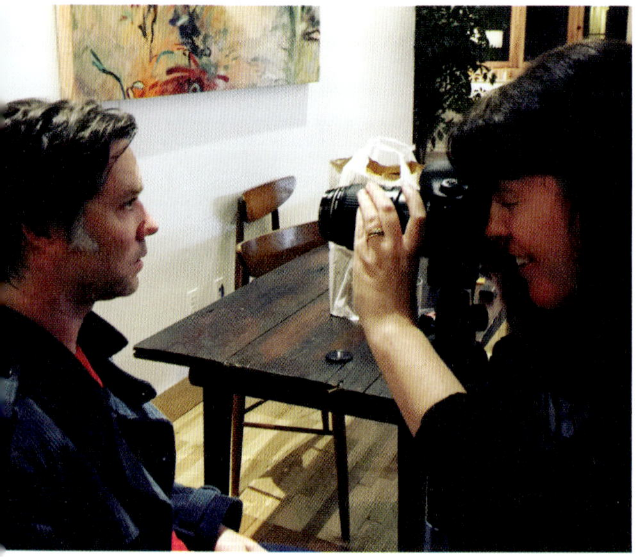

Rufus Wainwright has a serious musical inheritance but has managed to carve out a place of his own in popular music. There is an emotion and sometimes a raw sadness to his voice that I find powerful.

Rufus and I have several friends in common, so I've met him before. I photographed him in a recording studio in midtown Manhattan. He was in the middle of recording so I grabbed a few shots while he was between takes. I fortunately got to hear his album while in progress.

I've spent enough time in recording studios with musicians that I understand the intense focus that is required. I shot Rufus while he was listening to a playback of a vocal take. The photo is a side view of his eye intensely focusing someplace else. I see it as his mind's eye peering deeply into his music. There's something intriguing. You wonder what he's thinking.

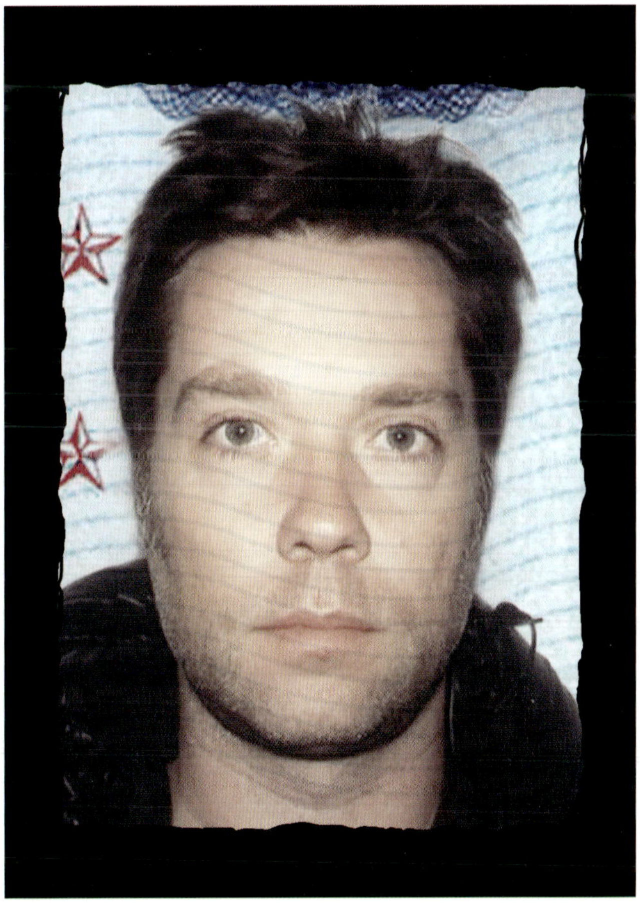

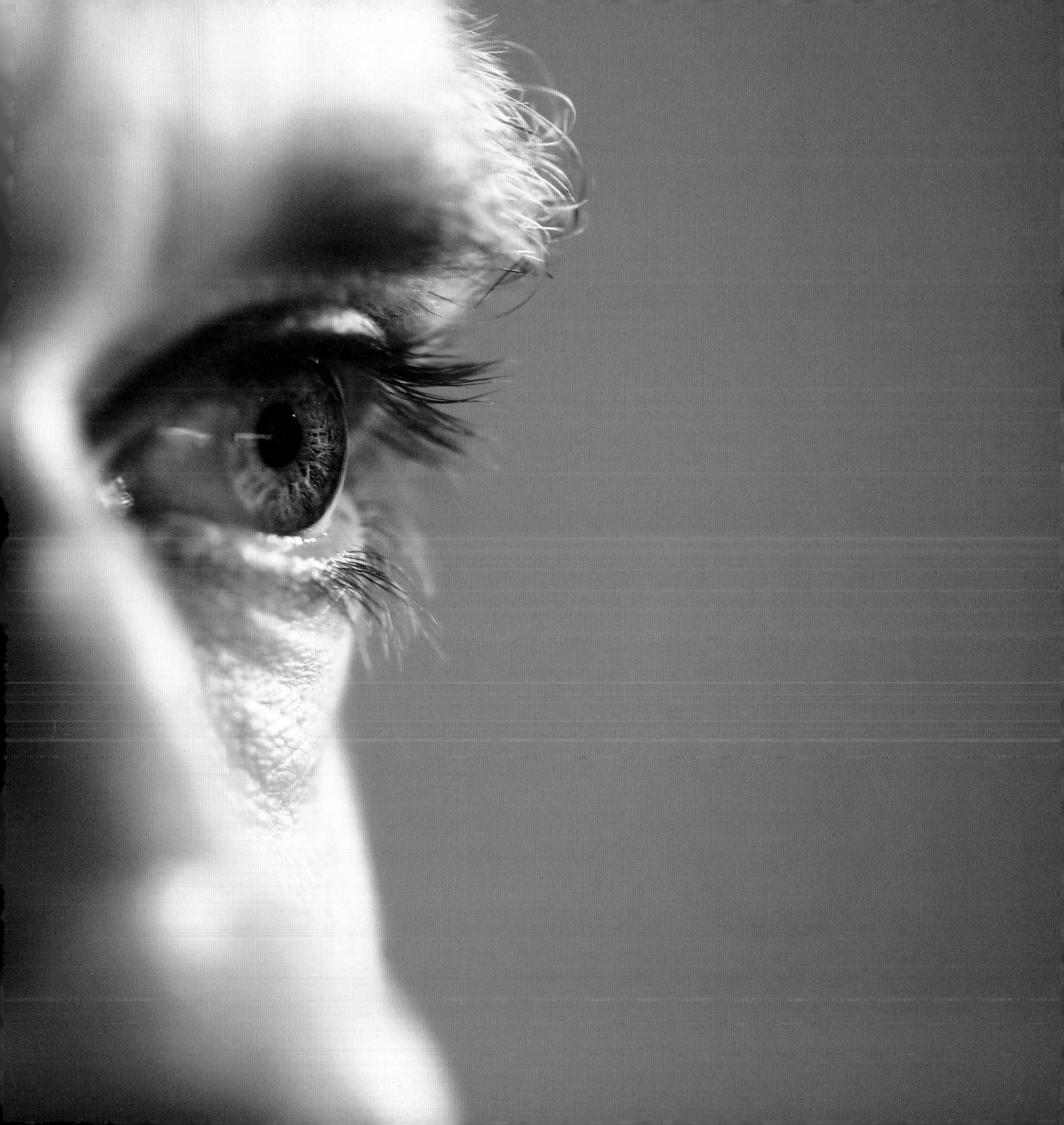

NILE RODGERS

Born in New York City, New York; September 19, 1952
Eyes: dark brown

Nile's music was my favorite to dance to as a teenager and I would always jump up on to the dance floor when Chic was played. In fact every song that Nile has written or produced made me want to move. Bowie's "Let's Dance" and Madonna's "Like A Virgin" were on constant rotation at my house. Nile has a kind of infectious, playful curiosity that just can't be stopped.

This shoot was the final one I did for the book, and I wanted something different, so I decided to bring some lights. All the previous shoots had been done with natural light. We met at Nile's Upper West Side apartment, which is a beautiful urban palace. He was in New York for a few days, but got stuck in town because of a snow storm so I was lucky enough to grab a moment with him.

I wanted to play with the dark and light in his eyes and I ended up with two images that I loved. There was one that shows his face and it's quite obviously him and there's one that I cropped where it's just his eye in the corner and the light makes it look almost tearful and emotionally dark. I let him choose which image he preferred, and he chose that more abstract one.

I really like the contrast in this shot, I feel like it's the most emotionally powerful image in the book. It looks like he's crying though he isn't.

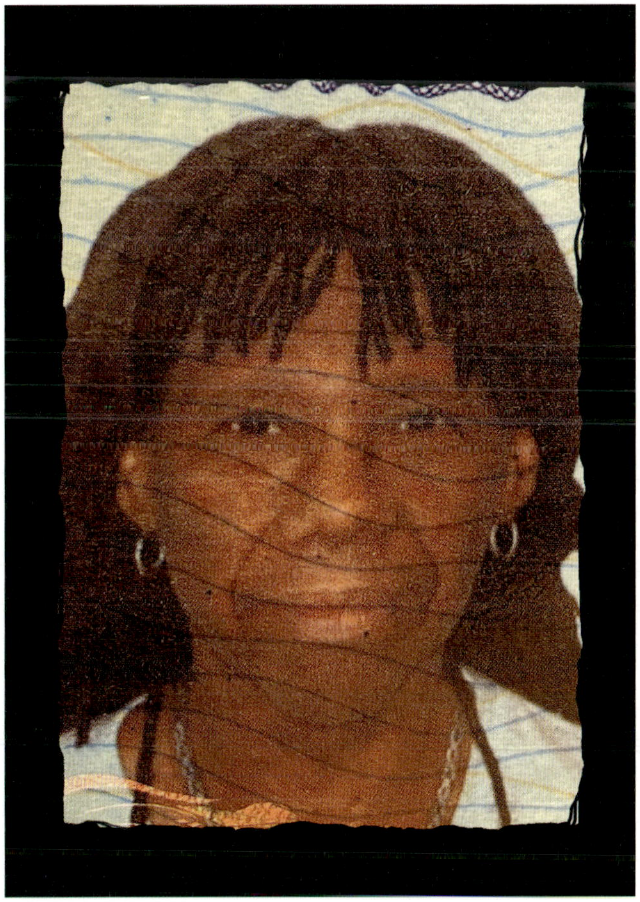

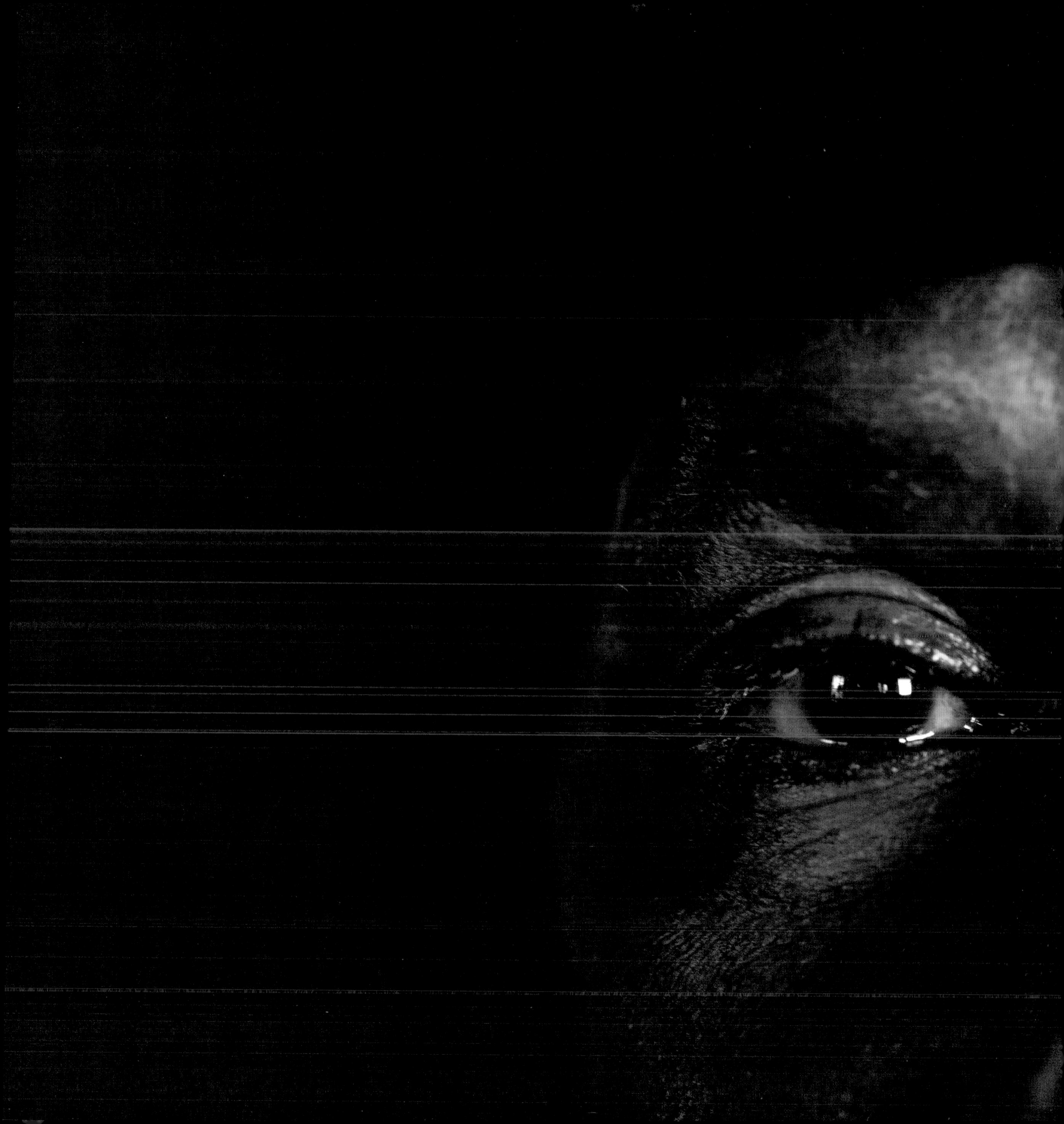

ADAM MASTERSON

Born in London, England; December 14, 1980
Eyes: dark brown

I felt it only fitting that I started this book with my father and end with my husband. Two musicians and two sets of eyes that see me to my core.

Adam is an incredible, charismatic musician with a moving soulful voice. He has a wonderful insight into life and people which he harmonically translates into songs. Yes, anyone reading this book should look him up right away.

To be an artist in this world is to follow your heart and open your mind to the universe around you. To live with an artist is to watch a vessel looking to be filled then pouring it out for others to take in. I believe music is an essential part of life and can heal, transform, calm, energise, communicate and touch us on a vibrational level. Music is a part of the energy that makes up this universe and our collective *Eye-D*.

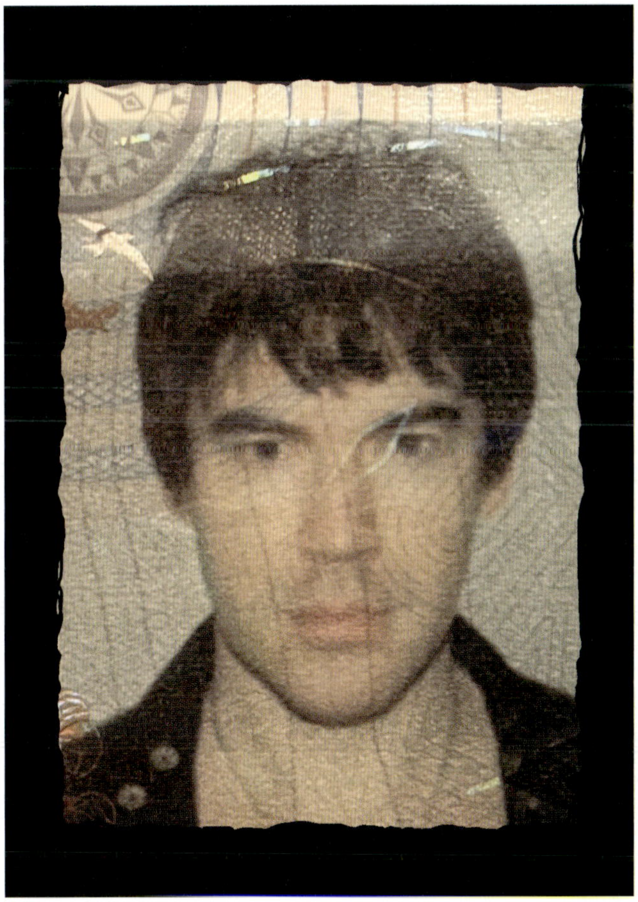

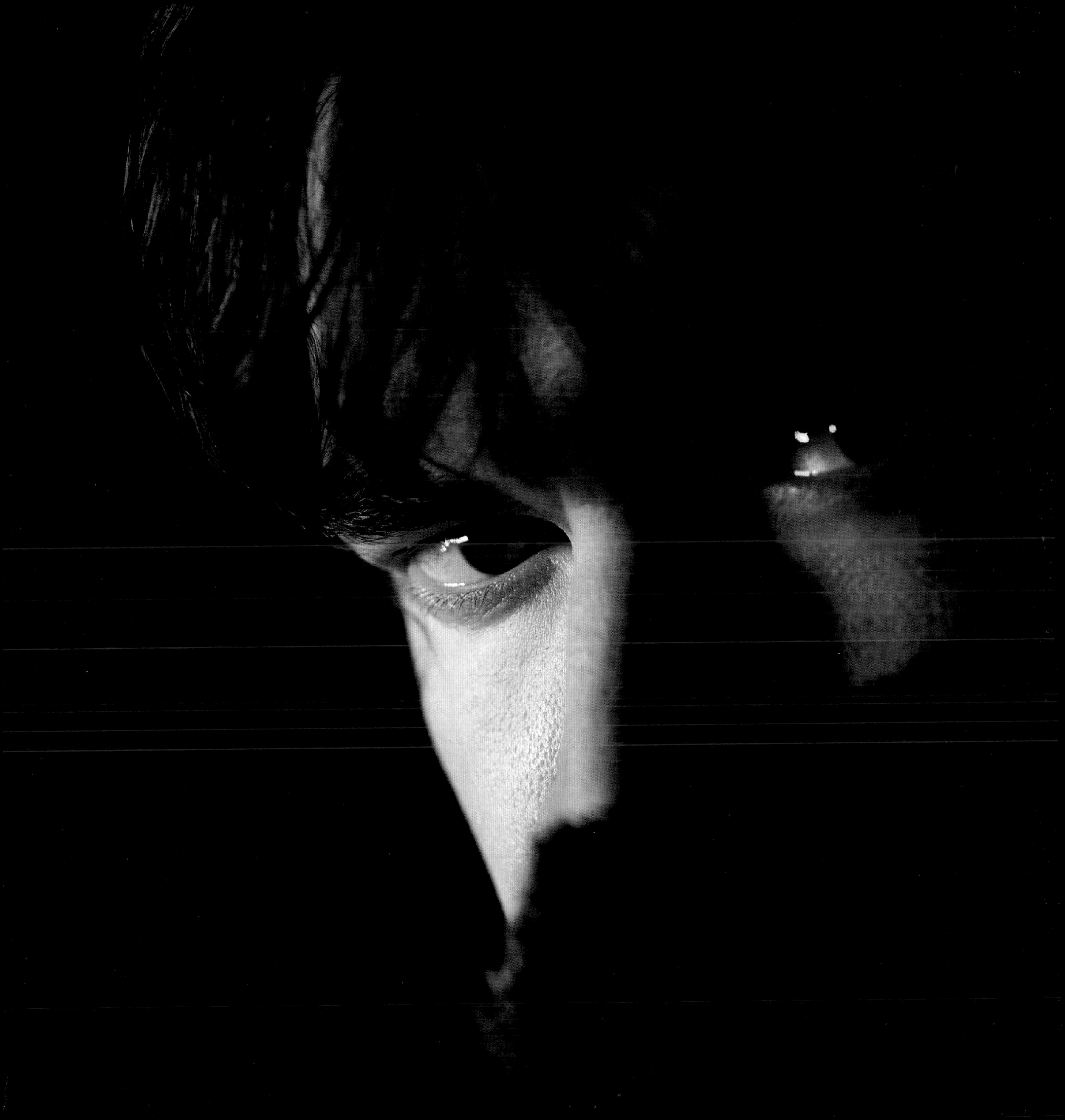

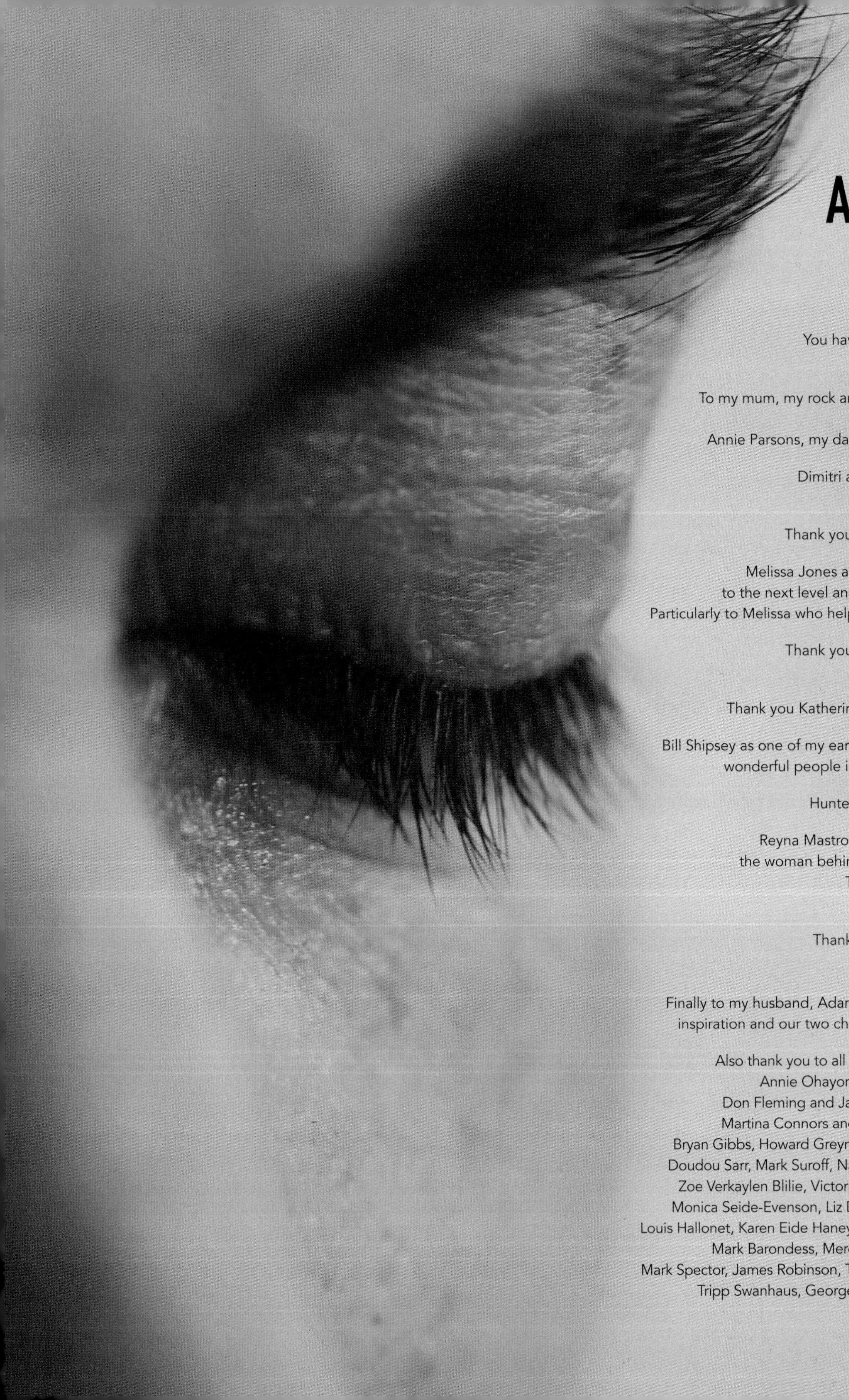

ACKNOWLEDGMENTS

Thank you to my dad who has always been my biggest support and inspiration. You have given me so many wonderful opportunities in my life. This project being one of them. Forever thankful.

To my mum, my rock and my support, I couldn't manage anything without you.

Annie Parsons, my dad's PA for many years, for helping with everything in life.

Dimitri and Greg Ehrlich, thank you for tireless work and sharing a lot of good conversations and laughs together.

Thank you Saul Palomo for all your help with the passport photos.

Melissa Jones and Ali Clarke and all at DTE Studio for lifting this project to the next level and creating beautiful box sets, website and deck designs. Particularly to Melissa who helped shop the project around and give wonderful advice.

Thank you to Karen Alinauskas for starting me out on this journey and helping with many connections and legal advice.

Thank you Katherine Latshaw at Folio for all the work you did on this book.

Bill Shipsey as one of my early supporters of the project and introducing me to some wonderful people in the book. You are an inspiration for using art for good.

Hunter Heaney my great friend, editor and secret ghost writer.

Reyna Mastrosimone, my dear friend and person I go to for all advice, the woman behind the scenes of most projects helping them take shape. Thank you for all the introductions to people in this book and being my partner in crime on many of the shoots.

Thank you Nancy Berry for all your help reaching out to artists and as a support from one photographer to another.

Finally to my husband, Adam, for being my rock, assistant, advisor, editor, writer and inspiration and our two children Max and Jasmine who give me the light in my life.

Also thank you to all the people who helped organise and set up these shoots: Annie Ohayon, Paul Stacey, Juanita Desilva, Steph Smith, Kyle Frenette, Don Fleming and Jason Stern, Susan Mieras, Amy Hairston and Bertis Downs, Martina Connors and Ray Hearn, Phil Chadwick, Tracy Bufferd, Tara Goldsmid, Bryan Gibbs, Howard Greynolds, Suzette Newman, Sooze Plunkett-Green, Zara Duffy, Doudou Sarr, Mark Suroff, Nathan Holmes, Dana Petty, Adria Petty and Annakim Petty, Zoe Verkaylen Blilie, Victoria Gilbert, Nicola Powell, Chantal O'Sullivan, Jean Hebrail, Monica Seide-Evenson, Liz Devlin, Gerry O'Boyle, Adrienne White and Paula Quijano, Louis Hallonet, Karen Eide Haney, Mike Gillespie, Kari Erickson, Anis Marks, Sarah Pearson, Mark Barondess, Merck Mercuriadis, Yannick Tardy, Georgia Villar, Helen Clarke, Mark Spector, James Robinson, Ted Kingsley, Kait Turner, Michael Hermann, Katie Semack, Tripp Swanhaus, George Acogny, Jonny Podell, Steven Rosen and Tommy Kessler

First published in 2021 in Italian under the title *EYE-D* by Rizzoli Lizard, an imprint of Mondadori Libri S.p.A.

rizzolilizard.rizzolilibri.it redazionelizard@rizzolilibri.it

This translation published in 2022 by ACC Art Books by agreement with Mondadori Libri S.p.A.

www.accartbooks.com

ISBN: 9781788841900

British Library Cataloguing-in-Publication Data
A catalogue record for this book is available from the British Library

The author and publisher gratefully acknowledge the permission granted to reproduce the copyright material in this book. Every effort has been made to trace copyright holders and to obtain their permission for the use of copyright material. The publisher apologises for any errors or omissions in the text and would be grateful if notified of any corrections that should be incorporated in future reprints or editions of this book.

Photography by Anna Gabriel
Text by Anna Gabriel with Gregor and Dimitri Ehrlich
Photograph retouching for passport photos by Saul Palomo
Behind the scenes photography by Adam Masterson and Reyna Mastrosimone
Paul Simon passport photo taken by Mark Seliger
Randy Newman passport photo taken by Robb Bradley
Debbie Harry passport photo taken by Guy Furrow
Maynard Keenan passport photo taken by David Goldman
Sting passport photo taken by Frank Ockenfels
Photographs on page 7 © 2021 Andrea Izzotti

Editorial coordination: Simone Romani
Design and layout: Paola Cannatella

Cover:
Photo of Sting by Anna Gabriel
Design by Roberto La Forgia

FSC
www.fsc.org
MIX
Paper from responsible sources
FSC® C106600

**Cover Photo:
Benjamin Zephaniah
By Anna Gabriel**

Printed in Slovenia by DZA Grafik
for ACC Art Books Ltd., Woodbridge, Suffolk, UK

www.accartbooks.com

ACC
ART
BOOKS

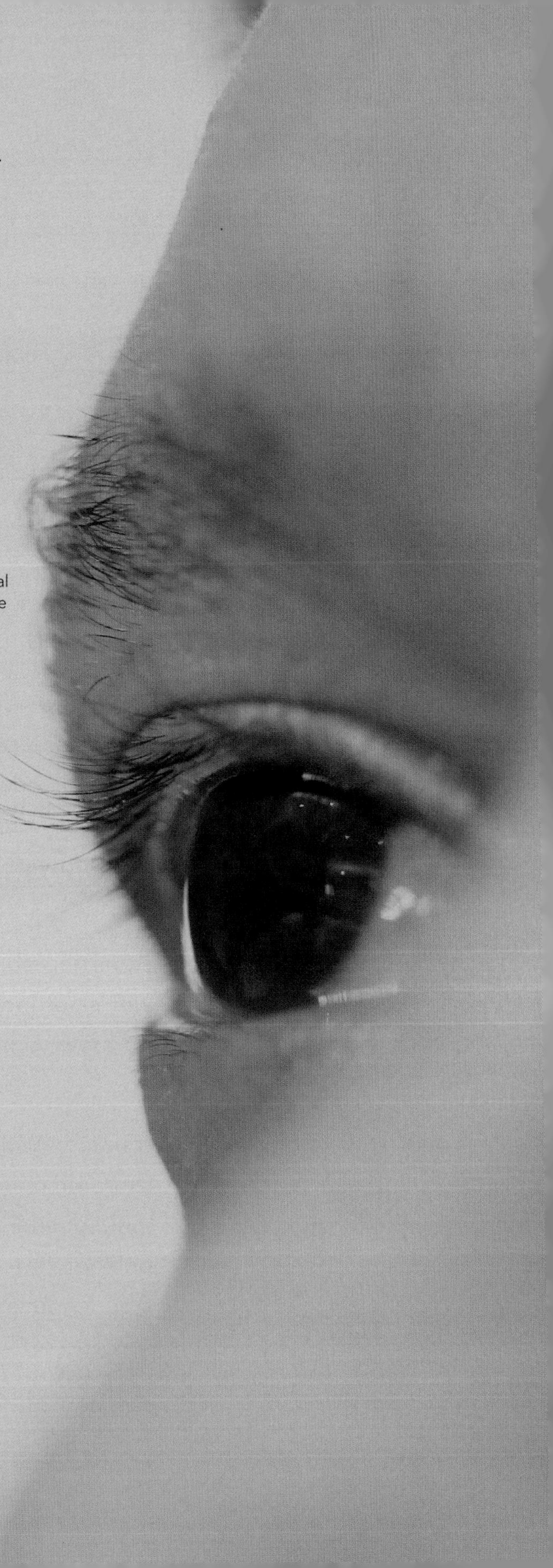

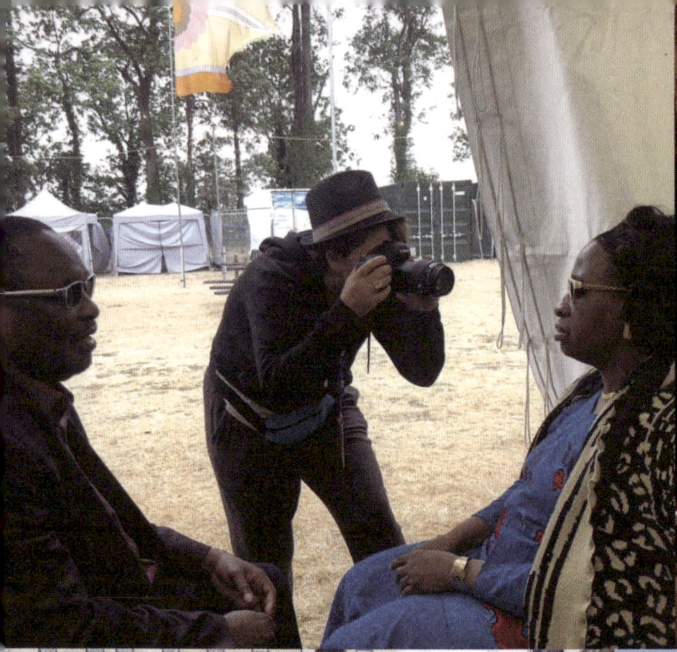
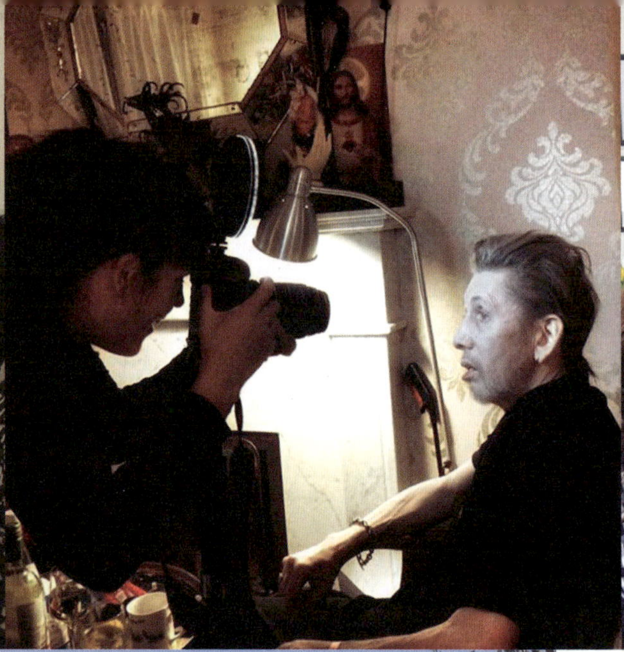
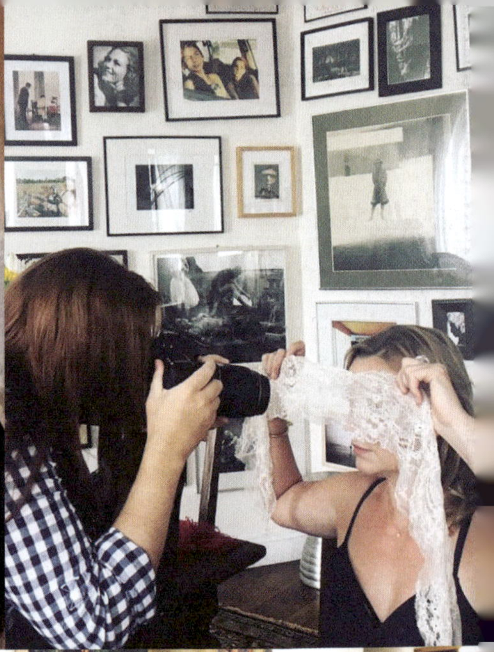
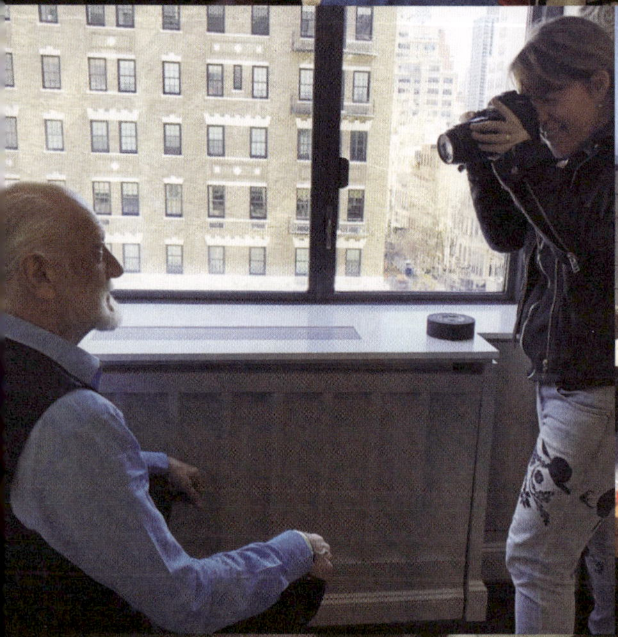
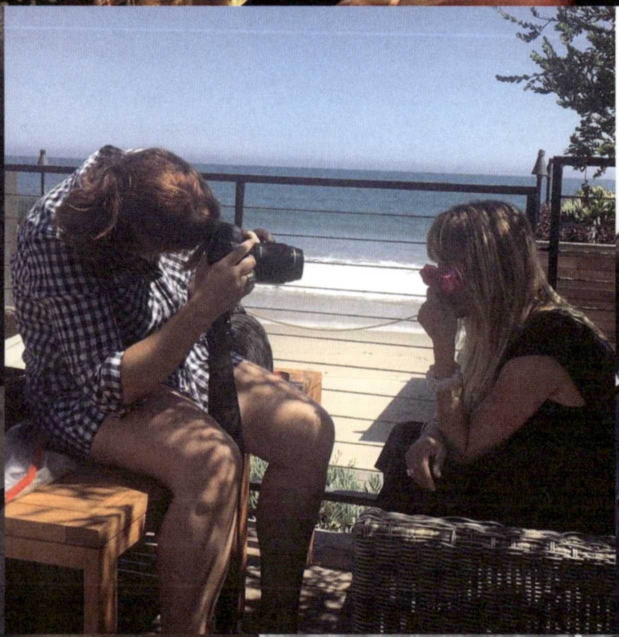
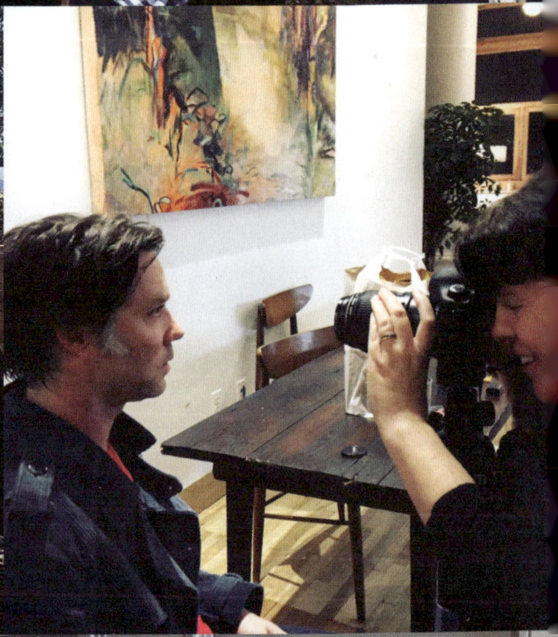
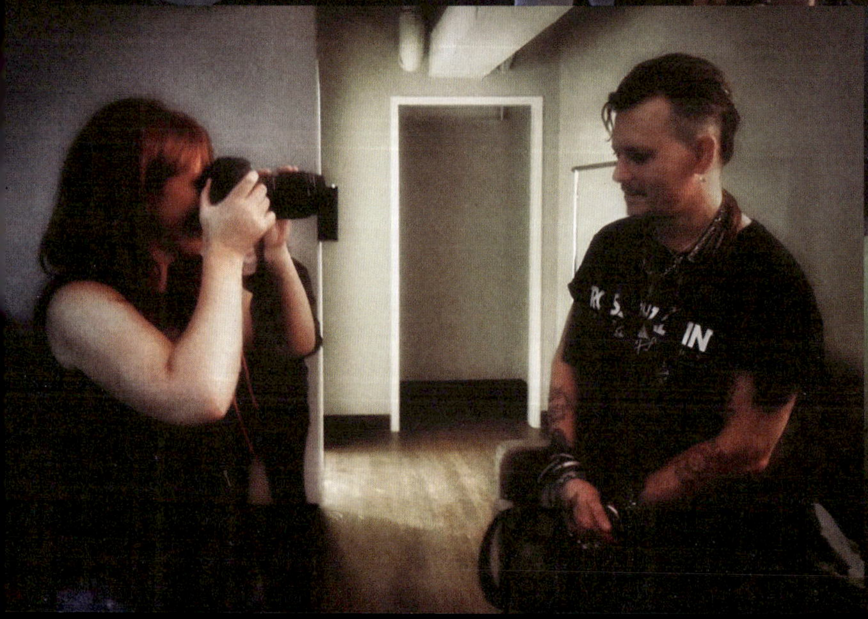
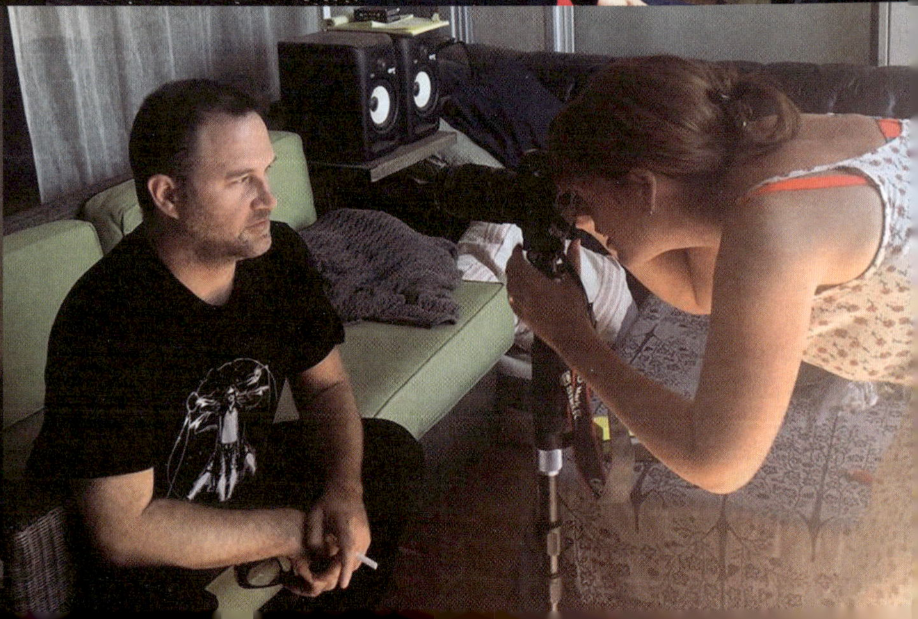